Did God Really Say That?

To Frank & Vicky,
Thank you so much for the delicious meal and your loving hospitality. We are so glad to have new friends across the pond! May God bless you all –
Eph. 1:17-19, John 8:31ᵇ-32

In the deep love Jesus,
Shawn & Jeanie Gibson

SHAWN GIBSON

Biblical Christian Beliefs book 1

Did God Really Say That?

A summary of the evidence supporting
the Divine origin of the BIBLE
and the existence of God

Biblical Christian Beliefs
Heavenly Truth for Down to Earth People
Find out more at shawndgibson.com

TATE PUBLISHING
AND ENTERPRISES, LLC

Published by Tate Publishing & Enterprises, LLC
127 E. Trade Center Terrace | Mustang, Oklahoma 73064 USA
1.888.361.9473 | www.tatepublishing.com

Tate Publishing is committed to excellence in the publishing industry. The company reflects the philosophy established by the founders, based on Psalm 68:11,

"The Lord gave the word and great was the company of those who published it."

Book design copyright © 2015 by Tate Publishing, LLC. All rights reserved.
Cover design by Eileen Cueno
Interior design by Manolito Bastasa
Illustrations by Florabela Nienaber

Published in the United States of America

ISBN: 978-1-63367-285-7
1. Religion / Christian Theology / Apologetics
2. Religion / Christian Ministry / Evangelism
15.06.10

I humbly dedicate this book to the following people, without whom it would not have been possible.

First, to my family, beginning with my wife, Jean, who has put up with and encouraged me for over forty years now; our daughter, Sarah and her husband John Brown, who used early booklet versions of this book in their missionary work in England and kept me refining, updating, and expanding my vision for this series; our son, Aaron, who was such a big part of our church plant in Winston-Salem, North Carolina, and his fiancée, Crystal; all of our grandchildren: Garrett, Savannah, Brooke, Noelle, Christian, Ayla, Abraham, Drew, and Alyssa, who keep us on our spiritual toes.

Also, to the small group of saints who allowed me the privilege of being their pastor for seven and a half years. This vision and these concepts were born in your service and allow me to continue ministering to all who will hear.

Acknowledgments

Special thanks to Janet Wooten, whose proofreading skills were truly an answer to prayer.

To Pam and Jerry Sheets, whose loving support helped us through some dark times and allowed me to finish this book.

And finally, Pastor Pete Mallinger at Calvary Chapel El Centro, who allowed me the privilege of teaching this material as a college course, which kept me busy refining and developing the content.

Contents

Abbreviations of Bible Books

When the names of Bible books are not spelled out, the following abbreviations are used:

Old Testament:

1. Genesis .... Gen	21. Ecclesiastes .... Eccl
2. Exodus .... Ex	22. Song of Solomon .... Song
3. Leviticus .... Lev	23. Isaiah .... Is
4. Numbers .... Num	24. Jeremiah .... Jer
5. Deuteronomy .... Deut	25. Lamentations .... Lam
6. Joshua .... Josh	26. Ezekiel .... Ezek
7. Judges .... Judg	27. Daniel .... Dan
8. Ruth .... Ruth	28. Hosea .... Hos
9. 1 Samuel 1Sam	29. Joel .... Joel
10. 2 Samuel 2Sam	30. Amos .... Amos
11. 1 Kings 1Kings	31. Obadiah .... Obad
12. 2 Kings 2Kings	32. Jonah .... Jonah
13. 1 Chronicles 1Chron	33. Micah .... Mic
14. 2 Chronicles 2Chron	34. Nahum .... Nah
15. Ezra .... Ezra	35. Habakkuk .... Hab
16. Nehemiah .... Neh	36. Zephaniah .... Zeph
17. Esther .... Est	37. Haggai .... Hag
18. Job .... Job	38. Zechariah .... Zech
19. Psalms .... Ps	39. Malachi .... Mal
20. Proverbs .... Prov	

New Testament:

1.	Matthew.................Matt	15.	1 Timothy.............1Tim
2.	Mark......................Mark	16.	2 Timothy.............2Tim
3.	Luke..........................Lk	17.	Titus.....................Titus
4.	John............................Jn	18.	Philemon...........Philem
5.	Acts.........................Acts	19.	Hebrews.................Heb
6.	Romans..................Rom	20.	James....................James
7.	1 Corinthians.........1Cor	21.	1 Peter.....................1Pet
8.	2 Corinthians.........2Cor	22.	2 Peter.....................2Pet
9.	Galatians.................Gal	23.	1 John......................1Jn
10.	Ephesians...............Eph	24.	2 John......................2Jn
11.	Philippians...............Phil	25.	3 John......................3Jn
12.	Colossians................Col	26.	Jude........................Jude
13.	1 Thessalonians....1Thess	27.	Revelation...............Rev
14.	2 Thessalonians....2Thess		

First Things First

What's so special about the
Biblical Christian Beliefs
book series?

What is a "biblical Christian?"

"Aren't all Christians biblical?"

Well, most try to be. But Christians usually tend to identify with their church background: "I am a..." Methodist, Baptist, Catholic, or whatever. As a result of their attendance, they learn the accepted beliefs or doctrines of their church or denomination. So, when they read and study the Bible, they begin with these teachings in mind and take special notice of the verses and passages that support them and ignore the rest. This is quite natural and is not necessarily bad, but the priority is backwards. The church or denomination is first, and the Bible is second. This bias can leave some Christians without "the whole counsel of God" on some important issues. A "biblical Christian" on the other hand, approaches the Bible without preconceptions (at least as much as is humanly possible), open to discover, and accept everything it has to say, even if it challenges the views of his/her church, thus making the Bible more important than church background in spiritual growth. A "biblical Christian" can belong to any church or denomination. He/she simply has a little bit different attitude toward learning and applying what the Bible teaches. More specifics on this balanced approach to studying the Bible are discussed in the *Did God Really Say That? - GPS (Godliness Placement System) Guide"* and other resources listed in the final chapter.

What is the *Biblical Christian Beliefs* book series?

The *Biblical Christian Beliefs* book series began as group of sermons aimed at intermediate discipleship that evolved into a systematic theology course, which I taught for an extension campus of Calvary Chapel Bible College. This, in turn, gave birth to these books. Although there are already many excellent books and college courses that do a more thorough job with these topics than I do, I believe God called me to present this academic and, what many think is boring material in a way that is simpler, more understandable, and more enjoyable for young people and folks who just consider themselves "theologically challenged." And, of course, I want to present it from the balanced biblical perspective that I mentioned above.

Take this first book as an example. Everyone, without exception, should know certain basic facts about the Bible and be aware of some of the main evidence supporting its divine origin. But, because of the academic nature of the topic, it is almost never included in the Sunday sermons, Sunday school lessons, and home Bible studies that are the educational backbone of most churches. A person needs to take a university course in Bibliology or buy college-level textbooks in order to find much of the information presented here. But most believers and seekers do not have the time or mindset to deal with the heavy theological and scientific language and breadth of content typical of these courses and books. This book is for people like this.

So, you can expect brief, simplified summaries of theological and sometimes scientific material presented in a way that is interesting and, hopefully even fun, with plenty of documentation and recommendations for further study. I will champion generally accepted views of Evangelical Christian doctrine (teachings), but I will also acknowledge some differences, especially if there is some biblical support, and I will even try to explain the pros and cons when warranted.

With this in mind, here is an overview of the *Biblical Christian Beliefs* book series:

Book 1: *Did God Really Say That?*—is a summary of the evidence supporting the divine origin of the Bible. Our source of truth is the logical place to start.

Book 2: *Is God Really Like That?*—presents the surprising nature and character of the God of the Bible, which will completely blow your mind!

Book 3: *Are We Really Like That?*—looks at the biblical view of man; how God knows we are less than perfect by nature, but loved us enough to solve our nature problem and its consequences.

Book 4: *Is the Church Really Like That?*—shows that the Church is *not* a man-made organization, but a spiritual *organism* that should play an important role in a believer's life and vice-versa. This book includes a chapter on angels, one on spiritual warfare, and one on the future of the Church in the end times.

GPS *(Godliness Placement System) Guides* will soon be available for all of the books in this series.

- ✓ Additional bonus material.
- ✓ Designed for group or individual study.
- ✓ Divided by maturity/interest level: new believer/beginner, intermediate, and advanced discipleship.
- ✓ Group discussion starters.

- ✓ Designed to teach students how to use Bible study resources, such as Bible handbooks, dictionaries, concordances, etc.
- ✓ Handy, condensed "Inductive Bible Study" reference pages.
- ✓ "Inductive Bible Study" templates and sample exercises.
- ✓ And More!

It is my prayer that *Biblical Christian Beliefs* will help provide a healthy foundation for your faith and inspire further study and growth in Christ. And please visit me at shawndgibson.com and sign up for my blog and newsletter.

WHAT'S THE BIG DEAL ABOUT THIS BOOK?

It is not often you find a book about the Bible with this much scientific information in it. I wrote it this way because, most of the books I've read on these subjects, many of which I have used as resources, left me with questions that I found answered in other books. But none of them seemed complete, at least as far as my inquisitive mind was concerned. This is because books on the Bible tend to focus on the theological aspects, paying little or no attention to science. And the scientific books, usually focusing on evolution, tend to ignore the theological aspects. So I have tried to make this book a hybrid, gathering information from a stack of books two or three feet high, adding some material from sermons, lectures, and the web, and then summarizing their wisdom in one place.

I also understand that many people are intimidated by scientific and theological books. So, I have tried to simplify difficult concepts and explain them with examples taken from everyday life. I have also tried to make this book at least somewhat entertaining with cartoons and humor scattered throughout. All of this was done to make the book as user-friendly as possible. It is my prayer that God will bless you through it.

I have also included a glossary at the end of the book to explain or give relevant background for important or confusing scientific, historic and biblical words. I encourage you to take advantage of it. There are a few very important words that I ask you to look up in the glossary. Please check them out because the way a word is used may have a different definition than the common understanding. For example, most of the time, when I use the word *believe*, it is with the normal definition in mind. But when it occurs in scripture, it can have a very different and important meaning.

A Different Look for Friends, Sources, and Scripture

You will notice the use of different typefaces for different purposes. The setting is a small home Bible study with various friends making comments and asking questions. For this reason, I have chosen to write the book in conversational language. Questions and comments by these friends will be in a typeface that looks like this, *"friend quote"*, except when their questions are used as headings. When I quote one of my sources, it will look like this, "source quote". And, finally, when I quote from the Bible, it will look like this, *"Bible quote"*. I hope that this variety will help enhance clarity, comprehension, retention and, of course, your interest.

Some Other Things You Should Know

You will also notice that within scripture quotes, some personal pronouns are capitalized when they refer to God (He, His, Him, etc.). These capitalizations are a tradition used in more formal Bible versions as a way of honoring God. But many recent translations have opted for an informal style and do not follow this tradition. I have chosen to use the informal style in the text of this book. But keep in mind as you read that when I quote from the Bible, the translation I am quoting from will determine if those pronouns are capitalized or not. Hopefully, this will give you a feel for the various versions utilized in this book and help form your own preferences when you select a Bible for your personal use.

And, finally, you will see the word *LORD* or *Lord* in some Bible quotations. This is also a tradition held over from the ancient Hebrews, who, when it came time to read the proper name of God (Jehovah or Yahweh), couldn't bring themselves to speak it. So they would substitute the word *lord*. When you see it in lowercase, it is the real word for *lord*. But when you see it in all caps or small caps, it is being substituted for God's proper name.

Well, that does it for the preliminaries. Now, on with the show!

Did God Really Say That?

WHAT WOULD YOU SAY?

If you are a Christian (if not, you may be a spectator for a moment), consider this imaginary story told by Dr. H. L. Willmington about a dinner party:

> Let us suppose that you are invited to an important social function in your hometown. Attending this gathering are people from all over the world. As the introductions are being made, it slowly dawns on you that the only professing Christian there is yourself. You are subsequently introduced to a Buddhist, a Confucianist, a Shintoist, a Muslim, and other individuals, all belonging to various non-Christian religions. After a pleasant dinner, the conversation gradually turns to matters of religion. Your hostess, realizing this subject to be of general interest, suddenly announces:
>
> "I have a wonderful idea! Since everyone here seems to have a great interest in religion, may I suggest that we share with one another by doing the following: Each person will be allowed to speak uninterrupted for ten minutes on the subject, 'Why I feel my faith is the right one.'"

The group quickly agrees with this unique and provocative idea. Then with no warning she suddenly turns to you and exclaims, "You go first!" All talk immediately ceases. Every eye is fixed on you. Every ear is turned to pick up your first words. (After picking yourself up off of the floor...) What would you say?

1. You couldn't say, "I know I'm right because I feel I'm right! Christ lives in my heart!" This, of course, is a wonderful truth experienced by all believers, but it would not convince the Buddhist, who would doubtless feel that he was right too. (And besides, how can anyone say that feelings are the final authority on truth, anyway?)
2. You couldn't say, "Christianity has more followers in this world than any other religion." This is simply not true today.
3. You couldn't say, "I know I'm right because Christianity is the oldest of all religions." The Confucianist might contend that Confucius presented his teachings centuries before the Bethlehem scene. What could you say?

   You could hold up your Bible and confidently proclaim the following: "Look at this! I know I'm right because the Author of my faith has given me a book which is completely unlike any of the books of your faiths."[1]

It's true, by far, the most convincing proof of the Christian faith and ultimately of the existence of God, is the Bible. And it's a shame that more people are not aware of this. If they were, they would find the answers to some of life's most basic questions. Questions that might well be on the minds of some of the people like those in the story above.

Let's consider a few of these questions by taking a look at Genesis 3:1. *"Now the serpent was more crafty than any of the wild animals the LORD God had made. He said to the woman, 'Did God really say…?'"* (NIV) And I'm sure you know the rest of the story. How Satan had entered the serpent, enticed Eve to eat the forbidden fruit, she gained Adam's participation, and the rest is history. Regardless of whether you think this really happened, I want to use it to introduce our main question: "Did God really say… (that)?" There are actually three parts to this question.

1. **"Did *God*…"** *"Is there even a God at all?"* That is the million dollar question. Many people wrestle with this or reject the idea of there being a God altogether. If you are a Christian, what could you say to such a person that would either answer that question or at least encourage further research?

2. **"Did *God* really *say*…"** *"I think there's a God, but why would he want to talk to me? I'm sure he's much too busy to be interested in the affairs of my life!"* A lot of people feel this way. Again, if you are a Christian, what could you say to someone like this who needs to know that God loves them and is personally interested in his or her life?

3. **"Did *God* really *say*… *(that)?"*** This was the real issue with Eve. She knew God, knew that he had spoken to her and Adam, and she knew exactly what he had told them. Satan, however, was crafty and essentially told her, "Okay, you know God, and you know what he said, but did he tell you the truth?" Then he promptly offered her an alternative "truth" (lie). She thought, *Well, there's only one way to find out…Chomp!*

A Gazillion Alternative "Truths" (lies)

I'm sure you are aware that there are many "holy books" that claim to contain the truth about God or "the gods," the meaning of life, and life after death. That means that we, like Eve, have also been given an ark-load of alternative "truths" to choose from.

"Are they all true or are there some that are lies?"

"Do we have to pick all of the different "fruits" and 'chomp' on them to find out?"

These are great questions. And, in the midst of them all, we have the Bible that claims to be the *only true holy book from the only true, living God!*

"How in the world can we ever find out if its claims are true? It seems hopeless."

Fortunately, God has not left us without hope. He has actually given us a ton of evidence supporting the Bible's claims.

THE ONLY TRUE "HOLY BOOK"?

"But, why should I believe that the Bible is the only true holy book from God? I was told that 'all paths lead to God.'"

"Yeah! How can anyone be so arrogant as to say that one way is true, and another is false? After all, if you just pay attention to what all religions have in common, it's easy to see that they are all the same!"

Elephants, Goldfish, and Religions

First, let me address this idea of only looking at the common elements of religions. Let's say you are doing a study on various animals and you happen to notice that there are many things that elephants and goldfish have in common. You find, to your astonishment, that they both have mouths; they both have eyes; they both have backbones, a heart, a tail, and dozens of other similarities! But, in spite of your findings, would you conclude that they are really the same animal?

"That's ridiculous! Of course not!"

Why?

"Because they're so different."

Exactly! In spite of their many common features, elephants and goldfish also have some *very big differences!* And if you really want to know the *truth* about them you will have to take note of their differences as well as similarities. And the same is true of religions. If you really want to understand the truth about them you need to understand their differences. Saying that all religions are the same is like trying to cram an elephant into a goldfish bowl. It doesn't work, because *it's just not true.*

The Meaning of "Holy"

Second, we have to understand that the word *holy* means pure. In order for a book to be truly holy it must be pure truth in every sense. That means error free. We are about to put the Bible through some tests to see if it qualifies. It's beyond the scope of this book to do the same for all of the other "holy books", but I will give some examples for you to consider.

Belief and Truth

Next, I'm afraid I have to get all philosophical on you. That's because in order to answer the main question above, we need to examine the nature of belief and its relationship to truth. We all have the *right* to believe whatever we want, don't we?

"Of course."

But does the fact that I freely choose to believe something automatically make it true? If I choose not to believe in gravity, will I start floating around the room? If I choose to believe that the world is flat, does that make it so?

"No, that's silly!"

Right. You see, there really is such a thing as universal, absolute truth. Let's face it, as fun as it might be to float around the room and freak out my friends, I'm not ever going to get that chance, unless I fill my shirt with balloons or something (in my case a whole lot of balloons). That's because I can't change gravity through my beliefs. In other words, what I believe about gravity has no impact on the truth of gravity. But my beliefs concerning it can certainly change me and my relationship to it. They shape my attitudes, behavior, and future relative to gravity, but not the truth about gravity itself.

Here's another example, let's say I'm on vacation, happily on my way with my family to a week of fun when I'm stopped by a patrolman, informed that a bridge is out up ahead, and he directs me to a detour. And let's say that this setback will delay our schedule for a full day. In spite of the inconvenience, lost time, and lost fun, shouldn't I still be glad to learn the truth that keeps me from driving into the river? Or should I get mad, refuse to accept the truth about the bridge, and stubbornly continue on as I had planned, believing that "mind power" will save us? Isn't it wiser, after learning the truth about the bridge, to act accordingly regardless of what I may *want* to believe?

"Yes, that's true."

My point has two parts: first, our beliefs do not change the truth; and second, it is wise to allow the truth to change our beliefs. So, find the truth first then believe that.

Beliefs do not change truth; truth should change beliefs!

"But, those are physical things. Spiritual things are different."

True, we have been talking about physical examples. But what makes you so certain that the spiritual realm is any different than this one? If the same God that made the physical universe also made the spiritual realm it only stands to reason that they would be similar. So, if there are physical laws that are true—no matter what—there must also be spiritual laws that are also true regardless of what I believe about them. And, I think you'll agree that there's nothing more important than finding the truth about God's existence or nonexistence and his personality, because what we believe about these things could have eternal consequences.

The Truth About God

So, taking what we've learned, I think it's safe to say that *if* God exists, then he *is* the way he *is*, and you and I can't change him by believing anything.

"Okay, I'll buy that."

You see, even though I have the right to believe whatever I want about God, it doesn't give me the right to force God to be the way *I want* him to be. That's like changing places and turning me into his god. Since my life is all I have to go by, I would automatically think, *"If I were God, I'd be like this and do that."* That's a critical mistake, because the God of the Bible is quite a bit different than I am. (My wife just shouted, "Amen!") God addressed this issue in Psalm 50, *"You may have thought I was just like you; but I will rebuke and indict you to your face."* (Ps 50:21, CJB) You see, I don't have his perspective from outside of time, so I can't see the future in this life or the next. I don't understand the way he dishes out perfect justice in this life and the next. And even if I tried to change him, he insists that he won't, *"For I am the LORD, I do not change."* (Mal 3:6, NKJV)

So, on one hand, the Koran is telling me that I can have up to four wives, that I can divorce and remarry at will, but my wives cannot divorce me and this is because men are superior to women (Surah or chapter 2:228), and I can even beat them if I want (Surah 4:34).[2] But, on the other hand, the Bible is telling me, *"There is no longer Jew or Gentile, slave or free, male and female. For you are all one in Christ Jesus."* (Gal 3:28, NLT) *"And you husbands, show the same kind of love to your wives as Christ showed to the Church when he died for her."* (Eph 5:25-26, TLB) So, which is right and which is wrong?

And I have the Hindus telling me to devote myself to one of their many gods and do good deeds and the prescribed rituals so I can be reincarnated in better and better lives until I am finally saved by achieving "nirvana."[3] And on the other hand, I have the Bible telling me, *"And as it is appointed for men to die once,* but after this the judgment, so Christ was offered once to bear the sins of many." (Heb 9:27-28a, NKJV) "For by grace you have been saved through faith, and that not of yourselves; it is the gift of God, not of works, lest anyone should boast." (Eph 2:8-9, NKJV) Now, I'm very sorry, but if one is right, then the other is wrong! And it is vital that I find out which is which, because, according to the Bible, if I worship false gods and try to earn my way to heaven, I'll end up spending eternity in a very bad place called hell.

God's Text Message to Us

"Okay, I know it's important to find the truth about these things, but I still don't see how we can do that."

I know, it seems like trying to herd cats. And the main difficulty is that wherever God is, we can't get there from here. He is the one who has to initiate communication with us. So, here's the deal, if there is a God, even if he might be busy, isn't it at least possible that he may *want to communicate* with us? Why do we think that is so weird? And, if that is the case, he is certainly smart enough to figure out a way of sending us a message, isn't he?

"I suppose so."

Well, the Bible claims to be that message, "the book of Truth" according to Daniel 10:21. (NIV) It is full of phrases like, "Thus says the Lord." The apostle Peter said, "There is no prophecy of scripture that is a matter of personal interpretation, for no prophecy ever came through human will; but rather human beings moved by the holy Spirit spoke under the influence of God." (2Pet 1:20-21, NABRE) Jeremiah reports, "This is what the LORD, the God of Israel, says: Write in a book all the words I have spoken to you.'" (Jer 30:2, NIV) And Paul told Timothy, "Every scripture is God-breathed (given by His inspiration)." (2Tim 3:16, AMP) And we could go on and on with examples like this!

Putting the Bible to the Test

"Okay, but how do we go about finding out if all that is true?"

Well, God made his holy book in such a way that it stands out from all the false alternatives. The measures he has taken are testable and easily expose the counterfeits while providing powerful evidence that the Bible is exactly what it claims to be! While there are many more proofs that we could examine, we're only going to look at the Bible's "unity" and four more of its main characteristics:

1. **The Bible is a History Book.** It is full of specific dates, geographical descriptions, names, and accounts of people, places, nations, kings, empires, and more. So, if it is from God, all of these references would be accurate, right? If, on the other hand, it's just a collection of legends, then the discoveries of archaeology should easily discredit it. With this in mind, we are going to examine the Bible in the light of history. And, to be fair, we will apply the same standard to the other "holy books" as well. We will survey both the Old and New Testaments.

2. **The Bible is a Prophetic Book.** It makes hundreds of predictions concerning actual people, places, events, and nations. Therefore, if it is not from the only true, living God, a simple comparison of its predictions with history would easily prove it to be a hoax. On the other hand, if it is from God, its record of fulfilled prophecy could prove to be the very signature of God himself. Likewise, all of the other contenders would have to stand up to the same scrutiny.

3. **The Bible Refers to Nature and Science.** Although it certainly is not a science textbook, the Bible is, nonetheless, full of references to nature and science. So, if it is a message from our creator, then every scientific statement would have to be accurate. On the other hand, if it is not from God, it would most certainly be shot down on the basis

of modern scientific knowledge. And, as always, the other "holy books" would have to keep up.

4. **The Bible is a Living Book.** One more of the Bible's very unique and powerful qualities is the way that the only true, living God uses it in the lives of its readers.

PRESENTING FOR EVIDENCE, EXHIBIT I: THE BIBLE'S UNITY

But before we jump into all of this exciting stuff, I want to point out that the Bible's basic facts alone, make it clear that it is very different from all of the other "holy books". The Bible is a collection of sixty-six books, letters, and poetry, written by at least forty authors, from very different walks of life: from kings to peasants, from fishermen to statesmen, from shepherds to priests, and many others. It was written over a span of nearly two thousand years, on three continents; in three languages: Hebrew, Greek and Aramaic. In spite of all this, *it is one book* that tells one story, the love story of God for man. It has one doctrinal system, one moral standard, one plan of salvation, reveals one picture of the future, and presents a unified portrait of God's nature and attributes (what he is like). This is just one of many reasons that Christians who have taken the time to verify these claims believe that a very real God had a lot to do with the writing of this book.

To underscore the magnitude of this fact, Dr. H. L. Willmington has written another fascinating story about a religious novel:

> Let us imagine a religious novel of sixty-six chapters which was begun by a single writer around the sixth century A.D. After the author has completed but five chapters, he suddenly dies. But during the next 1000 years, up to the sixteenth century, around thirty amateur "freelance" writers feel constrained

to contribute to this unfinished religious novel. Few of these authors share anything in common. They speak different languages, live at different times in different countries, have totally different backgrounds and occupations, and write in different styles. Let us furthermore imagine that at the completion of the thirty-ninth chapter, the writing for some reason suddenly stops. Not one word is, therefore, added from the sixteenth until the twentieth century. After this long delay, it begins once again when eight new authors add the final twenty-seven chapters. With all this in mind, what would be the chances of this religious novel becoming a moral, scientific, prophetic, and historical unity? The answer is obvious—not one in a million. And yet this is the story of the Bible.[4]

"What about the other 'holy books'?"

Some of the other "holy books" were written by multiple authors over a span of centuries, but none can lay claim to the kind of unity we see in the Bible, not even those written by one author. James Orr summed up the comparison of the other "holy books" to the Bible when he wrote,

> Destitute of beginning, middle, or end. They are, for the most part, collections of heterogeneous materials, loosely placed together. How different everyone must acknowledge it to be with the Bible! From Genesis to Revelation we feel that this book is, in a real sense, a unity. It is not a collection of fragments, but has, as we say, an organic character.... There is nothing exactly resembling it, or even approaching it, in all literature.[5]

How do we account for the Bible's unity?

1. **Coincidence?** *"Could the Bible's unity be due to chance?"* Well, as Dr. Willmington stated above, the odds of that are "not one in a million."
2. **Conspiracy?** *"Well then, did the authors conspire to write the Bible?"* The lack of contact due to the distances and time involved, as well as language and cultural barriers make this option pretty far-fetched as well.
3. **Common Source?** As it turns out, the only known cause of unity in the midst of this much diversity is that all of the authors had a common source. And the only possible way this could happen is if the source was of a supernatural nature. But wait, there's a lot more evidence we need to consider.

THREE QUESTIONS REVISITED

But, before we go on, let me revisit the three questions that we talked about earlier:

"Is There a God?"

First, "Did *God* really say… (that)?" If we were honest, I think we all have had our doubts about the existence of God at one time or another in our lives. If you have doubts about this, I believe the most powerful research you can do is to pray and ask God to reveal himself to you in some way. Hey, if he's really real and answers prayer the way he claims, what have you got to lose? However, he does see your heart. If you ask in defiant anger with a chip on your shoulder, he will ignore you. Nor would I expect him to appear in a blinding blast of light with roars of thunder and an earthquake. But if you are willing to ask him that question in sincerity with a willingness to follow his lead, he has made this promise to you: *"Ask, and it will be given to you; seek, and you will find; knock, and it will be opened to you. For everyone who asks receives, and he who seeks finds, and to him who knocks it will be opened."* (Matt 7:7-8, NKJV) In other words, he will be faithful to make himself known to you in a way that you will recognize. After all, he did lead you to read this book, did he not?

"Is God Interested in Me?"

Second, "Did God really *say*… (that)?" If you believe there is a God, but have no assurance that he would be interested in you, consider this: the Bible presents God as existing outside of the limitations of time; it has no bearing on him at all. This means that he can enter and leave time at will. So, it is possible for him to be present with me throughout my life, leave time, re-enter it again at a previous date and be involved with you in your life, as well. He could then leave time again, reenter it at another previous date, and spend someone else's life with them, etc.[6] And the Bible says that he created us for this very purpose! In fact, here are some other things about God that I want you to consider.

1. **God Knows You.** He knows all about you. David put it this way, *"You number my wanderings; put my tears into your bottle; Are they not in Your book?"* (Ps 56:8, NKJV)

2. **You Are of Value to Him.** Jesus said, *"Are not five sparrows sold for two copper coins? And not one of them is forgotten before God. But the very hairs of your head are all numbered* (not just counted; the Greek word means, assigned a number). *Do not fear therefore; you are of more value than many sparrows."* (Lk 2:6-7, NKJV)

3. **God Is Thinking of You.** And David, again acknowledged, *"You made all the delicate, inner parts of my body and knit me together in my mother's womb. Thank you for making me so wonderfully complex! Your workmanship is marvelous—how well*

I know it. You watched me as I was being formed in utter seclusion, as I was woven together in the dark of the womb. You saw me before I was born. Every day of my life was recorded in your book. Every moment was laid out before a single day had passed. How precious are your thoughts about me, O God. They cannot be numbered! I can't even count them; they outnumber the grains of sand!" (Ps139:13-18a, NLT)

4. **Jesus Is Calling to You.** "Look! I stand at the door and knock. If you hear my voice and open the door, I will come in, and we will share a meal together as friends." (Rev 3:20, NLT)

"What is the Truth about God?"

Thirdly, "Did God really say (*that*)?" Truth is the fundamental issue for all of us. As we view a brief survey of the evidence, I challenge you to consider what you will do with it.

That which was from the beginning, which we have heard, which we have seen with our eyes, which we have looked upon, and our hands have handled, concerning the Word of life – ... (1Jn 1:1, NKJV) This is the message which we have heard from Him and declare to you. (1Jn 1:5a, NKJV)

The Bible and History

"How can we find out if the Bible's historical record is accurate?"

There are actually three other questions tied in with this one when we study ancient books. First, where did these books come from? Second, how do we know who wrote them, or how "genuine" is the authorship. For example, how certain are we that the real Moses was the one who wrote the first five books of the Old Testament? Third, how can we tell if they've been tampered with over the centuries? And then we can finally deal with how to validate the Bible's historical accuracy or the "authenticity" of it's content.

Secular historians that are considered reasonably accurate by modern standards did not begin to appear on the scene until just a few hundred years before Christ. And even after that, the reliability of some historic accounts is questionable. Dr. Henry Morris describes writings of this time as being "a mixture of philosophy, religion and mythology, interwoven with uncertain amounts of history."[1] This makes it pretty hard to separate legend from the truth in these writings. It's no wonder, then, why so many people are suspicious of the Bible's historical record, especially when it includes miracles that are entirely outside of our modern experience. The similarity between the Bible's miracle-filled history and the mythology of other ancient writings is inescapable.

This is where the scientific field of archaeology comes in. These are the guys who dig up really old stuff to study. The main thing they look for in determining if something actually happened is what they call "corroborating evidence." That is, two or more pieces of evidence and/or testimonies that agree concerning the person or event in question. So, our test of history is really a test of archaeology. We need to compare what reliable ancient historians have written and what archaeologists have found with what the Bible says and see if they support the Bible's historical record or shut it down as a hoax.

PRESENTING FOR EVIDENCE, EXHIBIT 2: THE HISTORICAL ACCURACY OF THE OLD TESTAMENT

The Old Testament is a collection of thirty-nine books that Jewish rabbis, other ancient historians, Jesus Christ, and the authors of the New Testament have all recognized as being the inspired Holy Scriptures of the Jewish people.

Exhibit 2a: The Method of Collecting the Old Testament Books

The Family Project
"So, how did we get this collection of books?"

Well, I like to call it a "family project." When you live with someone for a few years, you get to know quite a bit about them. You know if they like anchovies on their pizza, if they wear jeans with holes in them, if they watch *Duck Dynasty* on TV, things like that; things that a stranger couldn't possibly know. This is the way it was with the Bible. You see, God is a person and, therefore, he can be known just like any other person. So, as God started revealing Himself to Abraham, Moses, and the other Old Testament prophets, they would write their experiences down in books to share with the rest of God's family. And the people of God knew firsthand that their prophets were also a part of God's family. So, their writings were accepted as being authentic and valid right from the time they were written. They were immediately considered sacred and were copied, and passed around to the synagogues. So, the thirty-nine books of the Old Testament were actually in use for centuries before they were "officially" recognized by the Jewish rabbis at the Council of Jamnia in AD 70.

This means that outsider critics, who question their genuineness and authenticity, must somehow prove that the authors were false prophets and fakes who were just pulling off a con job. This actually shouldn't be very hard, given the abundant amounts of prophecy contained in almost all of these books. We'll examine that in the next chapter. But if the authors were just con men, how come their writings gained such widespread acceptance without any argument? For example, if Moses didn't write the first five books of the Old Testament, why is this possibility not discussed in any of the ancient rabbinical writings? Surely the people that Moses brought out of Egypt would have known if he wrote anything or not. And how could some rabbi con men introduce fake books centuries later, when they contain a radical structure for both religious and social life? Do you really think that the entire Jewish nation would just automatically go along with it? The fact is that the ancient rabbis unanimously attribute these books to Moses and give them the weight of scripture. Now, there actually were a handful of Old Testament books that were questioned by the rabbis after they had come into use. But in every case their genuineness and authenticity were quickly confirmed.

"But, why only these books?"

It's true that there were plenty of other ancient books written during this time period with religious content. The books of the Apocrypha are a good example.

"So, why didn't the Jews consider them to be scripture?"

Because it was a "family project." Let's say that you have a brother, and you were raised in the same home together. Then your brother joined the Navy and shipped out to sea. And, let's say that the two of you began to correspond with each other by writing letters. Of course, you would save his letters because they would have special meaning to you. And let's say that someone wanted to trick you and wrote you a fake letter, supposedly from your brother. You would be able to tell that it was fake in a number of ways. You could tell if there was a difference in the vocabulary used, if there was a difference in the signature, by the postmark, or if certain details didn't line up with what you knew, like the ship's name and captain. And if, after checking Naval records, you discovered that your brother's ship never was at the port this letter claimed to be written from, that fact would also tell you it was a fraud. So, if a number of these things tipped you off, you would not fall for the prank, and you'd throw that letter out and disregard everything written in it! Right?

Likewise, God's people used similar means to detect and reject writings that they suspected were frauds. They found these other books to be full of historical, geographical, and prophetic errors. Furthermore, the teaching contradicted what was taught in the books that they knew were from God, so they were tossed out. Read them if you like; some are interesting. But the Jewish people have never considered them to be a part of their inspired scriptures. And, on that same basis, most Evangelical Christian churches reject them as inspired scripture as well.

Exhibit 2b: Tamper-Proof Copying Practices to Ensure Accuracy

Unfortunately, no originals of the Old Testament books have survived; we only have copies. (This note explains why God allowed this.[2]) These manuscripts are few in number because the Jews only kept one copy per synagogue and buried the old one when a new copy was made. They also burned copies that were damaged or had errors in them.[3]

Picky, picky, picky!

The Jewish scribes, however, used ultra-extreme-fanatical practices to ensure accuracy. Each column on every page had between forty-eight and sixty lines with exactly thirty letters per line. The letters and words on each page of each book were counted and checked. And the middle letter and word on each page had to match as well. So they didn't just copy word for word, they literally copied letter for letter! In modern terms, we would say that they were trying to produce a photographic copy. Two mistakes by a scribe (copyist) could be corrected, but if he made a third, it was "three strikes and you're out!" The whole scroll was burned, and he had to start all over![4]

The Jews burned copies that were damaged or had errors in them.

Masorites to the Rescue

In AD 500, a group of Jewish scribes, which called themselves Masorites, put together an "official" text of the Old Testament. This is called the "Masoretic Text." About one thousand ancient copies still exist. They sorted and compared all of the manuscripts that they had up to that time. Besides the copies of the Hebrew Old Testament they also used: a Latin translation, which had been written around AD 400; a Syrian version from around AD 200; a Greek version, which goes back to three hundred years before Christ (This was the Bible that Jesus and his apostles used.); and a Samaritan version of the books of Moses, which was from about 400 BC. They recorded all of the differences between these manuscripts in the margins, which came to about twelve hundred. This is less than one difference per page of the Hebrew Bible. The vast majority of these are variations in the spelling of names and places, and the rest are minor, having no impact on any doctrine or important event.

The Dead Sea Scrolls

The oldest manuscripts we have of the Old Testament are the Dead Sea Scrolls. Almost all of the Old Testament books were found among them. Some scrolls date back over a hundred years before Christ. This is within just a few hundred years of when the last books of the Old Testament were actually written! Amazingly, there are no significant differences between these and the Masoretic Text.

Compare this with the fact that the oldest surviving manuscripts of the Hindu Vedas (the main holy books of the Hindu religion) date to only the eleventh century.[5] And not one ancient manuscript has *ever* been found of the Book of Mormon, which claims to have been written centuries before Christ. So, there is no way to verify this claim or check the books accuracy.

Rabbinical Writings

Besides the manuscripts themselves, there are numerous ancient writings (the Talmud and other commentaries) by Jewish rabbis that quote and analyze Old Testament passages. This is an excellent way of verifying the details in the Old Testament text.

So, when we consider the family project that validates the genuineness of the authorship, the fanatical practices of the scribes, and the abundance of really old manuscripts available to examine, there is no reason to doubt that the Old Testament has been handed down to us accurately.

Exhibit 2c: The Old Testament's Historical Precision

"So, now are we ready to see how well the Old Testament remembers history?"

Yes we are. I'm sure you are aware that there always have been and always will be critics that try to discredit the Bible. Many historians used to deny the existence of a lot of biblical people and nations like the Hittites, Edomites, Belshazar, and others. But archaeological discoveries have embarrassed them into submission. The Bible's historical accuracy is now widely accepted in the field of archaeology. Here are just a few examples of discoveries, selected from hundreds, that support historical statements made in the Bible:

1. **Abraham's original hometown**: Genesis 11 says that Abraham was born in a city called "Ur". (Sounds funny, doesn't it? As in, "ur... um... uh...") It has actually been found and excavated.[6] The site is located on the Euphrates River near the Persion Gulf in what is now Iraq.

2. **Bricks without straw**: Exodus 5 gives an account of the Egyptian Pharoah punishing the Israelites because Moses asked him to let them go. At first, the taskmasters forced them to gather their own straw for bricks. Then they were

forced to make bricks without straw. Excavations at the ancient site of the city of Pithom (one of Pharaoh's storage cities in lower Egypt) reveal a change in the amount of straw used in the bricks. The lower levels have an abundance of straw, the intermediate levels have less, while the upper levels have none.[7] This is an example of how detailed the Bible's historical accuracy is.

3. **The Balaam Inscription**: Numbers 22-24 tells the story of the prophet Balaam. While the Israelites were on the way to their promised land, the Moabite king, Balak, freaked out because of them. So he sent and hired Balaam to curse the Israelites for him. But Balaam blessed them instead. In the ruins of an ancient building in Deir 'Alla, Jordan, was found an inscription on plaster fragments which reads, in part, "Warnings from the Book of Balaam the son of Beor. He was a seer of the gods…" The place where this was found is within 30 miles from the spot, in the plains of Moab, where Balaam gave Israel God's blessings.[8]

4. **King Solomon's Stables**: 1 Kings 9-10 tell us that Solomon kept horses at Megiddo, among other places. The remains of his stables there have been found among the ruins of an ancient fort.[9] Israel has even turned the site into a national park. If you ever visit Israel, you can see them for yourself.

5. **King Ahab's Ivory Palace**: 1 Kings 22:39 says that King Ahab had a fancy ivory palace. Archaeologists found its ruins, which had all kinds of ornate carved ivory inlays and tiles. Also among the relics unearthed were his Queen Jezebel's cosmetic saucers. The fact that she *"put paint on her eyes"* is recorded in 2 Kings 9:30 (NIV).[10] Is that enough exact detail for you?

6. **King Hezekiah's Tunnel**: King Hezekiah dug a tunnel to divert a nearby spring to provide Jerusalem with water during the Assyrian siege. This is recorded in 2 Kings 20 and 2 Chronicles 32. It is a tourist attraction to this day.[11] If you'd like a YouTube tour, here is an address to put into

your browser: www.youtube.com/watch?v=boC7lOV-1PU (as of 6-11-14).

7. **The repentance of Nineveh**: The story of the disobedient prophet, Jonah, is recorded in the book that bears his name. God sent him to the capital city of one of Israel's most bitter enemies, Assyria. But Jonah ran away and boarded a boat for as far away from Nineveh as he could get. He would much rather have seen God destroy the city in judgment. So, God arranged a storm to prod the crew into throwing Jonah overboard. A big fish then swallowed him and spit him up on shore. Luke 11:30 states that this was a sign to the Assyrians, implying that some of them saw Jonah come out of the fish and reported it to their fellow Ninevites. The city was so freaked out that Jonah's evangelistic efforts were rewarded by their repentance. Archaeologists have now confirmed that during the time of Jonah, Nineveh turned from worshipping many gods to the worship of one supreme God.[12] Additionally, the three kings that ruled Nineveh right after this backed off from the traditional Assyrian lust for conquest, which allowed Israel to recover much of her lost territory (2Kings 14:25).[13]

8. **You ain't seen nothin' yet!** There are hundreds of other inscriptions and artifacts from Israel and surrounding areas that name biblical kings, people, places and/or describe biblical events and *all* of them confirm the Bible's historical accuracy! All of the major cities mentioned in the Bible have been found and excavated and about 60 people that the Bible names have been identified and verified as legit.[14]

Dr. Nelson Glueck, once president of Hebrew Union College, the Jewish institute of religion, and considered the "dean of Palestinian archaeologists," made this amazing remark about the Bible:

> It may be stated categorically that no archeological discovery has ever controverted a Biblical

reference. Scores of archeological findings have been made which confirm in clear outline or in exact detail historical statements in the Bible. And, by the same token, proper evaluation of Biblical descriptions has often led to amazing discoveries. They form tesserae (see glossary) in the vast mosaic of the Bible's almost incredibly correct historical memory.[15]

William Albright, one of the most respected archaeologists of all time, agrees:

> The reader may rest assured: nothing has been found to disturb a reasonable faith, and nothing has been discovered which can disprove a single theological doctrine... We no longer trouble ourselves with attempts to 'harmonize' religion and science, or to 'prove' the Bible. The Bible can stand for itself.[16]

Even *U.S. News & World Report* has chimed in:

> In extraordinary ways, modern archaeology has affirmed the historical core of the Old Testament—corroborating key portions of the stories of Israel's patriarchs, the Exodus, the Davidic monarchy, and the life and times of Jesus.[17]

Exhibit 2d: Substantiating Old Testament Miracles

"But how can you consider the Bible's miracles to be historically accurate?"

Well, if there's no such thing as miracles, there's no such thing as God, and *that is the issue!* If this is a supernatural communication from an all-powerful Creator, it seems to me that there'd *better* be some accounts of miracles! The Bible tells how God used miracles to prove his identity. For example, he delivered Israel from Egypt by miracles so the Israelites would know that he was better than all the Egyptian gods that they had been worshipping. Think about it, would you really want to worship a god that can't even wipe his nose, like all those dumb idols? So, in light of what it claims to be, miracles don't make the Old Testament less believable at all. In fact, they actually add to its credibility. Here are a few examples of dozens of archaeological discoveries that support miracles recorded in the Old Testament.

1. **The creation of Adam and Eve**: Genesis 2 and 3 records the story of Adam and Eve. How God created them as the original human couple; how they fell from a state of immortality and bliss into a state of mortality and trouble (which we inherited) due to their sin of disobedience. God then drove them out of their original garden paradise. The very existence of this couple demands a creative miracle.

    An abundance of very early Babylonian inscriptions have been found that chronicle this same event in eerie detail. Two ancient seals have also been unearthed that portray this incident in picture: one on a Babylonian tablet, the other from Assyrian archives. Similar traditions have been discovered in the records of nearly every ancient civilization, including Egypt, Persia, India, Greece, China, Mongolia, Tibet, and more.[18]

    The details of the story of Adam and Eve differ from civilization to civilization and include mythical content. Nevertheless, the sheer universality and similarity of these accounts of early human history by civilizations that were separated by vast distances cannot be ignored! This corroborating evidence is a powerful testimony that some form of this event actually occurred.

And why aren't there any legends, not even one tiny hint in any ancient traditions of men descending from ape-like ancestors? There's not so much as a single cave drawing that depicts this! Why are *all* of the ancient records skewed towards creation? What is the best explanation for this discrepancy? Could it be that we humans did not descend from apes after all?

2. **Early accounts of really old guys**: Going along with the Adam and Eve traditions is the fact that many of them include accounts of people living a very long time before a devastating flood, just as recorded in Genesis 5. Obviously, life spans in excess of nine hundred years are miraculous. (Although there are some scientific possibilities, which we will explore in the chapter on Science.)

Berosus, a third century Babylonian historian, wrote three books about early human history based on many ancient inscriptions that he had at his disposal. Some of these inscriptions have been found that verify his accounts. His history includes a list of ten pre-flood kings that reigned for thousands of years each, and then "the Great Deluge occurred".

Excavations at the ancient Sumerian city of Nippur yielded about thirty thousand clay tablets in a library. Among the historical accounts documented by them are traditions of creation, Noah's flood and long-lived pre-flood kings and kingdoms.

The Weld Prism, a Babylonian cuboid stone made of clay, records a history of Sumeria that includes a list of pre-flood kings reigning for thousands of years each, then "the Flood overthrew the land".

Of course, thousands of years is an exaggeration according to the Genesis account. But these inscriptions also list the cities where these kings reigned, most of which have actually been found and excavated![19] Again, corroborating evidence is a powerful witness that there must be some basic truth to these records.

3. **Noah's Flood**: I'll have a lot more to say about this in the chapter on science. But, for now, here is some of the general evidence supporting a worldwide flood.

✓ **Worldwide flood traditions:** Egypt, India, Greece, and virtually every major early civilization has a flood tradition. These appear to be almost universal as the list includes jungle tribes in Africa, South America, and even the American Indians. Probably the best known of these is the ancient story of Gilgamesh (see glossary) interviewing the Babylonian Noah, which, once again, is eerily similar to the account in Genesis 6-9.[20]

✓ **The Euphrates Valley flood layer:** All of the Euphrates Valley dig sites have exposed an eight foot layer of sediment, containing no human artifacts, that is between layers that are full of them. This presents convincing evidence of a massive flood. Another striking fact is that the civilizations above the flood deposit are noticeably different from the one underneath. And, the pre-flood layers reveal an incredibly advanced civilization![21]

✓ **Sediments that are regional and continental in scope.** Sediments up to hundreds of feet thick that extend for hundreds of thousands of square miles with little or no evidence of erosion between layers are all over the planet. Some of these layers cover up to 60 percent of entire continents. If this magnitude of sedimentary layering were taking place today it would be a major global disaster! Entire populations of millions of people would be buried under hundreds of feet of mud! Thankfully, this extent of layering is not taking place with today's geologic processes.[22]

✓ **Huge fossil graveyards** indicate catastrophic and very quick burial. These graveyards are abundant on every continent and cannot be formed by the slow, day-to-day processes occurring in our present environment.[23]

✓ **Worldwide planation surfaces** are evidence of massive sheet erosion. The flat tops of buttes and mesas are examples of planation surfaces (the tops were planed, or sheared off flat). If you do an Internet search for aerial views of Monument Valley, you'll see some great examples. You will notice that the flat tops of the highest mountains are all at the same level. This indicates that the entire area was once flat at that elevation. Present processes do not create flat surfaces that are continent-wide. In fact, present erosion processes destroy flat terrain. These surfaces are on every continent. For example, 60 percent of Africa is made up of planation surfaces. Many geologists believe that the entire Earth was once generally flat. One of the baffling features of these surfaces is that they are littered with water-smoothed rocks and boulders. Many of these rocks have percussion marks, indicating that they were once being tossed about in turbulent rushing water. Some of these boulders have been deposited at extremely high elevations up to eight hundred miles from their known source of origin. These kinds of wide-ranging flat surfaces are only caused by the kind of massive sheet erosion that would take place during the initial receding stages of a global flood. That is, unchanneled water moving swiftly in sheets as the flood water receded, similar to how an ocean wave retreats back into the sea. Planation surfaces are not being formed on this scale today. [24]

✓ **More evidence of sheet erosion** is the slashing out of ridges and high mountain cliffs. Using the angles of sediments, geologists have computed the amount of sediment that has been sheared off. Average erosion from the Colorado Plateau is twelve thousand feet. Twenty thousand feet of sediment has been eroded from the

Appalachian Mountains. Other areas, worldwide, have lost between five thousand and twenty thousand feet.[25]

✓ **Erosional remnants** such as Devils Tower and and the buttes and mesas in Monument Valley are formed only when large volumes of water cut out channels that broaden into valleys but leave some places high and dry. This obviously happened quickly and catastrophically because these sharp, boxy formations cannot be formed by present geologic processes. Slow erosion is eliminated as a possibility because it can only produce smooth, rounded formations. Erosional remnants on this scale are not being formed today.[26]

✓ **The Grand Canyon** is flanked by planation surfaces that are ten thousand feet lower at the beginning of the canyon than at the rim's highest point. This is called the Kaibab Upwarp. As the water was flowing off of the uplifting Rocky Mountains, it began cutting out a broad gap in the upwarp that narrowed to cut out the canyon through sediments that were still soft. Thus, the Grand Canyon was formed in a matter of weeks. This is confirmed, once again, by the fact that slow erosion of solid rock makes smooth, rounded formations, it cannot create the jagged, boxy formations that are the main features of the canyon. Those features require quick, catastrophic erosion through soft sediments.[27]

✓ **More geological evidence** can be seen in *Flood by Design* by Michael Oard, which is detailed in the bibliography. There are also two good videos of his seminars at the 2011 Seattle Creation Conference, complete with photos and illustrations, available for free viewing at: www.nwcreation.net/videos/Worldwide_Evidence_for_Noahs_Flood.html and www.nwcreation.net/videos/Earth_Shaped_By_Receding_Floodwater.html (as of 6-11-14)

4. **Sodom and Gomorrah go boom!** Genesis 18-19 tells of the miraculous destruction of Sodom and Gomorrah. Dr. Steven Collins found the ruins of the city of Sodom eight miles northeast of the mouth of the Jordan River as it enters the Dead Sea. This is not the traditional location of this city, but it actually fits the biblical description much better. There is evidence of immense heat, such as sand turning to glass similar to what happens in an atomic bomb blast. Pottery shards were found with their surface turned to glass. These things can only happen with temperatures in excess of two thousand degrees Fahrenheit. Charred, disfigured human bones were found as if they were thrown by a blast against the western side of their houses. And the age of the destruction layer fits perfectly with the Bible's account.[28]

5. **The walls of Jericho collapse.** Joshua 6 records the fall of the city of Jericho by means of the miraculous destruction of its protecting wall. The Bible says *"the wall fell down flat."* (Josh6:20a, NKJV) Then Joshua's army rushed in and burned the city. Excavations at Jericho found that the city was destroyed in around 1400 BC, just about the time of Joshua's conquest. Archaeologists found that the wall that surrounded the city fell from the inside out, down a hill. So, it was not penetrated by the battering rams that were typically used at that time. Evidence suggests an earthquake was to blame. A layer of charcoal and ash and bricks burnt red by fire is all that remains from that time period. This is all consistent with the Bible's account.[29]

6. **Joshua freezes time:** In Joshua 10 we find the story of five kings that united to drive the Israelites out of the land God had promised them (sound familiar?), but Joshua surprised them and sent them running. Then he asked God to make the sun stand still to give him time to finish the job. So God froze time for a whole day, insuring a complete victory for Joshua's army.

I don't have a problem with God doing this by supernatural means. But it is curious that many astronomers think that the Earth and Mars were once in resonant orbits—that is, they crossed each other's path. Once a century or so they would pass so close to each other as to cause all kinds of irregularities, including wobbles and changes in their orbital paths. It is possible that God timed such an event in order to cause a wobble giving Joshua the long day he prayed for.

Research reveals that many other ancient civilizations also document a long day. Most notably, Chinese records tell of a long night at the time of Joshua's conquest.[30] (I could use a long day or night every once in a while myself!)

History and the Rest of the "Holy Books"

I'm afraid that *all* of the competing holy books of other religions either contain numerous verified historical errors, unverified or unverifiable historical accounts, or no historical content at all. A complete analysis of all of the other holy books is beyond the scope of this book, but here is a small sampling.

1. **Koran confusion**: Historical errors fill the Koran (Quran). It denies the crucifixion of Jesus, one of the most well attested-to facts of ancient history. It also calls Alexander the Great "a righteous servant of Allah" when he himself claimed to be the son of one of the gods of Egypt. And, his idolatrous and immoral behavior is well documented in other historical works. He would have been severely punished under Sharia Law (the Muslim system of criminal and civil law).[31]

2. **Mysterious Mormon mythology**: A great ancient civilization in North America with huge walled cities is detailed in the Book of Mormon. But, curiously, the cities all vanished without a trace—none have ever been found to excavate. There is no mention of this civilization in Indian folklore

and no archaeological discoveries have ever supported a single statement it makes. Add to this the fact that no manuscript evidence exists and the conclusion is clear, the book is pure fiction.

3. **The Apocrypha**: As I said before, one of the reasons that many of the Apocryphal books are not included in the Old Testament is because of their historical mistakes.

4. **Move along, there's nothing to see here!** Many holy books lack real world historical content altogether.

- **Hinduism:** The Hindu scriptures are primarily composed of mythology, a history of make-believe about gods and goddesses living in a spirit world. Archaeologists can't verify stuff like this.

- **Confucianism:** The writings of Confucius are philosophical in nature. In fact, many scholars don't even consider Confucianism to be a religion at all. It's more of a collection of wise sayings for life.

- **Buddhism:** Buddha focused on meditation and other techniques for reaching a state of "nirvana," which is an absence of suffering.

Exhibit 2e: The Testimony of Jesus Christ

Finally, especially for Christians, we have the testimony of Christ. Jesus and the apostles accepted the Old Testament as historically accurate, authentic, reliable, and inspired by God. They taught and preached from it. There are over 320 direct quotes from the Old Testament in the New, and hundreds more allusions. The four hundred verses of Revelation alone contain almost eight hundred quotes or references to Old Testament prophecies and events!

1. **Old Testament Authorship**: Jesus had a lot to say about who wrote the Old Testament books.

   - ✓ **The Word of God:** He called the Old Testament *"the Word of God"* and then said, *"The Scripture cannot be broken."* (Jn 10:35, NIV) He also said, *"And it is easier for heaven and earth to pass away than for one tittle of the law to fail."* (Lk 16:17, NKJV) He taught from the Old Testament. *"And beginning at Moses and all the Prophets, He expounded to them in all the Scriptures the things concerning Himself."* (Lk 24:27, NKJV)
   - ✓ **The Books of Moses:** He accepted the books of Moses. *"Do not think that I shall accuse you to the Father; there is one who accuses you—Moses, in whom you trust. For if you believed Moses, you would believe Me; for he wrote about Me."* (Jn 5:45-46, NKJV)
   - ✓ **The Book of Daniel:** He ascribes the book of Daniel to Daniel in Matthew 24:15.

2. **Historic Accounts**: Jesus held the historic accounts of the Old Testament to be true.

   - ✓ **Creation and Adam and Eve:** In Matthew 19:4 he accepted the account of creation, including Adam and Eve.
   - ✓ **Abel and Zechariah:** He accepted the accounts of Abel and Zechariah. *"That on you may come all the righteous blood shed on the earth, from the blood of righteous Abel to the blood of Zechariah."* (Matt 23:35, NKJV)
   - ✓ **Noah and Lot:** He refered to both Noah and Lot, *"As it was in the days of Noah, so it will be also in the days of the Son of Man."* (Lk 17:26, NKJV) Then, a couple of verses later, he said, *"Likewise as it was also in the days of Lot:..."* (Lk 17:28, NKJV)

3. **Miracles**: Jesus also accepted the reality of many Old Testament miracles.

- ✓ **Sodom:** He said, in *"But on the day that Lot went out of Sodom it rained fire and brimstone from heaven and destroyed them all.* (Lk 17:29, NKJV) A few verses later he said, *"Remember Lot's wife."* (Lk 17:32, NKJV)

- ✓ **Manna:** He used manna as an illustration, obviously accepting its provision as a literal event. *"I am the bread of life. Your fathers ate the manna in the wilderness, and are dead. This is the bread which comes down from heaven, that one may eat of it and not die."* (Jn 6:48-50, NKJV)

- ✓ **The Bronze Serpent:** Numbers 21 tells the story of how Moses, at God's command, made a bronze serpent and put it on a pole for the people to look at so they could be healed of poisonous snake bites. In John 3, Jesus explains that this was a prophecy of his crucifixion. Jesus said, *"And as Moses lifted up the serpent in the wilderness, even so must the Son of Man be lifted up."* (Jn 3:14, NKJV)

- ✓ **Elijah and Elisha:** He accepts several miracles in Luke 4. *"But I tell you truly, many widows were in Israel in the days of Elijah, when the heaven was shut up three years and six months, and there was a great famine throughout all the land; but to none of them was Elijah sent except to Zarephath, in the region of Sidon, to a woman who was a widow. And many lepers were in Israel in the time of Elisha the prophet, and none of them was cleansed except Naaman the Syrian."* (Lk 4:25-27, NKJV)

- ✓ **Jonah:** He even accepted Jonah being swallowed by the great fish. *"For as Jonah was three days and three nights in the belly of the great fish, so will the Son of Man be three days and three nights in the heart of the earth."* (Matt 12:40, NKJV)

The Evidence Is In!

So, we got the Old Testament books by means of a family project, which was also how their genuineness was verified. We discovered that the contents have not been significantly changed or altered since the very day they were written. And critics have yet to prove a single statement to be historically inaccurate while hundreds, if not thousands, of archaeological finds have supported biblical accounts of historic events and individuals including some of the Bible's miracles. I think it's safe to say that the Old Testament passes the test of history with flying colors, while not one of the other holy books even comes close to this awesome record! Well actually, there is one exception—one other ancient collection of writings matches it. We call it the New Testament.

PRESENTING FOR EVIDENCE, EXHIBIT 3: THE HISTORICAL ACCURACY OF THE NEW TESTAMENT

Exhibit 3a: The Method of Collecting the New Testament Books

"Okay then, how did we get the New Testament?"

Jesus Freak Pack Rats

Well, it should come as no surprise when I tell you that it, also, was a "family project." The early church came out of Judaism, so it automatically considered the writings of the Old Testament to be scripture and began collecting copies of those books. Then the apostles began writing accounts of Jesus's life and teachings, as well as letters to distribute among the churches that they had founded. So, the churches started copying and collecting these writings as well. Of course, the churches had no problem accepting the apostles that founded them as being part of their own church families. So it was a very natural process.

I know this is difficult to imagine, especially for young people, but back then they didn't have smart phones, computers, or the Internet. Back then you couldn't just download the book of Matthew to your tablet. They didn't even have overnight mail delivery.

"Wow! You mean they couldn't text? How did they ever...like...survive!?"

I'm sure it was difficult for them. Since they lacked all modern means of communication, and the different regions of the Roman Empire were separated by great distances, the first collections of these writings were incomplete and varied from region to region. Matthew, James, and Hebrews first appeared in Palestine; 1 and 2 Corinthians, Philippians, 1 and 2 Thessalonians, and Luke appeared in Greece; Titus in Crete; Mark, Acts, and Romans in Rome; and the rest in Asia Minor. The early church was also vigorously persecuted by several Roman emperors, which prevented organized church counsels. So, the process of standardizing the New Testament took over two centuries.

Are We There Yet?

When Constantine became emperor of the Roman Empire, one of the first things he did was to order the copying of fifty Bibles from a bishop named Eusebius. This occurred around AD 310. Eusebius used the tests of genuineness and authenticity as the primary justifications for selecting the New Testament books for these Bibles. That is, did an apostle really write the book or letter and is the teaching in harmony with the other accepted books? Since he knew it was a "family project", he checked around to find out which books were accepted in the regions where they first appeared. In the end, he selected the same twenty-seven books that we have in our New Testament today. This collection was finally "officially" ratified at the Council of Carthage in AD 397. This means that the New Testament books are considered to be either the writings of, or writings that were accepted by the men who were personally trained by Jesus.

"Again, why only these books?"

There were also many other religious letters and books written during this period that were not, ultimately, included in the New Testament. Some were found to be forgeries. Others were rejected because they are full of doctrinal, historical, and/or prophetic errors. A few are accurate and have some historical and devotional value, but they were rejected as scripture because of limited acceptance by the early churches in the regions where they appeared and the authorship was questionable. These books are kind of like the books written by Billy Graham. I highly recommend his books as valuable additions to any family library, but I would never claim that they were equal to scripture or include them in the Bible.

Exhibit 3b: An Ocean of Copies and a Sea of Quotes

"But, how we can be certain that these writings haven't been altered over time?"

Well, even though the Church came out of Judaism, the scribal traditions for ensuring accuracy were not automatically inherited. But the concern for care in copying was. It turns out that the method of ensuring the accuracy of the New Testament is unique in all of literature. That is, the vast number of ancient manuscripts that are available for our examination. There are about five thousand copies of New Testament portions in Greek and fifteen thousand in other languages. This is more than all other ancient documents before printing combined. There are individual differences between some of these, but the great number of copies available provides an excellent way of tracing them, and finding out what the original documents said. Once again, the great majority of these differences are in the spelling of names and places, and the rest are irrelevant, having no impact on any vital facts or teachings. I discuss this further in the final chapter.

Besides the manuscripts themselves, there are over thirty-six thousand New Testament quotes contained in letters, sermons, and other documents that were written by leaders of the early Church in the second and third centuries. These are so extensive that if the best early manuscripts were ever lost, the New Testament could be completely reconstructed using nothing but these quotes, with the exception of eleven verses!

The earliest portions of the Gospel of John date to within sixty years of the actual writing of the book. This is convincing evidence that the New Testament books we have today are identical to the ones that Christians used at the end of the first century. This also means that the events in the life of Christ, which are recorded in the New Testament, could not possibly have been gradual exaggerations over time.

Exhibit 3c: The New Testament's Historical Precision

"How accurate is the historical record of the New Testament?"

This is a significant question. Is it a collection of myths and embellished legends, or did the events and words recorded in the New Testament concerning the life and teachings of Christ and his apostles really happen?

One of the things that makes Christianity unique is that it is not just founded on moral, philosophical, or doctrinal instruction, but on historical events like healings, miracles, and Jesus's crucifixion and resurrection. As Paul said, *"If Christ be not risen, then is our preaching vain, and your faith is also vain."* (1Cor 15:14, KJV) This means that if the New Testament can be considered valid historically, equal to other ancient, reliable historical writings, then we can also consider its account of the life and teachings of Jesus to be accurate.

When we compare known history of the first century with the New Testament we find exactly the same phenomenon that was true with the Old Testament. That is, no archaeological find has ever contradicted a single statement in the New Testament. In fact, hundreds have been confirmed. And, as is the case with the Old Testament, many archaeologists have used it to guide them to important dig locations.

Sir William Ramsey, who for many years was the professor of humanity at the University of Aberdeen, Scotland and the foremost expert on the geography and history of ancient Asia Minor (Turkey), was an unbeliever when he began his career. But after undertaking an intense historical analysis of the books of Luke and Acts, also authored by Luke, he turned into a steadfast supporter of the New Testament's historical record. He said, "I take the view that Luke's history is unsurpassed in regard to its trustworthiness...you may press the words of Luke in a degree beyond any other historian's and they stand the keenest scrutiny and the hardest treatment."[32] Here are just a handful of the many archaeological finds that support statements made and events recorded in the New Testament.

1. **The Mother Lode:** Jerusalem is the "mother lode" of New Testament archaeological digs, many of which are still in progress. Among the finds are Herod's Temple (see glossary), the pools of Siloam and Bethesda, the burial box of Caiaphas (the high priest who tried Jesus), and the empty tomb of Jesus and the site of his crucifixion. There are so many artifacts and sites to be seen that Holy Land tours are a huge part of the local economy.

2. **The Synagogue at Capernaum:** Luke 7:1-5 states that a Roman centurion built the Jews a synagogue at Capernaum. Mark 1:21-22 tells us that Jesus preached there. This synagogue has been found and excavated.[33]

3. **The "Holy Grail":** The cup that Jesus drank from during the last supper may actually have been found in the ruins of a cathedral in Antioch. An ornate silver goblet was unearthed that sports carvings of Jesus and his apostles entwined in grape vines. It has been dated to the first century. This goblet was specifically made to hold something else, evidently more precious, a simple silver cup. Many scholars believe that the last supper was held in the home of Mark's mother in Jerusalem. It is known that Mark visited Antioch frequently during his many travels with Paul, Barnabas, Peter, and others. Antioch was a primary hub for missionary work during the first century. It is very possible that Mark brought the cup Jesus used at the Last Supper from his mother's house and presented it to the church at Antioch as a gift.[34]

4. **The Pilate Inscription:** "Pontius Pilate, Prefect of Judea" was discovered inscribed on a stone dedicating a building to Tiberius Caesar at Caesarea Maritima.[35]

5. **The Record of Josephus:** Flavius Josephus was a highly regarded secular Roman historian who was born just after Jesus's death and resurrection. By the time of his writing, there were many eyewitnesses of Christ's miracles and resurrection still alive, which he had the opportunity to interview. Here is what he said concerning Jesus:

> Now there was about this time Jesus, a wise man, if it be lawful to call him a man; for he was a doer of wonderful works, a teacher of such men as receive the truth with pleasure. He drew over to him both many of the Jews and many of the Gentiles. He was [the] Christ (Greek for the Hebrew word Messiah). And when Pilate, at the suggestion of the principal men amongst us, had condemned him to the cross, those that loved him at the first did not forsake him; for he appeared to them alive

again the third day; as the divine prophets had foretold these and ten thousand other wonderful things concerning him. And the tribe of Christians, so named from him, are not extinct at this day.[36]

6. **The Testimonies of Other Secular Historians**: Besides Josephus, almost a dozen other ancient writers gave a general outline of the life of Christ in their documents. These include Tacitus, Suetonius, Pliny, Trajan, Hadrian, the authors of the Talmud, and others.

Exhibit 3d: Supporting New Testament Miracles

"Now wait just a minute! How can you consider all of the stories of Jesus doing miracles and healings to be historically accurate?"

This is a very good question. But let me remind you what we said about the Old Testament miracles. A denial of miracles is a denial of God, and *that's the point!* Now, the implications of the genuineness of the New Testament are, indeed, staggering! It claims that Jesus is the Jewish Messiah (Christ or Savior), that he is God come in human flesh for the purpose of rescuing us from sin and death by dying on a cross and resurrecting on the third day. And the New Testament claims to be the accounts of eyewitnesses concerning his life and teachings.

In light of this, we must make an appeal to the character of the New Testament authors. Were these guys sincere or were they a bunch of power hungry con men plotting to establish themselves as the leaders of this new religion? Were they sane, or were they crazy, or victims of hallucinations? Were they sincerely blinded by their devotion to Jesus, thinking that he was God, when he wasn't? Were they gullible to the extent that Jesus was able to intentionally deceive them into thinking he was God? Or was Jesus himself deluded, perhaps persuaded by others of his divinity? Let's see if we can't find some answers to these questions.

1. **"Okay, just how sincere and honest were the New Testament authors?"** Were Peter, John, Matthew, Paul, and the others a bunch of fakes, guilty of fraud and conspiracy? Let's consider five facts:

   ✓ **Time and distance:** The New Testament was written by at least eight different authors, who wrote at different times and in places that were far away from each other. And since they didn't have phones, e-mail, or other modern means of communication, collaboration would be virtually impossible. They were also surrounded by so many eyewitnesses that one of them would certainly have blown the whistle if fraud were involved.

   ✓ **Character and style:** Also, the character and style of their writings are so different that there are places where it seems like they contradict each other. It takes careful reading of the passages in their original languages to resolve the issues. This is a powerful argument against the con man theory.

   ✓ **Specific accounts:** In addition to this, the accounts they give are much too specific about times, places, and public events to make fraud possible. Consider the feeding of the five thousand for example. That's an awful lot of witnesses to bribe in order to support a lie.

   ✓ **Sincere conviction:** If they were after honor and power, why do they portray themselves as such buffoons in the gospels? If they did conspire, they are the greatest con men of all time!

   ✓ **The substance of their message:** Also consider the teachings that they spread throughout the world. Such things as love, mercy, forgiveness, and doing good to your enemies are not the kinds of things that power-hungry phonies would be preaching.

✓ **Martyrdom:** Perhaps the greatest test of their sincerity is their willingness to embrace martyrdom. Why would they be so willing to be tortured to death for what they knew to be a lie? Yet, after refusing to renounce their faith, the following accounts of the deaths of Jesus's apostles are recorded in *Foxe's Book of Martyrs*:[37]

† **St. Stephen:** "preached the Gospel to the betrayers and murderers of Christ. To such a degree of madness were they excited, that they cast him out of the city and stoned him to death."

† **James the Great:** ..."As James was led to the place of martyrdom, his accuser was brought to repent of his conduct by the apostle's extraordinary courage and undauntedness, and fell down at his feet to request his pardon, professing himself a Christian, and resolving that James should not receive the crown of martyrdom alone. Hence they were both beheaded at the same time."

† **Phillip** "suffered martyrdom at Heliopolis in Phrygia. He was scourged, thrown into prison, and afterwards crucified."

† **Matthew:** "The scene of his labors was Parthia and Ethiopia, in which latter country he suffered martyrdom, being slain with a halberd (a combination spear/battle axe) in the city of Nadabah."

† **James the Less:** "the brother of our Lord, was beat and stoned by the Jews, and finally had his brains dashed out with a fuller's club."

† **Matthias:** "was stoned at Jerusalem and then beheaded."

† **Andrew:** "was taken and crucified on a cross, the two ends of which were fixed transversely in the ground

(X-shaped). Going toward the place, and seeing afar off the cross prepared, said, 'O cross, most welcome and longed for! With a willing mind, joyfully and desirously, I come to thee, being the scholar of Him which did hang on thee; because I have always been thy lover, and have coveted to embrace thee.'" Other sources tell us that he preached God's love and forgiveness to his tormentors for three days before he finally died.

† **St. Mark:** "was dragged to pieces by the people of Alexandria."

† **Peter:** "was crucified, his head being down and his feet upward, himself so requiring, because he was (he said) unworthy to be crucified after the same form and manner as the Lord was."

† **Paul:** "Nero sent two of his esquires, Ferega and Parthemius, to bring him word of his death. They, coming to Paul instructing the people, desired him to pray for them, that they might believe, who told them that shortly after they should believe and be baptised at his sepulcher. This done, the soldiers came and led him out of the city to the place of execution, where he, after his prayers made, gave his neck to the sword."

† **Jude:** "was crucified at Eddessa."

† **Bartholomew:** "having translated the Gospel of Matthew into the language of India, he propagated it in that country. He was at length cruelly beaten and then crucified."

† **Thomas:** "preached the Gospel in Parthia and India, where, exciting the rage of the pagan priests, he was martyred by being thrust through with a spear."

† **Luke:** "is supposed to have been hanged on an olive tree by the idolatrous priests of Greece."

† **Simon:** "preached the Gospel in Mauritania, Africa, and even in Britain, in which latter country he was crucified."
† **John:** "was cast into a cauldron of boiling oil. He escaped by miracle, without injury. Domitian afterwards banished him to the Isle of Patmos, where he wrote the Book of Revelation. Nerva, the successor of Domitian, recalled him. He was the only apostle who escaped a violent death."
† **Universal Passion:** How do we account for such universal and purposeful passion among the followers of Jesus? All of this for what they would have known to be a lie?

…Riiiiiight!

2. **"But what about the sanity of the apostles? Maybe they went crazy and began hallucinating!"** The problem with this view is that the nature of the events they recorded make hallucinations impossible.

- ✓ **Public settings:** They occurred in crowded public settings, not in private or remote places.
- ✓ **Different times and places:** They consistently happened at differing times and places among people with various backgrounds and personalities, not in similar places with similar kinds of people, which is typical of hallucinations.
- ✓ **Not mentally weak:** The men who recorded these events would not likely have been mentally or emotionally weak. Consider that Paul was highly educated; Luke was a physician and very accurate historian; Peter and John were "tough-guy" fishermen; Matthew was a tax assessor; and the writing of James is extremely practical.

✓ **Persecution:** Plus, their writings were accepted by substantial numbers of people who, because of intense persecution, would certainly be motivated to challenge the things that these guys wrote about Jesus. And there were still many eye witnesses around to either substantiate or deny what the apostles said.

3. **Is that legal?** Based on what we've seen so far, I believe it is safe to consider the apostles to be perfectly sane, credible, sincere men who accurately recorded what they saw and heard. Therefore, we can consider their testimonies to be valid historical records. The famous professor of jurisprudence at Harvard School of Law during the nineteenth century, Simon Greenleaf, was challenged to apply the laws of the courtroom to the accounts in the four Gospels. He published the results in a book, *The Testimony of the Evangelists* (1874) in which he concludes,

> If they had thus testified on oath, in a court of justice, they would be entitled to credit; and whether their narratives, as we now have them, would be received as ancient documents, coming from the proper custody. If so, then it is believed that every honest and impartial man will act consistently with that result, by receiving their testimony in all the extent of its import.[38]

Their testimony is that Jesus Christ is God come in human flesh, that he did many miracles, that he triumphed over death by physical resurrection, ascended to heaven and is coming again to establish his kingdom on the Earth. If this is not true, how did these beliefs become so entrenched in the minds of the apostles? We only have one natural possibility left.

4. "They must have been duped by Jesus himself!" Many people think that Jesus was a master magician who just tricked his disciples into thinking that they had seen him walk on water, heal blindness, lameness, leprosy and countless other diseases! The apostles only imagined that Lazarus had risen from the dead after being in his tomb for four days. Jesus's crucifixion and resurrection were just illusions. And, of course, his ascension[39] must have been a mirror trick! But what kind of magician would he have had to be to pull off so many deceptions that John wrote, *"And there are also many other things that Jesus did, which if they were written one by one, I suppose that even the world itself could not contain the books that would be written. Amen."* (Jn21:25, NKJV) Remember, they lived with Jesus for three years. If he was a mere magician, surely, in that time span they would have found his "bag of tricks" or walked in on him bribing people to fake healings. Furthermore, if Jesus was such an evil deceiver, how is it that even his enemies admit him to be the greatest moral teacher that ever lived? Does that make any sense?

"What? No mirrors?"

5. **"But how could they be so naive?"** Oh, it gets much worse, because Jesus is also guilty of making a long list of absolutely bizarre statements about himself. How could Jesus's disciples have been so gullible as to believe such arrogant claims as these:

✓ *"I am the light of the world. He who follows me shall not walk in darkness, but have the light of life."* (Jn 8:12, NKJV) And the facts are that Jesus's life and teachings have inspired the world's most beautiful paintings, music, and greatest literature. And most hospitals and charitable institutions in the world have been founded, not in the name of Krishna or Buddha, but in the name of Jesus Christ. So, has it come true?

✓ *"Heaven and earth will pass away, but my words will never pass away."* (Matt 24:35, NIV) The facts are that no one's words have been more attacked, banned, outlawed, and burned as his have been over the centuries. Yet, in spite of this, after two thousand years, they remain the most loved, comforting and inspiring words ever spoken. So, was he right?

✓ *"And I, if I be lifted up from the earth, will draw all men unto me."* (Jn 12:32, KJV) Sure enough, they lifted him up on a cross and men and women from every country, race, vocation, educational level, age group, and economic condition have been drawn to him! How did he know?

✓ **But wait, there's more...**

 ➢ *"Come to Me, all you who labor and are heavy laden, and I will give you rest."* (Matt 11:28, NKJV)
 ➢ *"When He saw their faith, He said to him, 'Man, your sins are forgiven you.' And the scribes and the Pharisees began to reason, saying, 'Who is this who speaks blasphemies? Who can forgive sins but God alone?'"* (Lk 5:20-21, NKJV)

➤ *"I am the way, the truth, and the life. No one comes to the Father except through Me."* (Jn 14:6, NKJV)

➤ *"I am the resurrection and the life. He who believes in Me, though he may die, he shall live. And whoever lives and believes in Me shall never die."* (Jn 11:25-26, NKJV)

➤ *"Most assuredly, I say to you, before Abraham was, I AM."* (Jn 8:58, NKJV)

➤ *"He said to them, 'But who do you say that I am?' Simon Peter answered and said, 'You are the Christ, the Son of the living God.' Jesus answered and said to him, 'Blessed are you, Simon Bar-Jonah[40], for flesh and blood has not revealed this to you, but My Father who is in heaven.'"* (Matt 16:15-17 NKJV)

✓ **What are we supposed to do about all these absurd statements made by Jesus?** C. S. Lewis, in his classic book, *Mere Christianity*, shows us three options that these preposterous proclamations lead us to.

> I am trying here to prevent anyone saying the really foolish thing that people often say about Him: 'I'm ready to accept Jesus as a great moral teacher, but I don't accept His claim to be God.' That is the one thing we must not say. A man who was merely a man and said the sort of things Jesus said would not be a great moral teacher. He would be either a lunatic—on a level with the man who says he is a poached egg—or else he would be the Devil of Hell. You must make your choice. Either this man was, and is, the Son of God: or else a madman or something worse. You can shut Him up for a fool, you can spit at Him and kill Him as a demon; or you can fall at His feet and call Him Lord and God. But let us not come with any patronizing nonsense

about His being a great human teacher. He has not left that open to us. He did not intend to.[41]

✓ **How do we explain the impact** his life and words have had on human history? Dr. James Allen Francis summed this up rather eloquently when he said,

> He never writes a book. He never holds an office. He never raises an army. He never has a family of his own. He never owns a home. He never goes to college. He never travels two hundred miles from the place where he was born. He gathers a little group of friends about him and teaches them his way of life. While still a young man, the tide of popular feeling turns against him. One denies him; another betrays him. He is turned over to his enemies. He goes through the mockery of a trial; he is nailed to a cross between two thieves, and when dead is laid in a borrowed grave by the kindness of a friend. Those are the facts of his human life. He rises from the dead. Today we look back across nineteen hundred years and ask, 'What kind of trail has he left across the centuries?' When we try to sum up his influence, all the armies that ever marched, all the parliaments that ever sat, all the kings that ever reigned are absolutely picayune in their influence on mankind compared with that of this one solitary life.[42]

The Evidence is in

There is really just one logical conclusion. The authors of the New Testament were sincere, sane, credible, and accurately recorded the life and teachings of Jesus Christ. You might say they "nailed it!" And the accurate, historical nature of the writings of these men lifts the New Testament, along with the Old, high above all of the other holy books that the world has to offer!

> *That which was from the beginning, which we have heard, which we have seen with our eyes, which we have looked upon, and our hands have handled, concerning the Word of life-...(1 Jn 1:1, NKJV) This is the message which we have heard from Him and declare to you. (1Jn1:5a, NKJV)*

The Bible and Fulfilled Prophecy

CHECK IT OUT

One of the most powerful ways God ensures that his Word stands out from the wannabes is fulfilled prophecy. There is no question that the Bible is a prophetic book. According to J. Barton Payne in his *Encyclopedia of Biblical Prophecy*, there are 8,362 verses in the Bible that predict or predicted the future. That means that just under one fourth of the entire Bible is prophetic. A surprising amount of these predictions have already been fulfilled in history. This provides an excellent means of discerning whether a holy book is a con job.

God states his case in Isaiah 46. *"I am God, and there is no other; I am God, and there is none like Me, declaring the end from the beginning, and from ancient times things that are not yet done, saying, 'My counsel shall stand, and I will do all My pleasure.'"* (Is 46:9-10, NKJV) What God is saying is that *only he* knows and can shape the future.

The Only God That is Outside of Time

It is important to realize, when discussing prophecy that the God of the Bible lives outside of the time domain. As we will see in the next chapter, God created time and, therefore, exists independent of its influence. When God spoke with Moses from the burning bush, Moses asked who he should tell the Israelites had sent him, "*And God said to Moses, 'I AM WHO I AM.' And He said, 'Thus you shall say to the children of Israel, 'I AM has sent me to you.''* (*Ex 3:14, NKJV*) God is saying that he lives in an eternal present. Our past is *now* to him, as is our future. This same idea is expressed in Revelation 4:8 when the seraphim (super angels) are praising God by saying, "*Holy, holy, holy, Lord God Almighty, Who was and is and is to come!*" (NKJV) We also see this when Paul wrote, "*In hope of eternal life which God, who cannot lie, promised before time began.*" (*Titus 1:2, NKJV*) Since there is no other being or god who lives out there, his knowledge of our future is 100 percent accurate, unmatched and unmatchable! Thus, *the fulfilling of prophecy is the signature of the God of the Bible.*

God Challenges the "Junk Prophets"

God even issues a challenge in Isaiah to fortune-tellers, mediums, sorcerers, the "prophets" of other holy books, and anyone else who thinks they have supernatural abilities. "'*Present your case,' says the LORD. 'Bring forth your strong reasons,' says the King of Jacob.*'" (*Is41:21, NKJV*) "*Show the things that are to come hereafter, that we may know that you are gods.*" (*Is41:23a, NKJV*) The Bible says that these other "gods" are really demons and that fortune-tellers, psychics, and the priests of idols get their supernatural abilities from them. Have you seen those ads for psychic hotlines? You may have noticed that the only way the psychics validate themselves is by telling people what has happened in their past or what is happening presently. This is because demonic spirits have access to that information. Their predictive powers, however, are severely limited because they do not have the ability to engage in time travel. This is why the God of the Bible can issue his challenge with such confidence.

These modern-day "junk prophets" still try to answer God's challenge in the grocery store tabloids every year. But, so far their record has been pretty miserable.

1. **Jean Dixon**: Someone figured out that Jean Dixon's predictions failed 95 percent of the time. And, I'm afraid that the other "holy books" that have dared to try their hand at prophecy have met with a similar fate.

2. **Joseph Smith**: For example, many of Joseph Smith's prophecies failed, including one that predicted that the American Civil War would draw England and all other nations into worldwide conflict (Doctrine and Covenants 87:1-3). Was he right?

3. **Muhammad**: Among Muhammad's false prophecies is one that states that the Antichrist[1] would appear seven months after the conquest of Constantinople, which occurred in AD 1453, and that Medina would be in ruins by then (*Sunan Abu Dawud*. Book 37. Numbers 4281-4283). But when Constantinople was taken, Medina was not in ruins, nor did the Antichrist show up seven months later. But in other statements he has the supposed Antichrist appearing during his lifetime (*Sahih al-Bukhari*, Volume 9, Book 92, Number 453 and others). Add to this confusion the fact that Muhammad predicted the end of the world would come five hundred years after his life, which would have been sometime between AD 1070 and AD 1132.[2] So, even though he hedged his bet with a shotgun approach to prophecy, none of them turned out right.

The Test of a Prophet

"So, just how forgiving are we supposed to be before labeling someone a false prophet?"

Well, Moses said that a prophet of God must have a perfect "batting average" or be put to death!

But the prophet who presumes to speak a word in My name, which I have not commanded him to speak, or who speaks in the name of other gods, that prophet shall die.' And if you say in your heart, 'How shall we know the word which the Lord has not spoken?' – when a prophet speaks in the name of the Lord, if the thing does not happen or come to pass, that is the thing which the Lord has not spoken; the prophet has spoken it presumptuously; you shall not be afraid of him (or have respect for anything else he has to say).
(Deut 18:20-22, NKJV)

"A prophet of God must have a perfect 'batting average' or be put to death."

Although many are yet to be fulfilled, not one Bible prophecy has ever been proven false, while hundreds, if not thousands, have come true.

"But, how do you know that the prophecies weren't written after the fact?"

The Old Testament was translated into Greek three hundred years before Christ, shortly after the time of Alexander the Great. So the books of the Old Testament had to have been in common usage and gained universal acceptance by then, thus proving that many of the Bible's prophecies were written centuries before their fulfillments.

PRESENTING FOR EVIDENCE, EXHIBIT 4: THE BIBLE'S FULFILLED PROPHECIES

Let's look at a sampling of some of the Bible's astonishing fulfilled prophecies.

Exhibit 4a: Fulfilled Prophecies About World History

Nebuchadnezzar's Nightmare

Daniel 2 contains an awesome prophecy about world history. King Nebuchadnezzar had a dream in which he saw a colossal statue. Daniel is required to tell the King what he dreamt; we pick up the story in verse 32:

> This image's head was of fine gold, its chest and arms of silver, its belly and thighs of bronze, its legs of iron, its feet partly of iron and partly of clay. You watched while a stone was cut out without hands, which struck the image on its feet of iron and clay, and broke them in pieces. Then the iron, the clay, the bronze, the silver, and the gold were crushed together, and became like chaff from the summer threshing floors; the wind carried them away so that no trace of them was found. And the stone that struck the image became a great mountain and filled the whole earth. (Dan 2:32-35, NKJV)

Daniel's Interpretation

In the interpretation that follows, Daniel tells the king that this dream is about history's four remaining world-dominating empires. The Babylonian Empire is said to be the head of gold. Then he goes on in verses 39-40:

> But after you shall arise another kingdom inferior to yours (fulfilled by the Medo-Persian Empire); then another, a third kingdom of bronze, which shall rule over all the earth (fulfilled by Alexander the Great). And the fourth kingdom shall be as strong as iron, inasmuch as iron breaks in pieces and shatters everything; and like iron that crushes, that kingdom will break in pieces and crush all the others (fulfilled by the Roman Empire). (Dan 2:39-40, NKJV)

Daniel's nightmare

Another prophecy, given in Daniel 8, gives us some details regarding the silver and bronze kingdoms.

> Then I lifted my eyes and saw, and there, standing beside the river, was a ram which had two horns, and the two horns were high; but one *was* higher than the other, and the higher *one* came up last. I saw the ram pushing westward, northward, and southward, so that no animal could withstand him; nor was there any that could deliver from his hand, but he did according to his will and became great. And as I was considering, suddenly a male goat came from the west, across the surface of the whole earth, without touching the ground; and the goat had a notable horn between his eyes. Then he came to the ram that had two horns, which I had seen standing beside the river, and ran at him with furious power. And I saw him confronting the ram; he was moved with rage against him, and attacked the ram, and broke his two horns. There was no power in the ram to withstand him, but he cast

him down to the ground and trampled him; and there was no one that could deliver the ram from his hand. Therefore the male goat grew very great; but when he became strong, the large horn was broken, and in place of it four notable ones came up toward the four winds of heaven. (Dan 8:3-8, NKJV)

Then the angel Gabriel interprets the vision beginning in verse 20:

The ram which you saw, having the two horns—they are the kings of Media and Persia. And the male goat is the kingdom of Greece. The large horn that is between its eyes is the first king (Alexander the Great). *As for the broken horn and the four that stood up in its place, four kingdoms shall arise out of that nation, but not with its power.* (Dan 8:20-22, NKJV)

This, of course, was fulfilled after Alexander's death, when his four generals split his kingdom amongst themselves. How could Daniel, writing hundreds of years earlier, have known this? Or was it just a wild guess?

The Big Bad Bully

Going back to Nebuchadnezzar's dream, we now know that the fourth empire was Rome, symbolized as both the strongest, by iron, and that it would remain the longest, being represented by the legs. Continuing from verse 41 in Daniel 2:

Whereas you saw the feet and toes, partly of potter's clay and partly of iron, the kingdom shall be divided; yet the strength of the iron shall be in it, just as you saw the iron mixed with ceramic clay. (Dan 2:41, NKJV)

So, the legs also foretell the split of the empire into eastern and western divisions. Some scholars even believe that the knees represent a shift from political to religious power that is fulfilled in the Catholic and Eastern Orthodox churches.

Today

The present is indicated by the feet, which are said to be iron mixed with clay. Verse 42 says:

> And as the toes of the feet were partly of iron and partly of clay, so the kingdom shall be partly strong and partly fragile. As you saw iron mixed with ceramic clay, they will mingle with the seed of men; but they will not adhere to one another, just as iron does not mix with clay. (Dan 2:42-43, NKJV)

We have inherited many parts of our modern society from ancient Rome, including our legal, educational, and military systems. Most of the countries of the world, however, remain independent. The United Nations is an attempt at world unity, but isn't this passage an accurate way to describe its efforts?

Back to the Future

How could Daniel have been so accurate in his description of world history? And since the foretelling of the empires of the past have come true, isn't it reasonable to assume that the rest will be fulfilled as well? Daniel goes on, in verse 44, to describe the future:

> And in the days of these kings the God of heaven will set up a kingdom which shall never be destroyed; and the kingdom shall not be left to other people; it shall break in pieces and consume all these kingdoms, and it shall stand forever. Inasmuch as you saw that the stone was cut out of the mountain without hands, and that it broke in pieces the iron, the bronze, the clay, the silver, and the gold–the great God has made known to the king what will come to pass after this. The dream is certain, and its interpretation is sure. (Dan 2:44-45, NKJV)

The ten toes represent a ten-nation confederacy from the remnants of the Roman Empire, five from each division, that will provide the political and military platform for the Antichrist (fake Messiah, see the glossary). His end is foretold by the stone that becomes a mountain and crushes him, which represents the second coming of Christ and the establishment of his kingdom on Earth.

Exhibit 4b: Fulfilled Prophecies About Individual Nations

1. **"Edom? Never heard of 'em."**: Unless you are familiar with the Old Testament, you have probably never heard of the country of Edom. Edom was a small nation south of Israel and the Dead Sea, which descended from Jacob's brother Esau. Its capital, Petra, was a fortress city built in a rock cliff that was virtually impregnable. It remains a tourist site to this day. Edom was a constant thorn in Israel's side. Among the many prophecies given against it is this one in Obadiah: *"And there shall not be any remaining of the house of Esau; for the Lord has spoken it."* (Obad 1:18b, KJV) This is why so few people have heard of 'em before...there aren't any more Edomites.

2. **Philistia**: The Philistines were another of Israel's many neighboring enemies. It was a small country located on the Mediterranean that included the area we now call the Gaza Strip. They were a strong and prosperous people up until AD 1200. But centuries before Christ Zephaniah prophesied this concerning them: *"And what sorrow awaits you Philistines who live along the coast and in the land of Canaan, for this judgment is against you, too! The Lord will destroy you until not one of you is left."* (Zeph 2:5, NLT) The Philistines, as a people, have also vanished—another fulfillment.

3. **Assyria**: Assyria was one of the strongest of the ancient empires, yet Zephaniah said, *"He will stretch out His hand against the North, and destroy Assyria; and will make Nineveh a des-*

olation, as dry as the wilderness." (Zeph 2:13, NKJV) This, and many other prophecies against it have been fulfilled.

4. **Egypt**: The Bible does not predict the total destruction of Egypt. In fact, it is mentioned as one of the players at the end of this age and is even included as a favored nation when Jesus returns (Is 19:23–24). But Ezekiel wrote that, at least during the present time, "*it shall be the lowliest of kingdoms.*" (Ezek 29:15, NKJV) Although it once was a leading world power, it is now weak, impoverished, and in political turmoil. How did Ezekiel know?

Exhibit 4c: Prophecies Concerning Cities

1. **Babylon**: Babylon was surrounded by walls 350 feet high and 87 feet thick. Yet Jeremiah wrote: "*The broad walls of Babylon shall be utterly broken, and her high gates shall be burned with fire.*" (Jer 51:58b, NKJV) Despite Saddam Hussein's attempt to rebuild the walls and the city before his death, most of it is still in ruins and can be seen to this day.

2. **Tyre**: One striking prophecy concerns the city of Tyre, an extremely wealthy seaport of the Phoenicians located in what is now Lebanon. There are seven elements of this prophecy contained in Ezekiel 26.

   ✓ **#1—Many nations, one after another, to attack:** "*Therefore thus says the Lord GOD: Behold, I am against you, O Tyre, and will cause many nations to come up against you, as the sea causes its waves to come up.*" (Ezek 26:3, NKJV)
   ✓ **#2—Made bare as a rock:** "*I will also scrape her dust from her, and make her like the top of a rock.*" (Ezek 26:4b, NKJV)
   ✓ **#3—For spreading of nets:** "*It shall be a place for spreading nets.*" (Ezek 26:5a, NKJV)
   ✓ **#4—Nebuchadnezzar to be the first wave:** "*Behold, I will bring against Tyre from the north Nebuchadnezzar king of*

Babylon, king of kings, with horses, with chariots, and with horsemen, and an army with many people." (Ezek 26:7, NKJV)

✓ **#5—Tyre to be thrown into the sea:** "They will break down your walls and destroy your pleasant houses; they will lay your stones, your timber, and your soil in the midst of the water." (Ezek 26:12b, NKJV)

✓ **#6—Never to be rebuilt:** "I will make you like the top of a rock; you shall be a place for spreading nets, and you shall never be rebuilt." (Ezek 26:14a, NKJV)

✓ **#7—Surrounding nations to surrender:** "Then all the princes of the sea will come down from their thrones." (Ezek 26:16a, NKJV)

All Seven Have Come True!

✓ **#4, check:** In 586 BC, Nebuchadnezzar laid siege to the mainland city of Tyre and ultimately destroyed it in 573 BC. However, there was a fortified island a few miles north and a half mile offshore to which many of the people fled. He didn't have a navy, so he just left them. The city was rebuilt and prospered again.

✓ **#1, 5 and 7, check:** But 254 years later, Alexander the Great also came against it—#1 fulfilled. And this time, when the people went to their island fortress, Alexander had his army take apart the mainland town and use the rubble to build a jetty 200 feet wide out to the island that still stands today—#5 fulfilled. When the island fell, the surrounding kings surrendered without a fight—#7 fulfilled.

✓ **#6, check:** Tyre persisted in varying degrees of strength until the Muslims destroyed it in AD 1291. The ancient mainland site has never been rebuilt.

✓ **#2 and 3, check and double check:** Regarding its present state, Philip Myers, writing in a history book for colleges and high schools, says "The larger part of the once great city is as bare as the top of a rock, a place where fishermen that still frequent the spot, spread their nets to dry."[3]

3. **Prophecies of destruction**: Many ancient cities were promised devastation in varying degrees, including Memphis, the capital of lower Egypt; Thebes, the capital of all Egypt; Ashkelon, Ekron, and Gaza, all cities of the Philistines; Bethel; Capernaum; Bethsaida; and many more, that have all been fulfilled in detail. How could the Bible's prophets have been so accurate?

More About the "Junk Prophets"

Now, I want you to notice that biblical prophecy is detailed and historically verifiable. In fact, that's God's whole point. If the prophecy isn't clear and fulfillment can't be proven historically, God isn't even going to waste his time. Bible prophecy was not written in vague generalities that could mean almost anything, like the stuff that, what I like to call the "junk prophets" have written. Take Nostradamus for example, the father of all tabloid junk prophets. His mumbo-jumbo is deliberately written so that fulfillment is in the eyes of the reader. One person thinks one of his prophecies means one thing, while someone else thinks it means something entirely different. There is absolutely *no way* to nail it down to anything concrete. Add to this the fact that various disciples of his have deliberately mistranslated some passages to suit the supposed fulfillments. God is not the author of this kind of confusion! He reminds me of some recording artists in the '70s, who, on occasion, would throw a bunch of meaningless words together in the studio just to get an album finished. And then they'd laugh at the hippies who would get high on drugs and try to discover the deeper meaning in them. Like these hippie artists, Nostradamus and the other junk prophets write for the guys on drugs. And I'm afraid that some of the other "sacred writings" fall into this same category. They are so vague that they are historically unverifiable. They only appeal to those who have no idea what real prophecy is and what it looks like.

But God has made certain that there is *no comparison* between this junk and his Holy Word!

Exhibit 4d: Fulfilled Prophecies Concerning Israel

1. **Abraham to father many nations**: Several early prophecies to Abraham promised that he would father many nations and that one nation in particular would bring blessing to all of mankind (See Gen 12:1-3, 13:14-17, 15:1-7, 15:18-21, 17:1-8). Today, Israelis, as well as many other Middle Eastern people, claim to be descendants of Abraham. And certainly Israel has blessed all nations by giving us the Bible and Jesus Christ.

2. **Israel to go into slavery**: Just before Israel took possession of the land that God had promised them, Moses recorded several prophecies that warned them about backsliding into idolatry. The penalty was that *"the LORD will bring a nation against you from afar...whose language you do not understand."* (Deut 28:49, NKJV) *"You shall beget sons and daughters, but they shall not be yours; for they shall go into captivity."* (Deut 28:41, NKJV)

   ✓ **Seventy years in Babylon:** Centuries later, Isaiah added that this captivity would be at the hand of the Babylonians, who, at the time of his writing, were only a small city-state. *"And they shall take away some of your sons who will descend from you, whom you will beget; and they shall be eunuchs in the palace of the king of Babylon."* (Is 39:7, NKJV) Jeremiah then added that Israel would, *"serve the king of Babylon for seventy years."* (Jer 25:11b, NKJV)

   ✓ **The prophecy fulfilled:** Nebuchadnezzar waged three campaigns against Jerusalem as various vassal kings kept rebelling against him. Finally, in 587 BC, he destroyed both the wall and Solomon's temple, taking most of the people captive to Babylon, just as the prophets predicted.

✓ **Released by Cyrus:** Two hundred years earlier, while Jerusalem's wall and the temple were still standing, Isaiah wrote,

> Who says of Cyrus, He is My shepherd, and he shall perform all My pleasure, saying to Jerusalem, "You shall be built," and to the temple, "Your foundation shall be laid." (Is 44:28, NKJV).... "Thus says the LORD to His anointed, to Cyrus.... For Jacob My servant's sake, and Israel My elect, I have even called you by your name; I have named you, though you have not known Me." (Is 45:1a, and 4, NKJV)

Seventy years after their captivity began, a Persian king named Cyrus allowed the Jews to return and rebuild their temple. And some years later, Ezra led another migration of Jews back to their homeland. Still later, Nehemiah was also allowed to go back and rebuild the wall and the rest of the city.

3. **Israel to be scattered throughout the world:** This captivity was by one nation, but Moses also wrote that if they didn't learn their lesson the first time, "then the LORD will scatter you among all peoples, from one end of the earth to the other." (Deut 28:64a, NKJV)

✓ **The Fulfillment:** In AD 70, the Jews rebelled against Rome, and Titus Vespasian took Jerusalem in one of the bloodiest sieges in history. The Jews that remained were scattered throughout the Roman Empire to keep them from rebelling again.

✓ **The Return of Israel:** But Moses also wrote, "the LORD your God will bring you back from captivity, and have compassion on you and gather you again from all the nations where the

Lord your God has scattered you." (*Deut 30:3, NKJV*) *"Then the LORD your God will bring you to the land which your fathers possessed and you shall possess it."* (*Deut 30:5a, NKJV*) On May 14, 1948, Israel was gathered to her land and once again proclaimed her independence. It is unprecedented in all of history that a people could survive for nearly two thousand years without a homeland and still retain their national identity!

Exhibit 4e: Fulfilled Prophecies About the Jewish Messiah

1. **Prophecies fulfilled by Jesus's first coming:** Here are just a few of nearly three hundred:

   ✓ **The Messiah's Lineage** is predicted throughout the Old Testament and verified in the New. Matthew 1:1-17 proves that Jesus is the legal heir to the throne of David through Solomon to Joseph, being his adopted son. But there was an evil king, Jeconiah, in that line whose descendants God cursed. Luke 3:23-38, on the other hand, records Jesus's genealogy to David, then through another son, Nathan to Mary, being the wife of Joseph. Thus, Jesus is both the blood descendant of King David by Mary and has the legal right to the throne of David by Joseph. Some have argued that one of Joseph's other sons should actually be heir to the crown. But that point is made mute by the fact that *all* of Jesus's brothers and their descendants became Christians after His resurrection.[4] This means that the line to the throne of David leads to and ends with Jesus Christ! Therefore, Jesus is the Jewish Messiah, and there is no other alternative!

✓ **His birthplace:** *"But you, Bethlehem Ephrathah, though you are little among the thousands of Judah, yet out of you shall come forth to Me the One to be Ruler in Israel, Whose goings forth are from of old, from everlasting."* (Mic 5:2, NKJV)

✓ **The virgin birth** (see glossary): *"Therefore the Lord Himself will give you a sign: Behold, the virgin shall conceive and bear a Son, and shall call His name Immanuel."* (Is 7:14, NKJV)

✓ **John the Baptist:** *"The voice of one crying in the wilderness: 'Prepare the way of the Lord; make straight in the desert a highway for our God.'"* (Is 40:3, NKJV)

✓ **He would be rejected:** *"He is despised and rejected by men, a Man of sorrows and acquainted with grief. And we hid, as it were, our faces from Him; He was despised, and we did not esteem Him."* (Is 53:3, NKJV)

✓ **Palm Sunday:** *"Rejoice greatly, O daughter of Zion! Shout, O daughter of Jerusalem! Behold, your King is coming to you; He is just and having salvation, lowly and riding on a donkey, a colt, the foal of a donkey."* (Zech 9:9, NKJV)

✓ **His betrayal:** *"Even my own familiar friend in whom I trusted, who ate my bread, has lifted up his heel against me."* (Ps 41:9, NKJV) *"And the Lord said to me, 'Throw it to the potter' – that princely price they set on me. So I took the thirty pieces of silver and threw them into the house of the Lord for the potter."* (Zech 11:13, NKJV) (See Matt 27:3-10)

✓ **His scourging:** *"I gave My back to those who struck Me, and My cheeks to those who plucked out the beard; I did not hide My face from shame and spitting."* (Is 50:6, NKJV)

✓ **The piercing of his hands and feet:** *"For dogs have surrounded Me; the congregation of the wicked has enclosed Me. They pierced My hands and My feet."* (Ps 22:16, NKJV) Incidently, this prophecy was written hundreds of years before the Persians invented crucifixion.

✓ **His Resurrection:** *"For you will not leave my soul among the dead or allow your holy one to rot in the grave."* (Ps 16:10, NLT)

2. **The day of his coming**: But probably the most astounding prophecy about Jesus is one in Daniel that foretells the exact day of his coming to Israel as her king.

> Know therefore and understand, that from the going forth of the command to restore and build Jerusalem until Messiah the Prince, there shall be seven weeks and sixty-two weeks; the street shall be built again, and the wall, even in troublesome times. And after the sixty-two weeks Messiah shall be cut off, but not for Himself; and the people of the prince who is to come shall destroy the city and the sanctuary. The end of it shall be with a flood, and till the end of the war desolations are determined. (Dan 9:25-26, NKJV)

The Hebrew word which is translated, "weeks", means a seven-year period of time, like our word *decade* means a ten-year period in English. Verse 25 says that there will be sixty-nine of these "weeks" of years between the issuing of the command to rebuild the city and the coming of the Messiah. The Jews used a 360-day calendar at that time.[5] This comes out to precisely 173,880 days. Artaxerxes Longimanus gave Nehemiah the command to rebuild the wall and city on March 14, 445 BC. When we count down 173,880 days it brings us to April 6, AD 32. What happened on this day?

Luke 3:1 tells us that Jesus was baptized in the fifteenth year of Tiberius Caesar, who was crowned on August 19, AD 14. His fourteen-year anniversary was August 19, AD 28, which ended that year and began his fifteenth year. Most Bible scholars believe that Jesus's baptism took place in the fall, which would make it the fall of AD 28. We also know that his ministry covered four Passovers. The first would have been in the spring of AD 29, and the last, the day of his crucifixion, would have been April 10, AD 32. The Sunday prior would have been April 6, AD 32, which was Palm

Sunday. This was the day that this carpenter from Nazareth rode into Jerusalem on a donkey while the crowds waived palm branches and cried, *"Hosanna! (Save now!) Blessed is He who comes in the name of the Lord!"* (Mark, 11:9, NKJV) By using these Old Testament phrases, the people were hailing Jesus as their Messiah and king. The people had tried to make him their king on several other occasions, but Jesus always refused. This was the first time that he allowed them to do this, and it was the precise day predicted by Daniel centuries before. Coincidence?

3. **Messiah to be executed:** You will remember back in Daniel 9:26 it says that *"Messiah will be cut off"*. This is a judicial term in Hebrew, meaning that he was to be executed for some kind of crime. However, the next phrase states, *"but not for Himself."* For whom, then, was Messiah to be executed? We find the answer in another amazing prophecy concerning the Messiah in Isaiah 53.

> *Yet it was our weaknesses he carried; it was our sorrows that weighed him down. And we thought his troubles were a punishment from God, a punishment for his own sins! But he was pierced for our rebellion, crushed for our sins. He was beaten so we could be whole. He was whipped so we could be healed. All of us, like sheep, have strayed away. We have left God's paths to follow our own. Yet the Lord laid on him the sins of us all. He was oppressed and treated harshly, yet he never said a word. He was led like a lamb to the slaughter. And as a sheep is silent before the shearers, he did not open his mouth. Unjustly condemned, he was led away. No one cared that he died without descendants, that his life was cut short in midstream. But he was struck down for the rebellion of my people. He had done no wrong and had never deceived anyone. But he was buried like a criminal; he was put in a rich man's grave. But it was the Lord's good plan to crush him and cause him grief. Yet when his life is*

made an offering for sin, he will have many descendants. He will enjoy a long life, and the Lord's good plan will prosper in his hands. When he sees all that is accomplished by his anguish, he will be satisfied. And because of his experience, my righteous servant will make it possible for many to be counted righteous, for he will bear all their sins. I will give him the honors of a victorious soldier, because he exposed himself to death. He was counted among the rebels. He bore the sins of many and interceded for rebels. (Is 53:4-12, NLT)

This is confirmed by Jesus as he states his mission very clearly in the gospel of John.

For God so loved the world that he gave (a sacrificial term) his only and unique Son, so that everyone who trusts in him may have eternal life, instead of being utterly destroyed. For God did not send the Son into the world to judge the world, but rather so that through him, the world might be saved. Those who trust in him are not judged; those who do not trust have been judged already, in that they have not trusted in the one who is God's only and unique Son. (Jn 3:16-18, CJB)

The apostle John gives us this eyewitness account of an event that took place just a few years before Daniel's prophecy of Palm Sunday was fulfilled: "*The next day John (the Baptist) saw Jesus coming toward him, and said, "Behold! The Lamb (an animal of sacrifice) of God who takes away the sin of the world!"* (Jn 1:29, NKJV)

The fulfillment of these prophecies leaves little doubt as to the mission and identity of the Messiah. Jesus came from his Father with the intention of offering Himself as a sacrifice for our sins. God's wrath against all of our sin was poured out on his own Son so that he could show *us* mercy and offer *us* forgiveness. He was "cut off" for your sake and mine.

THE EVIDENCE IS IN

Chance? Consider the odds.

While it's true that a con man could possibly make arrangements to satisfy a few of these prophecies, the vast majority are dependent on conditions being achieved by outside influences. Back in 1958, Dr. Peter Stoner published a book titled *Science Speaks*,[6] in which he ran a number of now famous probability statistics on the fulfillment of a variety of Bible prophecies. He figured that the odds of someone fulfilling just eight of these nearly three hundred prophecies, which were fulfilled by Jesus, to be a staggering 1 in 10^{17} (1 with 17 zeros after it); sixteen fulfillments would be 1 in 10^{45}; forty eight takes it up to 1 in 10^{157}. That's a pretty big number considering scientists have estimated the number of electrons, protons and neutrons in the known universe to be a mere 10^{80}.[7] So, is chance the best explanation for this? I hardly think so. Dr. Stoner makes this comment as he closes his chapter on prophecy, "Any man who rejects Christ as the Son of God is rejecting a fact proved perhaps more absolutely than any other fact in the world."[8]

So once again, after all of the other "holy books" are put to the test of prophecy and their records are compared with the Bible's—it's not even close!

The Bible and Science

CHECK IT OUT

The next area of evidence supporting the Bible's divine origin is that of the Bible and science. I'm going to divide this chapter into three parts, each with its own purpose. The reason is that the biggest scientific objection to the Bible being the truth about anything is the theory of evolution, which has gained total world domination status. So I'm going to devote one section to an attempt to remove evolutionary theory as a stumbling block to someone believing the Bible. Charles Darwin, however, never officially dealt with the origin of life. So, we will examine that in the last part of this chapter. This will provide what is, perhaps, the strongest scientific proof of the existence of God. In the first section, we will look at the astonishing scientific accuracy of the Bible's description of our universe.

Note to rocket scientists: You rocket scientists need to know that I have chosen some *very recent* discoveries in order to be as current as possible. Some of these are so recent that many in the scientific community may not be fully aware that these things have actually been *proven as fact*. So if you have a scientific background and are not aware of some of these findings, I ask you to please do the research before throwing me under the bus. Thanks.

Note to traditional creationists: Also, for those who have heard or read material by creationist ministries on the "big bang" and evolution theories, you should know that I am taking a different approach in some areas with brand new and different data. These very recent discoveries have made some of the traditional creationist arguments obsolete. So I urge you to do the research as well before you throw me out in favor of your favorite ministry or speaker. After all, we are on the same team.

Additionally, we are about to discuss the big bang in somewhat favorable terms. But, this does not mean that I believe in the billions-of-years thing. There are simply some very recent discoveries that make a modified big bang a powerful ally of the biblical account of creation. I actually see creation as more of a carefully engineered "installation" rather than a random explosion, but since the common term in our society is "big bang," I will use it for communication's sake. That being said, I'm going to ask you to consider, with me, the "Big ~~Bang~~ Installation" in a whole new light.

The Nature of Science

Before we get into the "meat" of this chapter, however, we need to understand some things about the nature of science itself. Many people hold it up as if it were some kind of all-knowing god. They think that if it's not scientific it can't be true. But I want you to consider the following facts about the field of science, which most true scientists fully agree with.

1. **The turnover of truth**: First, scientific facts change, sometimes rapidly and drastically. It should really come as no surprise that as scientific knowledge advances, things that we thought were true yesterday, turn out to be false or

obsolete today. There are many examples of scientific facts that have been dealt their kryptonite and fallen into oblivion over the years: the flat Earth idea gave way to a sphere; the Earth-centered model of the solar system yielded to the sun-centered one; the velocity of light was thought to be infinite until Roemer and Bradley measured it; in 1959 most scientists believed that the universe was infinitely old and that there was no such thing as a big bang; living cells were once thought to be nothing but bags of jelly; and we could go on and on.

But the main problem is that many of us non-rocket-scientists make the mistake of assuming that scientific advances are always additive. That is, we think that old facts don't change, and new facts are merely added to the old ones. But this is not the case. After fifty years, only 25 percent of the scientific articles written by super-scientists on hepatitis and cirrhosis are still considered fully factual.[1] And a similar analysis can be made on virtually every other scientific subject. In fact, I became a victim of this while writing this book. The initial figure I had that science used to measure the expansion of the universe changed before I could finish. I had to go back and update all of my associated numbers. In recent years this turnover of scientific "truth for now" has accelerated exponentially, especially when applied to technology. Advancements are so fast that your new computer, smart phone, or tablet is obsolete before you even get it out the box. So, the bedrock of science is not just shifting sand—it's a full blown avalanche!

2. **The "box men" and their boxes**: Secondly, the definition of science varies and changes as well. There is a little-known group of super-scientists called "Philosophers of Science" that try to define boundaries between science and pseudo-science, and between the various fields of science, such as biology, geology, chemistry, etc. Think of them as box-makers. They have one big box called science with a bunch of

smaller boxes inside. The problem is that they are finding significant areas that overlap: microbiology involves chemistry and botany; paleontology involves geology and vice versa. They even discover truth that doesn't fit in any scientific box at all, so they have to make a new one. This was the case with psychology some years back. So there are things that are not considered science now that will be considered a new branch of science in the future. One philosopher defines the boxes one way and another defines them in a different way. This confusion makes the boxes kinda fuzzy and full of cracks that allow things to fall through.

- ✓ **All hail the "Empirical Method!"** So the empirical method can no longer be used as the standard that determines what is and what is not scientific. It has been defined as: (1) watch something; (2) look for patterns and figure out how to measure it, then describe it; (3) propose rules or a set of truths about what was seen; and (4) test the rules or truths by watching some more and see if anyone else has seen the same thing. Boiling it down, you've probably heard the phrase, "knowledge gained through observation and experimentation."
- ✓ **Oops! Now what?** The problem is that not all fields of science can use this method. The historical wings of science, like geology for example, cannot go back in time to watch events that happened in the past. So, they have to use different techniques altogether. (I will have more to say about this when we get to the section on evolution.) Scientists themselves are now expressing dismay at their failure to clearly define what science is. Dr. Stephen Meyer wrote:

> This diversity of methods has doomed attempts
> to find a single definition (or set of criteria) that
> accurately characterizes all types of science by

reference to their methodological practices. Thus, philosophers of science now talk openly about the "demise" of attempts to demarcate or define science by reference to a single set of methods.[2]

This sentiment is echoed by Philip Kitcher.

For the past half-century, philosophers have tried and failed to produce a precise account of the distinction between science and pseudo-science. We cannot seem to articulate that essential demarcation.[3]

3. **Shifting sand and fuzzy boxes**: So, as wonderful as it is, science is still defined by imperfect men who can't agree on its definition. And, contrary to popular opinion, they haven't even figured out all the rules yet. Not only are the definitions of their "boxes" dynamic and changing, the "truth for now" inside them is also dynamic and changing. No matter how much scientific "truth for now" is uncovered, it's really just a small part of the total picture and may not even last for a week. Science isn't even close to knowing everything, but our Creator does know everything pertaining to science, and he said, *"I am the Lord, I do not change."* (Mal 3:6, NKJV) The Bible *is* "solid bedrock" when it comes to its scientific statements. And, as we are about to see, new discoveries often just serve to prove what the Bible has been saying all along.

Ancient Airliners?

To emphasize the significance of what we will be talking about, I have included an illustration used by Mark Eastman and Chuck Missler in their book, *The Creator From Beyond Time and Space.*

> Imagine yourself on an archeological expedition in the Dead Sea region of Israel during which an absolutely astonishing discovery is made. In a recently discovered cave you find an ancient papyrus containing a complete set of plans which accurately describes the structure and function ... of a Boeing 747!... Would you be impressed?
>
> You turn the scrolls over to ancient manuscript experts who conclude that the scrolls were written in Hebrew nearly 2,200 years ago! Skeptical, you transfer the scrolls to the local university radiometric dating lab. The results are the same. The ink and the papyri are found to be from before the time of Christ!
>
> The press immediately reports the story and the academic community begins their analysis. Some assert that an advanced civilization of extraterrestrials took the plans back in time and planted them in the caves. The skeptics assert that the whole thing is an elaborate hoax. However, the evidence is clear. The scrolls are ancient. Still others declare that a supernatural transcendent being gave this twentieth-century scientific knowledge to the ancient scribes who recorded it, only to be found centuries later.
>
> Each of these analyses share a common thread. Each theorist knows that ancient scribes could possess no knowledge of 747s unless they were instructed by someone with twentieth-century scientific and engineering know-how.[4]

This may seem pretty bizarre, but it demonstrates the perplexing nature of the scientific statements made in the Bible. The other worldly knowledge that the Bible's authors demonstrate could only have come to them in one of two ways: either they had some kind of time machine, or they got their information directly from our all-knowing, unchanging Creator.

THE BIBLE AND COSMOLOGY

So, fasten your seat belts as we take a peek at the universe through the eyes of the Bible. In this section I want to, first, examine its description of the cosmos; secondly, the "settings" that make life possible; and finally, the limits of our universe.

Presenting for Evidence, Exhibit 5:
The Bible Accurately Describes Our Universe

Exhibit 5a: The Framework of Our Environment
Our entire universe exists within a frame-like structure that we call space and time. Within this framework, there is stuff, which scientists call matter. Things happen to this stuff, which, they tell us, requires energy. Scientists have also discovered that each of these four things are joined to each other in such a way that they can't exist by themselves. So they made up the word *continuum* to describe it. So, that's what they are talking about when you hear the term space-time continuum.

Incredibly, these general facts, as well as a host of clues pointing to fascinating details, are described accurately in the first verses of the Bible, which were penned by Moses thousands of years before man had any scientific knowledge about this framework.

> In the beginning God created the heavens and the earth. The
> earth was without form, and void; and darkness was on the

face of the deep. And the Spirit of God was hovering over the face of the waters. Then God said, 'Let there be light'; and there was light. And God saw the light, that it was good; and God divided the light from the darkness. God called the light Day, and the darkness He called Night. So the evening and the morning were the first day. (Gen 1:1-5, NKJV)

Now, the ancient Hebrews did not have a word for universe. When they wanted to make a sweeping reference to all of creation they would use the phrase, "the heavens and the earth." This seems pretty obvious, but there's a lot more.

Exhibit 5b: Elastic Space?

The first important point that we have to make about this framework is that scientists have proven that it has expanded away from a single point. You guessed it, the big bang. There is some discussion, now, as to whether it is still expanding. Some scientists see evidence that it has stopped and is now in an oscillation mode. But, at least they all agree that it expanded to its present size. And this is actually consistent with what the Bible teaches. There are no less than seventeen references to the fact that God "stretches (or stretched) out the heavens" (2Sam 22:10, Job 9:8, 26:7, 37:18, Ps 18:9, 104:2, 144:5, Is 40:22, 42:5, 44:24, 45:12, 48:13, 51:13, Jer 10:12, 51:15, Ez 1:22, and Zech 12:1).

Exhibit 5c: No Time, No Space, No Stuff

The second point is that this stretching or expansion includes time itself, because time and space are interconnected. Therefore, the universe must have had a beginning, just as the Bible says. In 1970, a group of British astrophysicists used Einstein's equations to prove that space and time did not even exist before this beginning! Of course, most scientists can't bring themselves to admit that this proves creation, so the big bang exploded onto the scene.

The eleventh-century Jewish rabbi, Rashi, in his commentary on Genesis, tells us that this insight regarding time is also stated in the first few verses of the creation account. Most English Bibles actually mistranslate verse 5 to read, "the first day." But Young's Literal Translation accurately renders the Hebrew, *"And there is an evening, and there is a morning–day one."* (Gen 1:5, YLT) Compare this to the end of verse 8 where we read, *"–day second."* (Gen 1:8b, YLT) The difference is that "day one" is absolute, while "day second" is comparatave. Rashi explains that "day one comes to teach us that time is created."[5]

There are several other places in the Bible that make this very clear. For example, Paul speaks of God's grace, *"which was given to us in Christ Jesus before time began."* (2Tim 1:9b, NKJV) He uses this phrase here and in Titus 1:2. This sheds a whole new light on what the Bible means by the term, "in the beginning," doesn't it?

Exhibit 5d: Time's Up

1. **Time and the stretch (expansion) factor**: Hang on, we're going to stretch our brains even further. The Bible tells us that creation took place in six days, and the rest of history until now is just under six thousand years. Scientists, of course, say that the universe is somewhere around fourteen billion years old.

   "Well, a difference as great as that can't be reconciled, can it?"

   Or can it? Scientists have been able to measure the expansion of the universe and reduce it to mathematical terms. The expansion factor is 900 billion, which affects both space and time. That means that a pulse of light lasting one second leaving that first moment of creation would not look to us like one second when it arrived here.

   "Why not?"

Because it would be stretched on its journey by the factor of 900 billion. For example, if you were to take a bungee cord and make two marks on it that are one inch apart. Then stretch it out to its maximum length and measure the distance between the marks again. They would be a lot farther apart than the one inch you started with, wouldn't they? That's because as the cord was stretched, the distance between the marks was stretched along with it. Applying our bungee cord example to our one-second pulse of light, we have to multiply one second by 900 billion. So, by the time it gets to us it would look like a stream of light lasting 900 billion seconds or 28,519 years.

Now translate that into full 24-hour days and here's what you come up with. We will assume that the expansion of the first six days brought the universe to near its present size. This means that the six days of creation would look to us like 14 billion years.[6] Sweet! So, the Bible is right and science just forgot about its own expansion factor. Of course this is probably selective forgetfulness since six thousand years doesn't allow enough time for anything to evolve. Uh-oh, is evolution getting some kryptonite? But wait, there's more.

2. **Breaking News: Light puts on its brakes!** There is now another consideration that validates the figures above, and that is the recently confirmed discovery that light has been slowing down. The speed of light is one of the values used in the formulas that determine the age of the cosmos. Barry Setterfield, an Australian physicist, was one of the first to notice that 164 measurements of the velocity of light over 320 years revealed a significant loss of speed. The rate of loss has been confirmed by the recent discovery that atomic clocks are also slowing down when compared to orbital clocks. Scientists have compared some 1,228 data points over 4,550 years to confirm this. Other confirmations come from the measurements of other speed-of-light depend-

ent formulas, which include 639 values. These are much too technical and beyond the scope of this book to tackle here. But resources are suggested later for you rocket scientists. All of these measurements indicate that light's slowdown is following a parabolic curve that made it ten million times faster before 3,000 BC. When scientists corrected atomic time, which is speed-of-light dependent, using this curve they were astonished to find that the universe is less than ten thousand orbital years old, just as the Bible has said all along![7] This also has an impact on the methods used to date rocks and fossils, which we will get into later. Of course there is a lot of pushback and fit-throwing denial from evolutionists—screaming, name calling, jumping up and down, throwing things, you name it, because this means that evolution never had the time it needed to work its magic. Maybe this *is* evolution's kryptonite! Stay tuned. (Do an Internet search for "light slowing down," and you'll find an abundance of articles by both creationists and secular scientists.)

Exhibit 5e: The Original Plasma

Genesis 1:2a reads, *"The earth was without form, and void."* (NKJV) The twelfth century Rabbi, Maimonides makes an interesting observation about the terms used to describe God's work on the first day. He admitted that they didn't have words to accurately relay the truth of what was happening. He said that the true meaning may not be the technical definition. So at this point in creation, the word *earth* may not be referring to the dirt clod we know and love, but to its building blocks—matter. Scientists tell us that very early during the big bang, or beginning, there weren't even atoms yet. Atoms are made of electrons, protons, and neutrons; and they are made of an even smaller array of sub-atomic particles such as quarks, gluons, and others. These particles were in the state of a super-heated plasma. A plasma occurs when a gas gets so hot that electrons break free from their orbits. The gas is then said to be ionized or in the state of plasma. You watch a plasma every day if you have one of those plasma TVs. Plasma is also in fluorescent light bulbs. Nevertheless, this plasma was so hot that the protons and neutrons couldn't even stay together. So, without form and void would be an understatement!

Exhibit 5f: The Special Forces

"Okay, so now we've got time, space, and plasma in this 'continuum' thing. What's next?"

Well, we're almost ready to add energy and let things start happening. But before we do that there has to be some regulating forces to manage it, otherwise there would be nothing but chaos. Scientists have discovered four force fields that do just that. They are gravity, the electromagnetic force, a strong nuclear force, and a weak nuclear force. It is remarkable that, not only does the Bible recognize these forces, it also explains their origin.

1. **Gravity**: Scientists tell us that gravity is the result of matter warping the fabric of space-time. (Ha ha ha ha! Oops, sorry, my brain just got warped there for a second.) Gravity is the force responsible for planetary orbits, like how the Earth and other planets in our solar system go around the sun. It would seem like the strongest of all the forces, but it is actually the weakest by a large margin.

   At a time when the ancient cultures and religions were describing the Earth as being flat and held up on the backs of elephants, turtles, or giants, Job confidently asserts, *"He stretches out the north over empty space, and hangs the earth on nothing."* (Job 26:7, NASB) Many Bible scholars believe Job to be the oldest book in the Bible. So, how did Job know about gravity and deep space? An ancient time machine maybe?

2. **Electromagnetism**: The Bible acknowledges the electromagnetic force by the simple mention of light, which is

the visible part of it. It is actually many times stronger than gravity, as we will see in a minute.

3. **The strong nuclear force**: Protons repel each other. (Kinda like the way I repelled girls in school.) This force is so powerful that if a teaspoon full of protons were placed on both the North Pole and South Pole, at that distance, ten thousand pounds would have to be set on top of each one to keep them in place. Unleashing that repelling force is what makes the explosion of an atom bomb. The strong force is what keeps the protons and neutrons tucked into the nucleus of an atom. It is the strongest of all of the force fields, yet only works inside the atom.

4. **The weak nuclear force**: The weak force, on the other hand, works on an even smaller scale. It works on the particles that make up the protons and neutrons in atoms. It's the force responsible for nuclear reactions like fission and fusion, as well as radioactive decay.

5. **The Bible and nuclear forces**: Paul mentions nuclear forces in Colossians. *"In him all things hold together."* (Col 1:17b, NIV) How did Paul know that things need to be held together? Another obvious reference to these forces is in the book of Hebrews, where it says that God *"upholds all things by the word of His power."* (Heb 1:3b, NASB) So, not only does the Bible state the need for nuclear forces, but also declares that they are God's power at work.

Exhibit 5g: Black Fire or Dark Energy

Continuing in verse 2 of Genesis 1, we read, *"And darkness was on the face of the deep."* (Gen 1:2b, NKJV) Since there wasn't light at this point, the Talmud tells us that the word *darkness* in verse 2 doesn't mean darkness the way we think of it. Instead, it says it means "black fire." The Talmud goes on to define it as energy so strong you can't see it.[8] Incredibly, science is just now catching up! Scientists have recently made a fascinating discovery that they call dark energy or zero-point energy. But bear with me, I have to set the stage for this one.

1. **Space, a pixelated grid?** Now, you would think that if you have a line a foot long that you could, theoretically, keep dividing it in half to infinity. At least that's what my geometry teacher said. But physicists have discovered that this is not the case in our universe.

   "Now wait a minute! What you talkin' 'bout?"

   Quantum physics is based on the shocking reality that everything is quantized, that is, divided up into super tiny units, kinda like the hard drive of a computer. A guy named Max Planck found out what the smallest limits of time, space, and other things are. They are called Planck's constants. He found that the limit in length is 10-33cm, which is so small it's almost nothing. And the time limit is 10-43 seconds. So, space-time is really composed of sub-microscopic units that make up a pixelated grid, of sorts. These units are so small that they can hold the tiniest pieces of pieces of atoms.

   A two-dimensional example of this grid would be the screen on your computer monitor or digital TV. It's made up of tiny squares called pixels. They are the little dots that change colors and make the pictures. Expanding that out to the three dimensions of space you might be able to imagine an array of tiny cubes that are the fabric in which we and all of the galaxies and stars move around in. Time then makes it a four-dimensional grid, which is a little hard for my pea brain to handle, but is true nonetheless.

2. **Dark or zero-point energy**[9]: This four-dimensional pixelated grid extends through the vacuum of empty space, which scientists have discovered isn't really empty at all. Each unit in this grid has properties that allow molecules of matter and forms of energy to travel around from one pixel to another and also allow the force fields to work on

matter and energy. One of these properties is called zero-point energy (ZPE for short). It is a constant amount of electromagnetic power native to every pixel in the space-time grid throughout the entire universe. This power is what holds electrons in their orbits and prevents them from spinning out of control. So this power had to be installed in the cosmos and turned on before atoms could even form.

Scientists call it zero-point energy because as they were experimenting with an empty vacuum in the laboratory they noticed that they were still getting heat measurements. So, they turned the thermostat down to absolute zero degrees Kelvin or -400 degrees Fahrenheit. To their astonishment, they were still getting enormous electromagnetic energy readings. Thus, ZPE was discovered.

Going back to your digital TV screen, the pixels are there but aren't active until the power is turned on. Once the power is on, each pixel is plugged in and ready for the show. Well, the same is true of our universe. It has literally been powered on, just like a big TV or computer screen! And guess who flipped the power switch?

It seems that the word *deep* in verse 2 might very well be referring to this space-time grid. So, let's review the first part of verse 2: *"The earth* (ionized sub-atomic particles) *was without form, and void* (unable to form atoms or molecules yet); *and darkness* (black fire or ZPE) *was* (installed) *on the face of the deep* (the space-time grid)." If it were to be written in modern scientific terms only, it might read, "The ionized sub-atomic particles were unable to form atoms or molecules yet. So God installed the zero-point energy in the space-time grid." Wow! That sounds wild, doesn't it?! (And I know I've got some Bible teachers coming unglued about now! Hey guys, I really am saved...really.)

Exhibit 5h: Matter Matters

1. **A cosmic egg?** The few scientists that still believe in an eternal universe call the original blob of matter the cosmic egg and claim that it is infinitely old. (I wonder if they believe in a "cosmic chicken?") I'll have more to say about this "egg" later. But what I want to bring up here is that the only other choice for the existence of stuff is that it was created from nothing along with space and time.

2. **Two models for matter and the cosmos—gravity vs plasma:** Plasma physicists have been quietly laboring in the shadows of their more popular and numerous gravity-model counterparts for decades, often having to endure scorn and mockery. One of the reasons has been that gravity is much easier to understand for the public and the politicians that fund scientific research. But the gravity-model of cosmology has been consistently coming up short of answers. There's just not enough of it to shape galaxies, let alone give birth to them. They are so desperate to find enough gravity that they dreamed up something they call dark matter, which is purely theoretical stuff for which there is no evidence. Plasma cosmology, on the other hand, is now providing a host of answers where gravity, by itself, has struck out. And this should make creationist ministries excited because it provides many of the very answers that have been missing in their models!

3. **The creative power of plasma:**[10] The original plasma was, at first, evenly dispersed throughout the small but expanding universe. It was like a giant, electrically charged, super-thick fog. Plasma in this state, at the unimaginably high temperatures that existed, does not let light escape. Another property of plasma in this state is that sound waves travel incredibly fast, at almost 60 percent of the speed of light! Both sound waves and electromagnetic forces cause plasma to react in breathtaking ways. Gravity's influence was very

minimal at this stage because of the extremely small size of the particles. The expansion eventually caused the plasma to cool and the black-fire ZPE to strengthen to the point that atoms were finally allowed to form. Lab experiments have proven that if even 1 percent of the atoms in a gas are ionized, the entire cloud will behave as if it were 100 percent plasma. As soon as neutral atoms made up a majority of the cloud, the plasma fog began clearing and light was able to pierce the darkness for the first time. Scientists have actually detected the remnants of the original plasma fog in the farthest reaches of space. They call it the Cosmic Microwave Background Radiation (CMBR).

4. **The heavy-elements problem**: According to the gravity guys, the plasma cloud eventually became a gas made up of 77 percent hydrogen and 23 percent helium. They say that the heavier elements, such as iron, had to be formed in the fusion furnaces inside of stars. Then, when the star dies and explodes into a supernova, all of the heavy elements it had produced are flung into space where gravity pulls them into another star or planet. But there are a couple of serious problems with this scenario.

First, this process takes an enormous amount of time—far more time than is available—even if the universe was fourteen billion orbital years old. But, as astronomers look into deep space and back in time to some of the earliest moments in the cosmos, they see iron and other heavy elements in the gas clouds around some of the oldest quasars and galaxies. In fact, the entire universe contains the same abundance of heavy elements that we see in our own Milky Way galaxy. The gravity guys have no explanation for this.

Second, they need gas and dust clouds to shrink into stars. But, as a gas cloud shrinks it heats up and tries to expand again. The heavy elements are actually needed to radiate the heat out of the shrinking cloud so it will continue to shrink.

These problems, however, are easily overcome by the plasma model. Ed Boudreaux, emeritus professor of chemistry at University of New Orleans, Louisiana has stated that, at temperatures of ten to twenty billion degrees, which existed early in the universe's expansion, all of the elements, in their known quantities throughout the universe, could have been created by electromagnetic forces working on plasma in about half an hour. There is just one condition that must be met before this could happen. The plasma cannot be made up of hydrogen and helium as the traditional big bang gravity guys insist. Instead, it must be made of the elements of water (H_2O), just as stated in Genesis 1:2c. *"And the Spirit of God was hovering over the face of the waters."* (NKJV)

5. **The problem of galaxy formation**: Research on the CMBR has revealed patterns that were produced by sound waves. Young's Literal Translation brings out something interesting in verse 2. It says, *"The Spirit of God (was) fluttering on the face of the waters."* (Gen 1:2c, YLT) The word translated *fluttering* means "to vibrate." Then in Genesis 1:3 God spoke. Remember I stated that sound, in this environment, travels at an outrageous 60 percent of the speed of light. So sound could quickly crisscross the entire small but expanding cosmos. In other words, God himself stirred up the plasma stew.

When the charged particles of a plasma cloud are moved around, they form electrical currents. All electrical currents have a magnetic field around them. As the currents become magnetized, they attract more particles for the current. A perfect example of this is lightning. When clouds rub together, extra electrons are collected. These free electrons are a type of plasma forming in the cloud. As they are stirred around by the wind, the charge in the cloud builds up until it forms a current. We call it lightning. There is a magnetic field that surrounds the bolt as it heads towards ground. This is what holds the electrons inside the current flow of the lightning bolt. In plasma physics, the bolt is called a filament, and the same thing happens in all types of plasma clouds. The original water vapor plasma, as it was being stirred up, began forming stringy, finger-like filaments or currents in the cloud, along with their surrounding magnetic fields. As more particles were attracted to the filaments, voids also started forming. The result is the stringy structures we see in space today. Do an Internet image search for "plasma filaments in space," and you will see some great examples. These structures cannot be produced by gravity *at all*.

In fact, if gravity alone were responsible for the formation of the universe, galaxies and galaxy clusters would not exist. That's why the gravity guys have to pretend there is dark matter. But in the laboratory, plasma filaments do some amazing things when they get close to each other and the magnetic fields start to interact. Dr. Anthony Peratt of the Los Alamos National Laboratory has had a lot of success in duplicating galactic structures in his plasma experiments. Some photos of one simulation can be seen at this web address along with a photo of galaxy M81 for comparison: http://www.thunderbolts.info/tpod/2004/images/040913plasma-galaxy.jpg. As the plasma filaments get closer, a chain reaction is set in motion that results in galaxy-like formations. Plasma physicists have discovered that the electromagnetic influence on plasma is consistent, no matter what size we are talking about.

One of the "signatures" of a newly formed galaxy is the quasar. Just before the center of the galaxy stabilizes, twin polar jets spew electromagnetically charged material into space in opposite directions, releasing an enormous amount of radio waves and light. When experimental principles are expanded to galactic sizes and corrections are made for atomic versus orbital time, the light from the quasar in the center of our galaxy would have reached the young Earth approximately (drumroll please...) halfway through day one, just as the Bible states! *"Then God said, 'Let there be light'; and there was light."* (Gen1:3, NKJV) Coincidence? Read on.

6. **"Are you crazy? Planets can't form before stars!"** Or can they? One of the biggest hurdles for creationists to overcome when defending the biblical account is that God created the Earth before the sun. And the sun and stars don't appear on the scene until day four. Now, I don't have a problem with my all-powerful God doing that by miraculous means. But amazingly enough, the plasma model of creation produces the Bible's account exactly!

As I said earlier, plasma filaments are currents that have a surrounding magnetic field. These filaments are susceptible to swirling, bending, and pinching, like in the illustration below. When this happens, the material in the pinch or bend becomes compressed into a ball, forming a star. Do an Internet search for "ant nebula," and you'll see a great example of this. You can clearly see the pinched plasma filament with a star forming in the middle. The spiral arms of galaxies are plasma filaments that form stars and solar systems one after the other like a string of pearls.

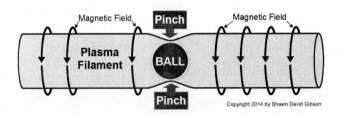

Copyright 2014 by Shawn David Gibson

The Pinching Effect on Plasma Filaments

It is not uncommon for these filaments to separate into a series of smaller filaments that are held together by their magnetic fields. Kind of like a large wire that is made up of smaller wires inside it. These smaller filaments form balls when pinched as well. On a stellar scale, this is how solar systems are formed. The ionized elements in the plasma layer themselves automatically. So the balls farthest from the center will have a lesser amount of heavy elements and larger amounts of gases. The balls form, moving in towards the center because the outer filaments feel the pinch sooner. As this happens, the heavier elements begin to predominate, just as in our solar system. Mercury, the planet closest to the sun, has the largest core of heavy elements proportional to its size. And the gas giants (Jupiter, Saturn, etc.) have much smaller cores of heavy elements proportional to their size. The balls orbit the center in the direction of the magnetic field. Because the pinch affects the outer filaments first, the planet balls form from the outside in. When the progression finally reaches the central and largest ball, gravity begins to exert enormous pressure on the elements until the ball lights up, and a star is born. So in plasma cosmology, it's the planets that form first then the central star.

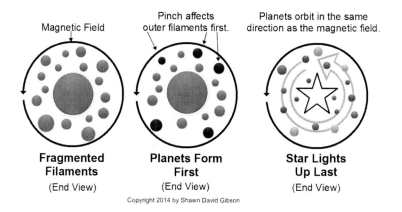

Magnetic Field	Pinch affects outer filaments first.	Planets orbit in the same direction as the magnetic field.

Fragmented Filaments	Planets Form First	Star Lights Up Last
(End View)	(End View)	(End View)

Solar System formation

7. **The creation of the Earth:** The separating of the filaments is probably what the second day of creation is all about.

> "Then God said, 'Let there be a firmament (space) in the midst of the waters (the plasma filaments would be separating here), and let it divide the waters from the waters. (That is, the water plasma that will be used to make the Earth from the plasma used to create the rest of the solar system and universe.) "Thus God made the firmament, and divided the waters which were under the firmament from the waters which were above the firmament; and it was so. And God called the firmament Heaven. So the evening and the morning were the second day." (Gen 1:6-8, NKJV)

Then on the third day we read,

> "Then God said, 'Let the waters under the heavens be gathered together into one place, and let the dry land appear'; and it was so. And God called the dry land Earth, and the gathering together of the waters He called Seas (water plasma finally becomes water). And God saw that it was good... So the evening and the morning were the third day." (Gen 1:9-13, NKJV)

8. **The Creation of the Sun:** Stars in the spiral arms of galaxies, like our sun, don't light up until sometime after the quasar has formed in the center of the galaxy. When laboratory observations are expanded to galactic proportions and corrections are made for atomic versus orbital time as well as other factors, our sun would have lit up (drumroll and fanfare please...) halfway through day four, just as the Bible says!

> "Then God made two great lights: the greater light to rule the day, and the lesser light to rule the night. He made the stars also. God set them in the firmament of the heavens to give light on the earth... And God

saw that it was good. So the evening and the morning were the fourth day." (Gen 1:16-19, NKJV)

Exhibit 5i: Multidimensional Multidimensions

In keeping with the recent discoveries that our universe is pixelated, the Bible speaks of the heavens or firmament in terms of fabric, rather than an empty vacuum. It says that spacetime can be "stretched" (Jer 10:12), "torn" (Is 64:1), "worn out" (Ps 102:25-26), "shaken" (Heb 12:26), "burnt up" (2Pet 3:12), "split apart" (Rev 6:14), and even "folded up" (Heb 1:12). These actions would require at least one more dimension. The Bible also speaks of a spiritual realm full of angelic beings that is connected to our physical realm, which would also require more dimensions.

A thirteenth century Jewish rabbi named Nahmanides, after carefully examining the Genesis account of creation, concluded that God created our universe with ten dimensions. But that only four are knowable to us.

Once again, science is finally catching up! Einstein solved the issue of time by adding it as another dimension. Physicists since then have followed his example in explaining the force fields we just talked about as well as some other things. Only recently have they been able to prove that our universe is contained in a framework of... (drumroll and fanfare please)... *ten* dimensions! This and some of the other discoveries we've mentioned prompted *Scientific American* to make this comment in their June 2005 edition: "Our universe is but a shadow of a larger reality."

It is astonishing how much the Bible has been confirmed by recent scientific discoveries. Of course, scientists have not proven the existence of the spiritual realm. But then, what's going on in all of those extra dimensions? You have to admit that these discoveries sure do *make room* for such a thing, don't they?

Exhibit 5j: Astronomical Observations

Now, let's look at a sampling of surprising remarks the Bible makes about astronomy.

1. **Uncountable stars:** Before the telescope was invented, the religions of many ancient cultures included the worship of the sun, moon, and stars. They had no idea what they were, but they were convinced that there was some kind of connection between them and their own lives. So, they would meticulously count and chart them. Roughly three to four thousand stars can be seen and counted with the naked eye. Yet, Jeremiah declares that *"the stars of the sky cannot be counted."* (Jer 33:22, TCB) This was taken figuratively until the invention of the telescope. Scientists have now given up counting. They now *estimate* that there are more than a hundred billion stars in our galaxy alone, and more than a hundred billion galaxies in the universe. The reason they gave up is that if they could count stars at the rate of ten per second, it would still take over a hundred trillion years to count them all. Can you blame them? And every time they make a bigger telescope that sees farther into space, they find more galaxies full of more stars. How could Jeremiah have known? A lucky guess? A time machine? Or, could it be that God told him?

2. **Orbits:** Ancient civilizations could see that the stars moved through the sky, but they had no idea about orbits. Yet, David said *"In them He has set a tabernacle for the sun. Its rising is from one end of heaven, And its circuit to the other end."* (Ps 19:4-6, NKJV) He describes the orbit as a circuit or circular path, which assumes that the sun goes all the way underneath the Earth and comes back up on the other side, implying that the Earth is a sphere. How did he know that?

   "Wait a minute! That's saying that the sun orbits the Earth!"

Well, it doesn't really matter what David thought, he was still right. Scientists know that the sun is indeed on a circular path as it races around our galaxy in one of its spiral arms. The Koran, of course, states that the sun sets in a swamp, which assumes a flat Earth (Surah or chapter 18:86). Which one do you believe?

3. **Our globe:** Isaiah asserts, *"It is He who sits above the circle of the earth, and its inhabitants are like grasshoppers."* (Isa 40:22, NKJV) The literal meaning of the Hebrew word translated "circle" is "sphere." How did Isaiah know that the Earth is a sphere? And Job adds that God *"hangs the earth on nothing."* (Job 26:7, NASB)

4. **Dumb luck?** So, the Bible clearly presents the Earth as being a sphere, suspended on nothing, and somehow involved in an orbit with the sun! Do you honestly think that several authors, writing centuries apart, in different places, just got that dumb lucky?

Flora Nienaber ©2013

The Bible says that the Earth is a sphere suspended on nothing!

Presenting for Evidence, Exhibit 6: The "Goldilocks Zone"

Although the Bible's account of creation and the big bang theory are similar in many ways, what the Bible describes is much different than a giant, violent explosion. The biblical account presents a carefully planned, skillfully engineered, and artfully orchestrated installation of a universe that is specifically fine-tuned for life on our little planet in a quiet corner of an average galaxy. Scientists call this the anthropic principle, and they have uncovered a long list of astounding facts that support this claim. There is little doubt that our environment on Earth, the Earth's position in the solar system, and even its position in our galaxy has been adjusted just for us. In fact, critics have *never* been able to present one shred of evidence to prove otherwise. That's because if they could, they couldn't because they wouldn't be here! And it wouldn't make any difference anyway because we wouldn't exist either. The amazing thing about all of this is, not that an individual "setting" is exactly right, but that if just one of literally hundreds of conditions is out of whack, even by a teensy-weensy bit—we go *boom*! Some scientists call it the "Goldilocks Zone", because everything is "juuust riiight". So, let's take a sampling of some of these "settings" required for us to exist.

Exhibit 6a: The Special "Special Forces"

We just mentioned that the Bible acknowledges the force fields that govern our universe. But now let's examine them in view of the Goldilocks Zone.

1. **The gravitational constant**: The force that gravity exerts on two objects depends on how much matter they contain and how close they are to each other. It primarily works on the really big stuff, like stars and planets. It is responsible for planetary orbits, and of course, it keeps our feet on

the ground and keeps the air we breathe and the water we drink in place.

Move the strength of gravity up by a little bit, and there would be too much ammonia and methane in our atmosphere for us to breathe; and the sun would burn too hot to support life here. If gravity was a lot stronger, our Earth would implode into a tiny black hole, which would be sucked into the sun as it imploded into a black hole, which would be sucked into the center of our galaxy and so on.

Move the strength of gravity down by a little bit, and the Earth would lose all of its water and dry up. (I'm thirsty already!) The sun would also burn too cool for life to exist. If it was a lot weaker, the universe would simply be a giant sea of hydrogen gas. Um...I like the strength of gravity where it is!

2. **The electromagnetic constant**: The electromagnetic force is many times stronger than gravity. It governs the laws of chemistry, it makes light, magnetism, X-rays, radio waves, and more. If electromagnetism were any stronger, molecules essential for life would not exist. If it were weaker, molecules essential for life would not exist. I guess we shouldn't monkey with this one either!

3. **The strong force constant**: The strong force is, by far, the strongest of the forces, but it only acts on the nucleus of the atom. This is what keeps protons and neutrons tucked into place so atoms and molecules can exist. This is also what makes the stars and our sun to shine, which is essential for life. If the strong force were stronger, heavy elements would dominate the universe. Lighter gases, such as oxygen, would either not exist or be so rare that there wouldn't be enough of the necessary concentrations to support life. If the strong force were weaker, all there would be is that giant sea of hydrogen gas again. No other elements could form. I don't think we need any more gas.

4. **The weak force constant**: The weak force is in charge of atomic instability. This is what creates the heat from the radioactivity in stars and nuclear power plants. If the weak force were stronger, there would be no lighter elements or heavier elements, which would throw the balance of elements out of whack and life could not exist. If the weak force were weaker, there would be an overabundance of light and heavy elements, with the same results.

Exhibit 6b: Earth

Our planet happens to have a multitude of other "settings" that, if changed, would prevent life. Here are just a few:

1. **The Earth's orbit**: Our distance from the sun is just right! If we were closer, we'd literally be toast. If we were farther, we'd be frozen stiff; the oceans would freeze over, the water cycle would come to a screeching halt, and the extreme permanent winter would make life a lot more impossible than it already is.

2. **The Earth's crust**: If our earth had a thicker crust, too much oxygen would be sucked into it, and we wouldn't be able to breathe. If it were thinner, the tectonic plates would cause constant earthquakes much stronger than those we experience now. And volcanic activity would go through the roof (literally) filling the atmosphere with a constant supply of volcanic ash and gas, which would have a drastic impact on the Earth's climate. And, guess what? We wouldn't be able to breathe!

3. **The speed of the Earth's rotation**: At first glance, it may sound like a great idea to slow down the rotation of the Earth. Then we'd have the proverbial "more hours in the day" that so many people wish for. But, there's a "gotcha." The temperature differences between the nightly lows and the daily highs would be so extreme that life would not be

possible. If the rotation were any faster, the atmospheric winds would be out of control, and we'd be blown away.

4. **The Earth's tilt:** If the Earth's axis were tilted more, either way, surface temperatures would be too high to sustain life, and we'd be crispy critters. No, thank you.

5. **The Earth's reflectivity:** If our atmosphere reflected more of the sun's heat, we'd have a permanent ice age. If it reflected any less, we'd have runaway global warming. Reflect on that for a while.

6. **The Earth's ozone level:** Ecologists are constantly warning us that a mere tenth of one percent change would result in the extinction of all life on our planet. They're right. If it were to drop that tiny little bit, UV radiation and surface temperatures would be too high. On the other hand, if it were any more than it is, we would plunge into a permanent ice age, which would not be cool.

Exhibit 6c: But wait...there's more!

Other factors that have a bearing on whether we live or die include: the Earth's magnetic field, the age of our sun, its mass, its color, its distance from the center of our galaxy, its position between the more dense arms of our galaxy, the number of stars in the universe, the distance between stars, the mass of the universe, its uniformity, and we could go on and on. If any *one* of these were slightly different, one way or the other, you would not be reading this book.

Multiverse to the Rescue!

Do we really need to compute the odds? It is obvious that all of these "settings" could not have just happened by accident. Yet scientific superheroes, who refuse to accept the overwhelming evidence for the skillful design of our universe and planet, have come up with the idea of the "multiverse." You see, they have to step up their game and find a way to shift the odds back in favor of life being an accident. They reason that if there are an infinite number of universes, surely one like ours would have to happen sooner or later. But, is there any real scientific evidence for such a thing? Uh…no, its just a fantasy—I mean a theory. There is, however, a biblical version that we will get to shortly.

The deeper question:

But there's a much deeper question here. How were all of these "settings" and laws that govern the universe "installed" in the first place? If a master engineer did not design and install the laws of physics, chemistry, biology, and the rest, why would you assume that there would be any laws or organization at all? An uncreated, unplanned, unengineered universe would, in fact, have *no* settings to tweak. There wouldn't even be enough structure for chaos! In fact, without a governing structure, there wouldn't be anything at all. This much orderly structure *demands* intelligent guidance!

Presenting for Evidence, Exhibit 7: Our Confined Cosmos

"To Infinity and Beyond!"

For centuries, scientists believed that the universe was of infinite size and duration. This is also a foundational teaching of most of the other holy books. The Bible is unique, however, in that it teaches that the universe is created and, therefore, limited in size, scope and duration. Sorry, Buzz fans. "To infinity and beyond!" ain't goin' to happen.

Exhibit 7a: The Little Big Universe

On the one hand, the universe is limited in largeness. Since it was created and is expanding (or has expanded), it is limited by its expansion. You can't get any bigger than that. On the other hand, there are also limits to smallness. We've talked about Planck's constants and the pixelated, powered-on grid that makes up space-time. One of the ways quantum physicists proved this limit is by observing that particles that got smaller than 10^{-33}cm lost a property that they call "locality" and exhibited "non-locality." That means that the particle fell through its individual place on the grid into a dimension where it became everywhere at once.

"WHAT!"

Yep! They've actually proved it in those supercollider things. But don't ask me to explain it; I'm as lost as you are. The point is, try as they might, they can't get anything smaller than 10^{-33}cm. Space has size limits. (Hmm…if a subatomic particle can be everywhere at once, surely God can do the same! Just sayin'…)

Exhibit 7b: Where Does the Time Go?

Not only did time have a beginning, but, since it is a physical property, the same as length or width, time has similar limits as well. In fact, time is so intertwined with space that to be in a different place in space is to be in a different place in time. You probably never realized it, but every time you walk down the street, you are engaging in time travel. Time is limited in largeness by the edge of the expansion of space, just like space itself. It is also limited in smallness. Planck measured that limit to be 10^{-43} seconds. (I wonder… if God could occupy a fraction of time smaller than 10^{-43} seconds, would that place him in an eternal present? Just sayin'…)

Exhibit 7c: The Perplexing Partial Perception Problem

One of the many apparent contradictions of quantum mechanics is what they call wave-particle duality.

"Huh?"

Take light, for example. It is associated with a particle called a photon. You've heard of those. But light also exhibits properties of waves. Now, every physicist knows that particles behave differently than waves do.

"So, which is it?"
Both.
"But that can't be!"
But it is.
"No!"
Yes! And it gets even worse. Scientists have found that light only behaves like particles when they are looking at it! Is that weird or what? This can only mean that we humans cannot see the whole picture. There are even limits to our ability to perceive the truth around us, which is why scientific "truth for now" is so shaky.

Exhibit 7d: All Charged Up and Running Down

The discovery of the laws of thermodynamics also supports the biblical view of a limited universe.

"Thermo-what?"

I know, scientists talk funny, but be patient. We've got to talk about keeping it and losing it.

1. **We're keeping it.** The first is the law of conservation of mass and energy, which says that stuff is no longer being created, nor is it being destroyed anywhere in the universe. It's a stability thing. Matter is converted into energy and vice versa, but nothing is being lost or added to the existing pool of matter-energy. This is stated in many places in scripture. *"And on the seventh day God ended His work"* (Gen 2:2a, NKJV), which means he stopped making stuff out of nothing. *"You alone are the LORD; you have made heaven, the heaven of heavens, with all their host, the earth and everything on it, the seas and all that is in them, and You preserve them all."* (Neh 9:6a, NKJV) *"I know that whatever God does, it shall be forever. Nothing can be added to it, and nothing taken from it. God does it, that men should fear before Him."* (Eccl 3:14, NKJV) That means we're keeping it, but…

2. **We're losing it.** The second law of thermodynamics is called the law of entropy. A simpler word is "decay." It states that,

although matter and energy are being conserved, as time advances, their structure is moving from a state of order to one of chaos, with a corresponding decrease in available energy. Like a battery-powered toy car—turning it on runs down the battery. When the battery dies, nothing physical has been lost; it just stops. Again, this idea is confirmed in the Bible. *"For the heavens will vanish away like smoke, the earth will grow old like a garment, and those who dwell in it will die in like manner."* (Isa 51:6b, NKJV) Jesus said, *"Heaven and earth will pass away, but My words will by no means pass away."* (Matt 24:35, NKJV)

✓ **Vanishing protons:** One intriguing form of entropy is what they call proton decay. At one time, scientists believed that subatomic particles were stable. Now, however, they know that every proton is made up of several smaller particles called quarks. (Did I just hear a cosmic duck?) Quarks decay into even smaller particles of useless matter and radiation. Although the rate of decay is very slow, eventually all protons will fall apart, all processes will stop, and the universe will return to a state of subatomic plasma, or "smoke," just as the Bible has said. This really scrambles that cosmic egg idea because it means that stuff can't sit unchanged forever. Even a cosmic egg would have to be charged up.

✓ **All bounced out:** One variation of the big bang theory says that the universe is oscillating with an eternal succession of big bangs. But the second law of thermodynamics dooms this for with every successive bang, the energy level available for the next will be less; like a bouncing ball, it too would eventually stop. Another problem with this theory is that the gravity exercised by all the matter in the universe is not enough to stop its expansion and return it to its "egg."

✓ **The universal chill:** Another form of entropy is what they call thermal decay. Something hot always cools down unless there is a source of energy being applied. If the universe was infinitely old all of the stars would be burned out and cooled down by now. The universe should be the same temperature everywhere. But this isn't the case, so, it can't be infinitely old. It had a beginning and will have an end.

✓ **Who charged up the cosmos?** Since the universe is "running down," there must have been a time when it was fully "charged up." But the law of entropy also says that it can't recharge itself any more than a toy car can recharge its battery by itself. So, *who charged it up?* And who told the authors of the Bible that it would run down? Dumb luck? A time machine? Klingons?

Who Gets the Last Laugh?

Mark Eastman and Chuck Missler summed all of this up quite well, "For centuries the biblical teaching of a finite universe was ridiculed by skeptics. Then came Einstein, Slipher, de Sitter, Hawking, Penrose and Ellis. They aren't laughing any more!"[11]

Scientists Respond to the Evidence

✓ **Paul Davies,** a former atheist, recently said, "There is for me powerful evidence that there is something going on behind it all....It seems as though somebody has fine-tuned nature's numbers to make the universe....The impression of design is overwhelming."[12]

✓ **George Greenstein,** an astronomer, wrote, "As we survey all the evidence, the thought insistently arises that some supernatural agency must be involved. Is it possible that suddenly, without intending to, we have stumbled upon scientific proof of the existence of a Supreme Being?"[13]

✓ **H. S. Lipson,** a physicist, also broke down in a fit of honesty when he wrote, "I think, however, that we must go further than this and admit that the only accepted explanation is Creation. I know that this is anathema to physicists, as indeed it is to me, but we must not reject a theory that we do not like if the experimental evidence supports it."[14]

✓ **Robert Jastrow,** a NASA astronomer and professed agnostic, eloquently summed up the implications of these things when he wrote, "For the scientist who has lived by his faith in the power of reason, the story ends like a bad dream. He has scaled the mountains of ignorance; he is about to conquer the highest peak; as he pulls himself over the final rock, he is greeted by a band of theologians who have been sitting there for centuries."[15]

"Where did decay come from, anyway?"

The Bible explains how entropy began. The Bible calls it death or corruption. And it was only after Adam sinned that God said, *"Cursed is the ground for your sake."* (Gen 3:17b, NKJV) In other words, entropy was not present in God's original creation. When God created the world, he said it was, *"very good."* (Gen 1:31, NKJV) That means it did not include corruption or entropy of any kind.

1. **God's promise:** But God has also determined to deliver us and restore the world to its original *good* state. *"For God so loved the world that He gave His only begotten Son, that whoever believes* (see glossary) *in Him should not perish, but have everlasting life."* (Jn 3:16, NKJV) That's a world without entropy once again! And read what Paul said:

> *For the creation was subjected to futility* (entropy), *not willingly, but because of Him who subjected it in hope* (God introduced death and decay to limit this life, so we might have a second chance at life the way

he intended it to be.); *because the creation itself also will be delivered from the bondage of corruption into the glorious liberty of the children of God. For we know that the whole creation groans and labors with birth pangs together until now.* (Rom 8:20-22, NKJV)

2. **The promise fulfilled:** The ultimate fulfillment of this promise will come in the biblical form of a multiverse or, more accurately, a "dualverse". Take a look at Revelation 21:

Now I saw a new heaven and a new earth, for the first heaven and the first earth had passed away. Also there was no more sea. Then I, John, saw the holy city, New Jerusalem, coming down out of heaven from God, prepared as a bride adorned for her husband. And I heard a loud voice from heaven saying, "Behold, the tabernacle of God is with men, and He will dwell with them, and they shall be His people. God Himself will be with them and be their God. And God will wipe away every tear from their eyes; there shall be no more death, nor sorrow, nor crying. There shall be no more pain, for the former things have passed away." Then He who sat on the throne said, "Behold, I make all things new." And He said to me, "Write, for these words are true and faithful." And He said to me, "It is done! I am the Alpha and the Omega, the Beginning and the End. I will give of the fountain of the water of life freely to him who thirsts. He who overcomes shall inherit all things, and I will be his God and he shall be My son." (Rev 21:1-7, NKJV)

This is what you and I were created for! This is life the way God intended it to be! Do you have the assurance that this kind of life is yours? Or does this seem far-fetched to you?

If so, consider this. I happen to play the guitar. If I were to tell you that I was going play a certain song, you may or may not believe me. But then let's say that I pick up my guitar and play the song for you, and thus I prove that I have the ability and skill to master it. And then I repeat my promise to play the song. What would you say then? Because I have already demonstrated my ability and skill, you would not have any trouble believing me, would you? Then why do you have trouble believing God's promise of a new universe when he has already demonstrated to you that he possesses the ability and skill necessary by creating this one? Your very existence is a testimony to his ability to create and sustain life! He's already played the song once. So, what makes you think that he can't do it again?

The Other "Holy Books"

I'm afraid that the attempts by all of the other major "holy books" to explain the nature of the universe make the fatal mistake of assuming that it is infinite in age and expanse. The Hindus, for example, believe that the universe itself is the supreme uncreated reality and that it is infinitely old. The Mormons also, believe it is infinitely old to accommodate their belief that there has been and will be an infinite succession of men achieving godhood so they can rule over their own planet (guys only; sorry, gals). But, as we have seen, the Bible says, and science agrees, that a universe of infinitude does not exist.

How do we explain the Bible's scientific knowledge about the universe?

Forty authors from all walks of life, writing over a span of sixty generations, on three continents, in three languages got incredibly ultra-super-dumb-lucky? Did they have a time machine? Did they conspire with space aliens? Or could this possibly be the fingerprints of our Creator? *"For since the creation of the world His invisible attributes are clearly seen, being under-*

stood by the things that are made, even His eternal power and Godhead, so that they are without excuse." (Rom 1:20, NKJV)

THE BIBLE AND EVOLUTION

"Oh yeah? Well, what about the dinosaurs?"

In spite of all the evidence we have already examined, someone will invariably ask that question. It seems that by far, the most prominent argument against the Bible is the belief that evolution has been proven by science and, therefore, the Bible and its account of creation is false. Evolution mania has swept the globe and is now firmly planted in the thinking of modern society. All types of science interpret their data so as to support Darwin's theory. Some churches have even caved in to the overwhelming tide of propaganda and now accept evolution as if it had been proven a fact.

"Well, doesn't the Bible deny the existence of dinosaurs?"

Not at all. The word *dinosaur*, which means "giant lizard," was not coined until the mid-1800s, long after the Bible was written. That's why that word isn't in the Bible. The Bible does mention some creatures, Behemoth and Leviathan, which might be dinosaurs, but we don't know that for sure. So for our purposes, we're going to conclude that the Bible is silent about them.

"What? How could that be?"

Well, the Bible is not a textbook on science or a catalogue of animal life. It is a love story about God and mankind in which the dinosaurs do not play a role, so the Bible simply ignores them. In fact, there are tens of thousands of living creatures that are not mentioned in the Bible. But this doesn't mean that it denies their existence. We can assume that when the Bible states that God created animals, the dinosaurs were included.

"But what happened to them?"

God knows all of that, but the truth is, he's far more concerned about what happens to you! So, his message isn't to
them or about them. His message is written to you and me.

Evolution and the Scientific Method

As I mentioned at the beginning of this chapter, science usually defines itself as "knowledge gained through experimentation and observation." But there arises a problem with this
when we begin talking about evolution. You see, neither creation nor evolution could be considered scientific on that basis.
Creation, of course, does not fit this definition because it cannot be observed. The Bible even says so. *"And on the seventh day
God ended His work."* (Gen 2:2a, NKJV) But, on that same basis, evolution from one species to another would not be considered
science either because no one has ever observed it. This has led
many to claim that evolution is really a philosophy that takes
as much faith to believe as creation does. We will see later that
some scientists have even agreed with this statement.

Philosophers of science (Remember those "box-maker"
guys we talked about?), in grappling with this problem, have
noted certain differences between the historical and experimental sciences, as well as differences in their methods.
Historical scientists work much like detectives. Using present
evidence to reconstruct the past, they evaluate their theories
by how well they explain the past causes or conditions. In
order for a theory to be valid, it must prove both that it has
the ability to cause the effect in question and that it was there
when it happened. And if the theory is the only known cause
of an effect, it automatically qualifies as the best explanation. But a thorough search must also be made to ensure that
all possible causes are being considered, which evolutionists fail to do because they *assume* that evolution is the only
known cause.

These methods actually lend themselves nicely to comparing creation with evolution because creation is an his-

toric event. The difference between them is that the evolution model attempts to explain the presence and variety of living things in terms of natural causes, while the Bible explains them in terms of supernatural causes. So, let's examine the existing evidence, and see which model explains things best. On one hand, we have the belief that life is the result of careful, intelligent design and engineering by a Creator. And on the other, we have the belief that life is the result of a whole lot of "dumb luck."

"Dumb luck?"

Yes. You see, *chance* is a word that scientists use to describe an event when there was no intelligent, reasoned selection involved. This is why I prefer the term *dumb luck* because it emphasizes that chance is void of intelligent, reasoned selection—it's dumb. I'm just telling it like it is.

Presenting for Evidence, Exhibit 8: The Execution of Evolution

"But doesn't evolution disprove the Bible?"

In order to tackle this question, I will first summarize some of the traditional creationist arguments regarding the relationships among species, the processes of genetic engineering, the fossil record, and the geologic ages. But the real kryptonite for evolution's superheroes is the new discovery that the speed of light and atomic clocks have been slowing down. I will revisit this at the end of this section. Then I will move on to present more new discoveries in the section on the origin of life. So, let's compare the evidence with both the creation and evolutionary models to see which one provides the best explanation.

Exhibit 8a: Relationships Among Species—the Boundary Question
First let's look at the relationships among species. Scientists have catalogued all known plants and animals into what are called taxonomic classifications, which include genus and species. The Bible says that God created each kind to reproduce only its own kind. But evolution says that as time goes by, living things are becoming better and more advanced. So, do the present relationships among species suggest that living things are staying the same or getting better?

1. **Boundaries...** First of all, we obviously see a lot of variation within species. There are many different kinds of dogs, for example. Some look really weird! We have a pug, we've had a bassett hound, a Doberman, and some mutts, all very different from each other. We do not, however, see variations that cross the boundaries of species. So far, my dogs have not sprouted wings and turned into birds, or cats, or horses, or anything else. No matter how weird a dog I've had, they've all been 100 percent dog. And we see this in all species. No one, in the history of the world, has ever observed one species even starting to evolve into another. So, does the existence of these boundaries suggest engineering genius or dumb luck?

2. **Or no boundaries? That is the question!** In fact, would the luck factor built into evolution produce taxonomic classifications at all? Darwin, himself wondered about this. "Why is not all nature in confusion, instead of the species being, as we see them, well defined?"[16] He thought it more reasonable to assume that living things evolving by dumb luck wouldn't have any classifications at all. Indeed, if all living things evolved from the same amoeba, they all should be able to breed successfully and produce offspring with all other living things. Evolution would tend to make every living thing one of a kind. We'd have octibirds and crock-

ephants! Is dumb luck really the only known cause of the order and organization we find in the classes of species?

Exhibit 8b: Evolution's Genetic Engine Breakdown

There are three things that cause genes to change, but only one can cause evolution. The three things that change genes are recombination, hybridization, and mutation. When evolutionists claim that Darwin's theory has been proven as a scientific fact they are referring to recombination. They then assume that mutation is a workable cause for a species to change into a different one. This is because they reject the existence of God and creation from the start. Therefore, in their view, evolution *must* be the *only* cause for the existence of life and must be considered factual on that basis alone. But a closer look at the genetic engine reveals a breakdown at a critical point.

1. **Recombination**: This process accounts for the variations within species, but it cannot produce a new one because it doesn't introduce any new genetic material. All it does is rearrange the genes that are already there. So, move along folks, there's nothing to see here.
2. **Hybridization**: This process produces some truly interesting animals, like the mule. But none of them can reproduce. Um…strike two!
3. **Mutation**: The only process critical to evolutionists is that of mutation because it is the only method that can add new material to the gene pool.

   ✓ **Birth defects?** The problem here is that almost all mutations are damaging. A more common term is *birth defects*. Our society considers them to be injuries. If mutations are so vital to evolution, why are they so feared and called defects instead of joyfully embraced as advances? Why are women who have abortions, because their babies might be deformed, allowed to do so?

Should they not be locked up in jail for preventing the betterment of mankind? No! The fact is, we instinctively abhor and fear the destructive process of mutation.

✓ *"But doesn't natural selection and survival of the fittest support mutants?"* No, natural selection and survival of the fittest do not support mutations, as some scientists claim; they actually weed out and eliminate them. For example, let's say that little bunny Fufu is born with a mutation that is good. In order to pass it on to his offspring, there would have to be a lady Fufu with the same or similar mutation in the same vicinity for him to mate with. What are the chances of that happening? Otherwise, if he mates with a normal bunny, his mutation will be watered down and disappear within a few generations. And even if he did find a similarly mutated mate, the offspring would have to inbreed with their brothers and sisters in order to continue propagating the mutation. Inbreeding, of course, is not even allowed anymore in both humans and domestic animals because it weakens the gene pool, causing all kinds of…(you guessed it) *defects*. Eventually Fufu's mutant bunny race would give way to these defects and become extinct.

✓ **Built-in walls and fences:** Thus, the processes of genetic engineering have a series of built-in walls and fences that do not allow living things to get better but keep each kind only reproducing after its own kind, just as the Bible says. And we still have to ask, once again, how these boundaries were installed in the breeding process in the first place? Which model explains this the best—engineering genius or dumb luck?

Exhibit 8c: The Missing "Missing Links"

"Well, what about the fossils?"

Good question. Do fossils really prove evolution, the way most scientists say they do, or do they just dig up more kryptonite?

The biggest issue with the fossil record is, what scientists call, the missing links. Darwin himself said that proof for his theory was totally dependent on the discovery of these transitional forms. And he even questioned why they are so scarce, "Why, if species have descended from other species by fine gradations, do we not everywhere see innumerable transitional forms?"[17]

The film *The Evolution Conspiracy* (available for free on YouTube) features several interviews with evolutionary scientists. Dr. Leo Hickey, director of the Yale Peabody Museum, and Preston Cloud, director of geological science at the University of California, Santa Barbara, both initially claim that there are many fossils that are half one species and half another. But when pressed for specifics, they both changed their tune and started making excuses as to why there were none.[18] Evolutionist author, Dr. Colin Patterson, director of the British Museum of Natural History, wrote this concerning these fossil links: "I will lay it on the line, there is not one such fossil for which one might make a water tight argument."[19]

"So, out of millions of fossils that have been dug up around the world, there is not one that links one species with another? But, I thought evolution had been proven!"

What the fossil record does show is that new species pop up unexpectedly, totally established, without any links between them and other species and stay unchanged until they become extinct. Present groupings of living things can be easily traced throughout the geologic ages. What is the best explanation for that?

Even the fossils of so-called early human ancestors have complications.

- ✓ **Ramapithecus** (Try saying that ten times real fast!) is now known to be an extinct variety of ape similar to the orangutan.[20]
- ✓ **Java Man**, or the "coffee guy" as I like to call him, is the result of wishful thinking. Dr. Dubois found a piece of a skull of what is likely an extinct ape, similar to a gibbon, in the same vicinity where he found a human leg bone. But he found human skulls in the area, as well. So, the only "proof" he really had was a piece of a skull. Given the fact that the fossils of all other transitional forms have yet to materialize, I'd like more proof than that! So much for the coffee guy.
- ✓ **Lucy,** according to Dr Charles Oxnard, professor of anatomy and human biology at the University of Western Australia, belongs to a group that is, "indeed, more different from both African apes and humans in most features than these latter are from each other."[21] He then concludes that this group is unique, and therefore cannot be considered a missing link between apes and man. ("Luuucy! You got some 'splanin' to dooo!")
- ✓ **Piltdown Man** is a complete hoax exposed by *Time* magazine in 1953. The bones were from three different species that were stained with an iron-acid solution to make them appear really old, and it even has filed teeth! (Huh…he musta been to my dentist.)
- ✓ **Neanderthal Man** was shorter than most people are today with thicker bones, but is now considered fully human. Neanderthals actually have a larger brain capacity than most people today, which is not at all what we would expect from evolution. Also, they had similar cultural practices as other ancient humans. So Neanderthals are simply an extinct race of fully human beings.[22]

✓ **Nebraska Man** was constructed from a single tooth, which belongs to a variety of extinct pig! (Oh, so now we've descended from Miss Piggy?) Fortunately, an honest retraction was made in the journal *Science* in 1927, which many evolutionists conveniently ignore.[23]

✓ **Monkey's uncle?** Instead of including God as a possible explanation, these supposed human ancestors were presented to us with the evolutionary presupposition that he does not exist. This intentional ignorance caused gross misinterpretation and, in some cases, falsification of the evidence. Seriously and for the (fossil) record, there is absolutely *no proof* that man evolved from apes or anything else!

"If evolution were true..."

Exhibit 8d: The Geologic Ages
"But, the geologic ages, don't they prove evolution?"

On the surface, this does seem to give evolution a strong argument. In general, it appears that "simpler" life-forms are buried deeper than more complex ones, which makes it seem like they evolved first. There are, however, a number of snags with this assessment, as well.

1. **Life is not "simple"!** First, as we will see in the next section, there really is no such thing as a *simple* life-form, even at the level of single cells. We now know that life-forms at the bottom of the geologic column rival the complexity of those at the top.

2. **Fossils rock!** Second, the only thing that determines the "geologic age" of rocks are the fossils contained in them and their pretend evolutionary relationships. But these relationships have never been established scientifically. Consider the following facts:

   ✓ **Fuzzy rocks:** There are no differences between the rocks themselves from age to age. All kinds of minerals and deposits are evenly mixed throughout the layers.

   ✓ **Fuzzy layers:** The boundaries between these geologic ages are not very well defined either. They are often gradual and can contain significant gaps. It is not uncommon for "older" rocks to be found on top of "younger" ones. These supposed ages can be present or missing, upside down, thick or thin, and so on. The Grand Canyon, for example, has hundreds of millions of years' worth of "ages" completely missing; nowhere in the canyon can they be found. How can that happen? Was the canyon on vacation during those ages or something?

   ✓ **Fossils rule:** Naming the layers of sediments is certainly legitimate, and associating them with assumed and unproven ages and projecting possible fossil contents is also okay as long as it's presented as a theory. But because the possibility of creation is ignored by scientists in general, this geologic column was accepted as hard, cold fact, before scientific processes were employed to prove or disprove it. For example, this was done long before radiometric dating was invented. But when the radiometric date dares to challenge the assumed age of a rock, which is quite often, scientists always reject the radiometric date and accept the assumed age. They base all of their decisions on fossil content, considering that to be more important than radiometric dating. Come on, man! How scientific is that?

✓ **The fossil merry-go-round:** So, the only real determining factor used to date the ages of rocks is their fossils, and the ages of the fossils are determined by their alleged evolutionary status. So when considering the geologic ages, the only proof for evolution is... (drumroll please) *evolution?* Um... isn't that circular reasoning? Oh but exceptions are always made in the case of evolution because that is science's sacred cow. It can't be questioned or subjected to true scientific processes, lest it be proved false. The evolution superheroes are on a mission to force it to be the "truth" regardless of the evidence!

3. **"But then, how do you account for the groupings of fossils?"** Here's a biblical idea—Noah's flood.

✓ **Day-to-day catastrophes?** But before we dive in to the flood, I need to mention one more thing about the evolutionary model. Since evolution is supposedly such a slow process that takes millions of years, fossils are assumed to be produced at regular intervals spread out over this extremely large time span in order to give us a complete record of the supposed development of the species. This is called uniformitarianism. But there's another problem aside from the time issue. Fossils are only formed in sedimentary rocks. The victim must be trapped and buried quickly by mud or volcanic ash. This means that catastrophes, such as Noah's flood, are what make fossils. The normal, day-to-day processes that we are experiencing now tend to decompose and destroy dead animals rather than preserve them through fossilization. This fact buries the uniformitarian model needed to substantiate evolution. It also demands that the geologic column be interpreted with catastrophies in mind rather than slow processes.

✓ **To review:** Let's briefly review the evidence supporting "Noah's flood" presented earlier in "The Bible and History" chapter. There are approximately five hundred flood traditions for virtually every ancient civilization worldwide. There are sediments up to hundreds of feet thick that extend for hundreds of thousands of square miles with little or no evidence of erosion between layers all over the planet that, thankfully, are not being formed today. There are huge fossil graveyards on every continent that would have required catastrophic and very quick burial. This is not happening on that scale today. Worldwide flat planation surfaces are evidence of massive sheet erosion that are not being formed by present geological processes. More evidence of sheet erosion is the slashing out of ridges and high mountain cliffs and shearing off of thousands of feet of sediment from every continent. Again, this is not happening today. Erosional remnants, such as Devils Tower and the buttes and mesas in Monument Valley, are only formed when large volumes of water cut out channels that broaden into valleys but leave some places high and dry. This is not being done on that scale today.

✓ **A variety of flood models:** Actually, some creation scientists believe there was a series of natural catastrophies beginning with the flood and culminating with the ice age that deposited the sediments and fossil graveyards we find today. There are a variety of brilliant flood models put forward by creation scientists, but it is not within the scope of this book to dissect them all. I encourage you to do that if you like. What I am presenting is sort of a hybrid from several models of the things that make the most sense to me, and I will mention some variations for you to explore. But I want you to know there is an ark load of material that I am leaving out or glossing over for lack of space. Although creationists disagree about some of the details, we all agree that the flood had a major impact on our present environment.

✓ **Here's mud in your eye.** Earlier I explained how sound and electromagnetic forces shaped the galaxies, stars, and planets very quickly from the original plasma. Before we go on, it's essential to understand a few things about the state that our Earth was in when it was first created, because plasma processes are different than what we are used to. And they take place with a very different timeline.

By the time the original elements were pinched together into a ball on day three, the continuing expansion of space-time had cooled off the original plasma quite a bit. The temperature was cool enough that God could gather water into a sea. This means that the Earth was formed cool at first. Even the Earth's core was relatively cool. Gravity had not yet had a chance to pressurize the harder elements into solid rock. And remember that the plasma was ionized water vapor, so the Earth was a soggy mud blob at first. Even the core was sopping wet. There were no tectonic plates to produce high mountain ranges, no volcanoes and no polar ice caps to drive winds. Verse 3 of Genesis 1 indicates that there was one continent and one ocean, probably what is now the Pacific, but much shallower. And because the heat that was needed to expand the core and separate the continents had not been generated yet, Earth's sphere was roughly 20 percent smaller than it is today.[24] The Bible says, *"The Lord God had not sent rain on the earth...but streams came up from the earth and watered the whole surface of the ground."* (Gen 2:5b-6, NIV) The place was so soggy that everything was watered from underneath. The water table was nearly ground level. By the sixth day, pressure from the warming core was beginning to build and water was being pushed to the surface. The Garden of Eden had a major spring that fed four rivers (Gen 2:10). The headwaters of the Mississippi are only six hundred feet above sea level. So major rivers don't need very high elevations to begin shaping the land surface. Lush river valleys, low-lying swamps and higher, slightly dryer rolling hill country were the major features of the topogrophy. There were no deserts as they are formed by high mountain ranges that keep the rain on one side while denying it to the other. The swamps would tend to attract certain kinds of animals and insects. The river valleys would attract other kinds of animals, while man and mammals would generally choose slightly higher elevations to get out of the mud.

One interesting point about the water coming from underground is that in order for fossils to form, mineral rich water must be present. It isn't enough for the victim to buried quickly. Minerals from water are what replaces the bones and tissues that become fossils. Once this condition is in place, a fossil can be formed in as little as ten to fifteen years.

Genesis 1:29 states that God planted trees and plants *"on the face of the whole earth."* (Gen 1:29b, NIV) And to be sure, fossils of tropical plants and trees have been uncovered from pole to pole.

✓ **Storage places of the deeps:** There are several references in the Psalms that add details to the way God formed the original Earth. *"For He has founded it upon the seas, and established it upon the waters."* (Ps 24:2, NKJV) And *"He gathers the waters of the sea as in a bottle; He puts the deeps in storage places."* (Ps 33:7, AMP) And finally, *"To Him who laid out the earth above the waters..."* (Ps 136:6a, NKJV) So, as the core and mantle (the layer of plasticized rock just beneath the Earth's crust) heated up from pressure and radioactive decay, more water was forced up towards the crust. Weak places in the upper mantle and crust allowed a great deal of water to be concentrated in underground and undersea caverns laid in storage for the great flood. Eventually molten magma also formed in the mantle setting the stage for volcanic activity.

✓ **Canopy models:** Several ancient civilizations, as well as early Jewish traditions,[25] depict an original paradise protected by a water or crystal canopy. Some creation scientists see this in Genesis 1:6-7 and suggest that there was a water or ice canopy over the pre-flood Earth. Such a canopy would have provided a layer of UV protection and turned the whole planet into a giant greenhouse/hyperbaric chamber. It would have caused uniformly warm temperatures and higher air pressure planet wide, causing plants, animals, and insects to grow to gigantic proportions as we find in fossils today. It might also explain the longevity experienced by humans in the pre-flood world. Research has found that the air of the pre-flood environment contained 35 percent oxygen as compared with 21 percent today. Some scientists have even concluded that certain dinosaur species suffocated when the atmosphere changed due to limited lung capacity relative to their size. The ozone layer or one of the other gas layers that surround our planet today may be remnants of such a canopy. Scientists have conducted experiments that prove the real possibility that such a thing could have existed. Creationevidence.org gives a long list of candidates and discusses the conditions that would have been necessary to support them. (But be warned, the language is full of scientese!)[26]

✓ **Man lived with dinosaurs?** There is a startling amount of evidence that man and dinosaurs coexisted in both the pre- and post-flood worlds. Of course, evolutionists have done their best to deliberately suppress this evidence because it counters their model. The truth is that human footprints, handprints and man-made artifacts have been found throughout the geologic column from top to bottom.[27] In Glen Rose, Texas, human and dinosaur footprints have been found in the same rocks. In South America, over ten thousand pre-Inca painted stones have been found, many of which feature men riding and/or hunting numerous kinds of dinosaurs. A lot of human artifacts have been found in coal seams, which are the remains of prehistoric jungles and forests. Cave paintings worldwide depict men and dinosaurs together. Likewise many ancient ceramic figurines and pottery paintings picture the same things. Widespread legends of a large variety of dragons in past centuries suggest that some dinosaurs were still around during the Middle Ages.[28] Add to this persistent reports of living dinosaurs sighted in the Amazon and Congo jungles.[29] All of this supports the fact that man and dinosaurs lived together right from the start.

✓ **The flood:** Genesis 6 tells us of the unchecked violence and evil things that people were doing to each other that provoked God's righteous wrath. So he determined to send judgment in the form of a great flood. But it also says that *"Noah found grace in the eyes of the Lord."* (Gen 6:8, NKJV) Then God told Noah to build the ark (Gen 6:13). Noah warned the people of God's coming judgment for 120 years, offering salvation to anyone who wanted to be spared. But they all refused.

Once the ark was finished and Noah, his family, and all the animals were safe inside, the Bible says, *"The fountains of the great deep were broken up and the windows of heaven were opened."* (Gen 7:11, NKJV) Pressure from the core and mantle continued to build until the Earth's crust cracked open like an egg and the tectonic plates were born. Then a chain reaction of cataclysms ensued.

First, scalding water under high pressure exploded through the cracks, taking hot mud and rocks with it high into the atmosphere where it fell back to Earth as muddy, rocky rain. Volcanic activity and tectonic movement always go hand in hand, so explosions of molten lava and ash were added to the mix. If there was a canopy, it too collapsed onto the Earth. The initial sediments were formed by what was probably very hot water and mud. Fossils aren't formed in this kind of environment. Organisms that died in the initial upheaval would have been cooked and mixed into the hot mud, leaving carbon-rich layers of sediment instead of fossils. And that is exactly what we find in the very lowest layers of strata. Some creationist scientists believe that this is all that the flood did and that the rest of the geologic column was laid down afterwards. I have great respect for this opinion as it seems obvious to me that the forces, which the flood set in motion continued for centuries after. You can visit www.setterfield.org to get a complete rendition of this model. But I tend to side with those who believe the flood itself was responsible for most of the fossils. I think that after months of being exposed to the cooler air and mixing with ocean and lake water, the floodwater would have cooled enough to fossilize its victims. The condensation of the clouds into rain is also a cooling process; and if there was a canopy of ice, that would have cooled things even further.

We get another peek into this event in Psalm 104. *"You covered it (the Earth) with the deep as a garment; The waters were standing above the mountains."* (Ps 104:6, NASB) *"The mountains rose; the valleys sank down to the place which you established for them."* (Ps 104:8, NASB) Until the flood, there were no high mountain ranges. But at this time the Earth was covered in hundreds to thousands of feet of mud in various layers. The water that was once below the surface and in the atmosphere was covering the land. The tectonic plates had been fractured and the interior of the planet was still expanding. Geologists tell us that the main movement of the tectonic plates is up and down. So that's what began to happen. The weight of the water and mud caused the sea floor to sink. As the underground caverns emptied their contents, many of them would have collapsed as well. At the same time other forces were causing other areas to rise up.

The Bible says that the waters rose for 150 days, or roughly five months. So, it is probable that it took several months for everything to die. This would also give the more mobile animals and people time to seek the rising areas of land. Slower marine animals and fish living in lakes and shallow seas would be buried first. Plants can't run, so they would be covered early. The next strata up would contain the swamp dwellers. Then the larger animals that lived in the river valleys would be buried. Mammals living at the higher elevations would be last. Birds would fly until exhausted, and humans would climb trees and cling to vegetation mats before being deposited on the top of the seafloor, where their bodies would be eaten by surviving fish or simply decay. As the waters were rising, great earthquakes generated huge tsunamis that inundated the land. Also, tides were adding their influence twice a day. So there was a lot of slish-sloshing going on.

As the Earth expanded, the Americas separated from Europe and Africa. As they slid away, the Atlantic Ocean opened its mouth and began swallowing the floodwaters. On the opposite side of the Americas, the continents were getting resistance as they slid westward and began to pile up mud like a bulldozer. Thus the Andes, Rockies, High Sierra, and other mountain ranges started to rise. Fossil oysters eleven feet wide have been found ten thousand feet high in the Andes. Fossil clams were found on the top of Mount Everest. These clams and oysters are in the closed position, which means they were buried alive because shellfish always open once they die. So the tops of these mountains were once under water.

If you've ever driven across country, you've undoubtedly seen severe twists and bends in the sedimentary layers of rocks that are in the cliffs along the road. If you haven't seen them, there are some great examples at this website: http://freddoty.com/ (as of 6-13-14) or do an Internet search for "bent rock layers." It is impossible for hard rock to be bent into sharp folds like this, except under very controlled laboratory conditions. Pressure that would cause that in nature would simply pulverize the rock into gravel and dirt. The only possible way to cause extreme folds in sedimentary layers is while they are still in a soft, pliable state. The forces unleashed by the flood were easily capable of doing just that.

As the ocean floors sank and the mountains rose, the water began to flow off the land into the ocean beds, which caused sheet erosion and then cut through the layers of mud to form great canyons. Tidal waves from earthquakes would have sheared off portions of these sediments and laid down new ones, which would have really mixed things up. This was a time of violent upheaval all over the planet. So, the Bible's account of a worldwide flood is an excellent explanation for the Earth's geologic formations and apparent order of the fossils.

✓ **After the flood:** It's logical to assume that the Earth remained unstable for centuries after the flood. After all, the tectonic plates are still moving around to this day. There were earthquakes as areas of land continued to settle and rise, mudslides, local floods as earthen dams gave way, tsunamis, etc. So, part of the fossil record was undoubtedly still in process. Some scientists believe that the tower of Babel event brought on more catastrophes. And the Bible says that *"the earth was divided"* (Gen 10:25b, NKJV) a few hundred years after the flood, which is probably a reference to the flooding of the remaining land bridges between the continents and the continuing separation of the Americas from Europe and Africa. The Earth was not a stable planet at this point.

✓ **The Ice Age:** With the protective canopy gone, the poles began freezing. As the warm seas came in contact with colder air, a great deal of evaporation would have taken place, producing an overabundance of snowfall. As the snow built up, glaciers formed, and the ice age was in full swing. Scientists have deduced that Earth's tilt was changed a couple of times shortly after the flood. Asteroid impacts are likely to blame. The first helped bring on the ice age and a second brought it to an end.

Exhibit 8e: The Young Earth

You will remember that in the section on cosmology we saw that science has proved that the universe is between six thousand and ten thousand years old. And, the same is true of the Earth itself. Of course, many scientists still say the Earth is much older. There are several, now-outdated methods they have used to determine this that I would like to address at this point.

1. **Layers don't count.** One way that scientists used to determine the Earth's age was by counting the layers of sediment in a canyon, assuming that each layer represents one year, similar to the rings in a tree. It is more reasonable, however, to assume that each layer represents a single storm. I have personally observed single storms that have put down many layers in a streambed. During the Mount St. Helens eruption, a stream of volcanic mud cut through one of the initial mudflows forming a canyon six miles long and four hundred feet deep. Scientists counted over a million layers. But they were all laid down in a matter of hours. Thus, scientific observation itself has disproved this method.

2. **Dating rocks!** The main method used to determine the age of planet Earth is the atomic decay rate of uranium^{238} to lead^{214}. This is an extremely slow process, which takes millions of atomic years (uncorrected for the slowing down of the speed of light), and is why they say the Earth is that old. But two faulty assumptions undermine this method: (1) that the decay rate has never changed, and (2) that all lead^{214} present with uranium^{238} was once uranium^{238}.

   Cataclysmic events, such as a nearby supernova or a magnetic field reversal, which scientists tell us has happened several times to the Earth, could easily increase this rate of decay, not to mention the slowing of the speed of light, which I will review shortly. Furthermore, active volcanoes, such as Mount St. Helens, have left deposits of lead^{214} and uranium^{238} together in the same rocks. It is curious that radiometric readings of these rocks suggest that they are millions of atomic years old, when, in fact, they are brand new. And, if the rock is that old, *all* of the uranium^{238} would have turned to lead^{214}. So, why are they both in the same rock to begin with?

3. **Blind dating:** The other dating methods have issues as well. The potassium-argon method often produces differ-

ent dates for the same rock and old ages for young rocks. Confusing, isn't it? Radiocarbon dating often makes mistakes in excess of 25 percent. What kind of grade would you get in science class with a percentage like that? Dr. John Morris of the Institute for Creation Research tells of sending samples to a lab from two lava flows, one from the rim of the Grand Canyon and the other from the bottom. The lab dated the bottom sample as being younger than the one from the top.

4. **If the Earth were billions of years old**...the world's population would be 150,000 humans per square inch. We would find hundreds of millions of supernovas (star deaths) instead of just three hundred. Comets would be extinct as they have a lifespan of ten thousand years. The Earth's magnetic field, which is slowly weakening, would be gone. Since the Earth's spin rate is gradually slowing, winds during the age of the dinosaurs would have been five thousand mph, making evolution impossible. The oldest reef would be millions of years old instead of just forty-two hundred years old. The oldest tree would be millions of years old instead of just forty-three hundred years old. The oceans would be so salty they would have turned to sludge. All of the mountain ranges would have eroded to the seas, and we could go on and on.

5. **Light's out!** But let me review the other consideration that affects all of the methods that rely on radioactive decay. That is the recently confirmed discovery that the speed of light is indeed slowing down. The speed of light is one of the values used in the formulas that determine these decay rates and in turn, the age of the rocks or fossils being tested. As I said before, when corrections are made that take this into account, the Earth turns out to be less than ten thousand orbital years old, just as the Bible has said all along. It also explains the old and inconsistent ages given by these dating methods because of the depend-

ence on the speed of light in their equations. Evolution has run out of time! This utterly destroys its foundation of millions and billions of years needed for it to perform its "magic." Checkmate…game over…the fat lady has sung… light's out!

And the evidence isn't even all in yet!

We have already witnessed the death of evolution at the hands of many logical and scientific assassins. But wait! There's still much more kryptonite to come…

THE BIBLE AND THE ORIGIN OF LIFE

Of course, the Bible tells us that God created all life-forms. Although he expressed some reflections in a letter to a friend, Darwin never officially tackled the origin of the first life-form in his theory of evolution. He limited it to the change of "simpler" species into more complex ones. It was the scientists after him that developed the theories involving the primordial soup and the simple cell. Back then, scientists thought cells were just tiny bags of jelly. (Pass the bread and peanut butter, please.) They had no idea how very wrong they were!

Presenting for Evidence, Exhibit 9: The Origin of Life: Dumb Luck or Creative Genius?

Exhibit 9a: The Unsimple Cell: Bag of Jelly or Engineering Masterpiece?

First, let's take brief look at the structure and makeup of a simple bacterium. These are the most uncomplicated life-forms known and are composed of about 10^{13} (1 with 13 zeros after it) atoms that are specifically arranged for necessary functions. Keep in mind that all other cells are even more complex. So, without further ado, let's take a look at the engineering genius behind the design of… (and let's give it up for…) the unsimple cell!

1. **The central library and administration complex:** The central region of the simplest cell is called the nucleoid. (It sounds like the name for a robot, doesn't it?) It acts as a central library and administration facility, housing the DNA molecule. Here are some of the things it does.

   ✓ **Administration, planning, and operations:** DNA provides the blueprints for the production of the proteins, enzymes, and other products the cell requires to live and reproduce. It also provides regulatory information and programming that works like a computer operating system. There is a whole range of vital services and instructions encoded in the DNA molecule that direct the way the various systems in the cell work.

   ✓ **A copy machine and shipping facility:** Also housed inside the nucleoid is the RNA-polymerase.
   "What in the world is that?"
   I thought that would get you. This thing acts like a copy machine, duplicating information from the DNA molecule and shipping the RNA copy to one of several tiny factories for protein production.

2. **Swarming city streets:** Inside the cell wall is a jelly-like substance called the cytoplasm. (Don't worry, I can't pronounce it either.) It's made up of water, salts, enzymes, and other organic stuff. It's the fluid that contains the nucleoid, the protein factories, and the other working systems of the cell. It also allows the army of microbots the freedom to move around and do their jobs. Here are just a few of things it contains.

- ✓ **Protein-building factories:** Amino acids are the building-block molecules of proteins. Out of the five hundred known amino acids, there are only twenty that make up the proteins in living cells, but they have to be arranged in a specific order for the protein or other genetic product to fold and work right. It's kinda like putting together a jigsaw puzzle. This arrangement is what determines the protein's function in the cell. There are a number of little factories called ribosomes scattered around the cytoplasm. (Is that a silly name or what?) The ribosome gets the RNA blueprint copy from the DNA molecule, reads it, selects the specific amino acid called for, and adds it to the protein chain it's building. When the puzzle is complete, the ribosome spits the protein or enzyme out into service.
- ✓ **Adaptive communication stations:** Another silly name science came up with is plasmid. These are smaller, independent portions of DNA that are located outside of the nucleoid in the cytoplasm. (Got that?) They have varied functions, one of which is to direct adaptive traits depending on the environment. They are sometimes copied and transferred to other bacteria in the colony so that the adaptation can be quickly communicated. So if it's getting cold, one bacterium can tell the others to put their little bacterium sweaters on.
- ✓ **Storage warehouses:** Extra food, energy molecules, and other things the cell wants to put away for a rainy day are stuffed in tiny bags and stored in a variety of granules. These are like little storage warehouses within the cytoplasm.
- ✓ **An army of microbots:** There are literally hundreds of thousands of types of molecular bots buzzing around in the cell. Think of them as the factory workers, garbage collectors, and others that perform maintenance and repair, defense, construction, message delivery,

proofreading, error correction, language translation and decoding, energy distribution, and hundreds of other cellular jobs. All skillfully directed by dumb luck of course.

✓ **Endospore:** This is a defense mechanism. It only forms when the environment gets dicey. An endospore is like a seed that contains a copy of the bacterium's DNA and other necessary components. It has a hard outer container that is resistant to severe conditions. If something bad happens to the bacterium, the endospore is released and will remain dormant until conditions improve. At that point, it will germinate, like a seed, and start a new colony. That's why bacteria can just keep coming back, like those bad guys in the movies.

3. **The great wall of bacteria:** The bacterium's cell wall is actually made up of three layers.

✓ **The capsule:** The outer layer is called the capsule, which provides the first line of defense. But it also serves as an anchoring point for some other cellular gadgets. There are dozens of little hairy tentacle things, called pili, attached to it that allow the bacterium to grab on to things. (Boy, the silly names just keep coming, don't they?) It also has one or more flagella attached. (Sounds like a fancy name for a whoopee cushion, but no...) These are whip-like limbs connected to rotary engines composed of about forty moving parts. Many scientists consider these things to be an engineering masterpiece. These are what give the bacterium the ability to swim around. And, of course, the capsule has openings for dumping out the garbage and the intake of food and oxygen.

✓ **The cell wall:** The middle layer is the *real* cell wall. This is the primary level of defense and security.

✓ **Route 66:** The inner layer is called the plasma membrane. It acts like a highway system for transporting food, oxygen, and trash to their destinations. This is also where sugars, oxygen, and proteins are broken down and converted into usable energy molecules and amino acids before being shipped to the specific locations that need them.

4. **Little riddles—which came first?** There is a serious puzzle for the evolutionist in these unsimple cells. The information processing system that resides in it is made by the proteins that the system builds. As David Goodsell puts it, "One of the unanswered riddles of biochemistry: which came first, proteins or protein synthesis? If proteins are needed to make proteins, how did the whole thing get started?"[30] And that's not all. The same thing can be said for every system in the cell! Take the digestive system—it produces the energy molecules needed to build the digestive system. So which came first, the energy or the system?

This presents the evolutionary super-scientist with more kryptonite: the sobering reality that all of the systems and microbots had to evolve all at once. If all systems are there except the digestive system, the cell dies. If everything is in place but the garbage collecting microbots, the cell dies. If all systems are go but the DNA molecule is missing the programming that tells the garbage-collecting microbots where the ports are to take out the trash, the cell dies. If the ability to reproduce is missing, the potential for a colony is cut short. If the cell is complete except the RNA copy machine, the cell dies. There are literally thousands of conditions that must be met to ensure the cell's survival that had to be evolved to perfection all at once. So, is that *simple* enough for you? Oh, but we're not done yet...

Exhibit 9b: DNA: The Brilliant Work of "Dumb Luck" or a Programming Masterpiece?

There have been some recent discoveries about DNA that have turned the scientific world upside down and have a direct bearing on how unsimple the simple cell really is.

1. **No junk here!** If evolution were true, there would be lefto-ver portions of the DNA molecule from failed trial and error processes. As recently as a few years ago, evolutionists hailed what they thought was the presence of junk DNA in every living thing as being *big time* evidence in their favor. But the rug has now been pulled out from under them. Oh, there are non-protein manufacturing sections of the genome, to be sure. But scientists have now learned that those sections have different purposes. They seem to work like a computer operating system, coordinating and regulating various services, formatting and indexing the location of information, directing the combining of dif-ferent sections of DNA for the RNA copy, and more. So, the concept of junk DNA has now been junked. But wait, there's more…

2. **Organized, compressed, encrypted and indexed informa-tion:** DNA storage is organized in a hierarchical system, similar to the folder structure on a computer hard drive. These "file clusters" are *arranged according to function in non-random, organized groups*, super-groups, sub-groups, sub-sub-groups, etc. Secondary information is embedded and sometimes spread across multiple genes to form a kind of compression, which reduces the amount of storage space required on the DNA molecule. Other data is placed in equal-distant-letter sequences, such as every third letter, or is read backwards, which are types of encryption (a tricky way to hide data). Thus, one gene is not just limited to the production of one protein, as was previously thought, but it can contribute to the production of thousands of dif-

ferent proteins and other products. And the entire DNA strand is indexed so the cell knows exactly where to look for the information it needs. This reveals why mutations are so destructive. A single letter change in the DNA strand doesn't just affect one gene—it could affect hundreds of them! But wait, there's even more...

3. **Automatic backup, error detection and correction functions**: Information for building a given protein is usually placed in several locations on the DNA molecule. So if one location is damaged, by a virus for instance, reference is made to the other locations and the error is corrected. Wow! Dumb luck sure is smart! There's maybe one computer programming engineer in a hundred that can write a program that features error detection and correction. And that's still not all...

4. **DNA on steroids**: There are also other genetic molecules in the cell, like plasmids, that store and utilize data. And there are "editor" molecules that splice and recombine RNA information so that many proteins can be formed by overlapping the genes. The structural context of the cell also provides a reference system for a lot of other information. DNA makes the parts, the proteins and other products, but where the parts end up and how they connect to the cell is guided by the 3D structure of the cell itself. Thus, some features can be inherited even though they aren't listed anywhere in the DNA library! The data storage capacity of the cell is now known to be thousands of times greater than once believed.

5. **Dumb luck or programming genius?** Uh...so...what is the best explanation for all of this highly advanced data storage/retrieval, operating system, auto backup, error detecting/correcting, adaptive programming that we find in the unsimple cell? Dumb luck or programming genius? More kryptonite?

Exhibit 9c: Trouble in the Test Tube
We've already talked about how amino acids are the building blocks of proteins and are essential to life. And, yes, scientists have been successful at creating a few of them in a laboratory. But there are a host of additional issues that scientists have not been able to overcome.

1. **Peek-a-boo amino acids:** You see, the very process that generates the vast number of amino acids needed to form a single protein also produces a massive amount of poison that destroys them. The only way to save them is to get rid of the toxins immediately. Scientists can do that in a test tube. But how is that supposed to happen in a primordial soup?

2. **The glass is half empty:** Another problem with these experiments is they fail to produce any of the nucleotides (the "letters" of the genetic code) that are necessary for the DNA strand. Nor do they yield the enzymes that copy information to the RNA strand. So, scientists have a long way to go before they can create life in a test tube.

3. **Left-handers only:** There is also the issue that amino acids come in both right-handed and left-handed varieties. All of the building blocks of the protein molecule are left-handed. A single right-handed amino acid destroys the whole physical shape of the protein. But these experiments produce amino acids in a 50/50 mix.

4. **The monkey god of evolution:** This spells serious trouble for the time factor that was hailed as the savior of evolution. Evolutionists often say that if you give a monkey a word processor and enough time, he will eventually type all possible combinations of letters, including *Webster's Dictionary* and *Encyclopedia Britannica*. They claim that this is how evolution works and why it takes so long. But, the 50/50 mix of right and left-handed amino acids changes the picture. The monkey would now have a word processor that

randomly switched back and forth from laying down letters to erasing them. Such a monkey would then put out just as much work in five minutes as he would in a billion years because he would eventually erase everything he wrote!

Exhibit 9d: Revenge of the Super-Scientists: The "Self-Organizing" Counterattack

In the face of the rising tsunami of evidence that reveals just how dumb "dumb luck" really is, evolutionists have come up with some innovative theories in an effort to counterattack. Summaries of these are listed below, but a more complete scientific presentation and evaluation is available in Stephen Meyers's fascinating book *Signature in the Cell*. I highly recommend it, but the language is definitely full of scientese.

1. **"Who's on first?"** The classic Abbott and Costello "Who's on First" comedy routine is about a baseball team whose players have such unusual nicknames that they produce hilarious confusion. As Costello tries time and again to find out the player's names, he always seems to end up at third base. This is also the case with the so called self-organizing theories. No matter how they start, they all end up at the same place—missing information. There are protein-first theories, DNA-first models, RNA-first models and theories that propose that lower-level molecules evolved into more advanced ones. But all of these just shift the main problem to other presumed and unexplained sources. That problem is the staggering amount of data stored in the unsimple cell and the extremely efficient and complex, highly advanced storage system it employs, not to mention the operating and other regulatory systems that are required. All of these models still assume the magic existence of all of this information and fail to address its origin.

2. **Dumb luck/dumb law models:** Some theories add various laws of nature to dumb luck in an effort to make it smarter and improve the odds. But laws produce order in a rigid sense. They allow no freedom to create and innovate. And this is what the detailed and highly specific nature of the information contained in DNA requires. They, too, fail miserably.

3. **Computers to the rescue?** Recently, a number of highly complex computer simulations of evolution have been attempted. But these also fail because they still require the programmer to insert data into the simulation artificially. They have to provide a target sequence of data for the simulation to "evolve" towards. And they also have to filter the results of each random attempt so that the target sequence is eventually reached. But these influences are simply not present in nature. Out here, in the real world, we call it cheating!

Exhibit 9e: Dumb and Not So Lucky

Earlier, I explained why I prefer the term *dumb luck* (because it emphasizes the fact that chance is void of intelligent, reasoned selection). But, what if the *truth* is that engineering genius *was* involved in the origin of life?

"Okay, so how can we tell if intelligence is a factor in something?"

1. **"Is engineering genius an option?"** Well, a guy named William Dembski wrote a book titled *The Design Inference*[31] in which he gives some guidelines for detecting purposeful design that are now widely accepted in the scientific community. Here is a snapshot of what he came up with.

   ✓ **Common sense is just common sense!** One of the points he makes is that we know instinctively how to recognize design and do so, without thinking about it, thousands of times every day. For example, let's say you are out for your morning walk and find a cell phone on the sidewalk. What do you conclude? Would you really think that the plastic, polished metal, circuit board, charged battery, memory chip, code for the operating system and apps, and personal data all came together by some natural "little bang" accident?

"Of course not!"

Why?

"Because that's ridiculous!"

That's right! You know full well how to recognize design when you see it, don't you? If you're honest, you'll navigate to the info page to find out how to return it to its owner.

"Oh but, isn't it possible, given millions and billions of years that sooner or later this exact arrangement of materials could happen by accident and fall on somebody's sidewalk?"

If you believe that, call me...there's a bridge I'd like to sell you!

✓ **Recognizing intelligent design:** Dembski gives a two-fold test that can determine if something is designed by an intelligent being: (1) extremely low probability, far outside the range of normal, reasonable expectations that the event or item in question occurred by chance; and (2) the presence of meaningful specification, or specific meaning that produces a working result. When something exhibits these two qualities, it's *reasonable* to conclude that engineering genius was the cause, rather than dumb luck.

For example, if you find a paper on your desk with the "Ten Commandments" on it, written out by hand, you can safely conclude that it was purposefully written by an intelligent being. Why? Because (1) the odds are extremely low that ink would randomly form out of thin air and drop on a piece of paper in the specific form and arrangement of the English letters and spaces that make up the Ten Commandments; and (2) the fact that what is written follows the specific rules of English spelling and grammar that successfully work to express meaning. You rightly deduce that it was created by a smart person because, in your experience, meaning and function are always the products of intelligence. Right?

✓ **Eliminating dumb luck:**

"So, when is it safe to cross 'chance' of the list as a possible cause of something?"

Well, to be fair, the tests that Dembski gives are not quite enough. We must also consider the "probabilistic resources" available. That means we have to consider if sufficient time exists to allow the number of attempts required, and if the environment is capable of facilitating the event.

Let's say I want to roll a one with a six-sided die. So, I get out a board game and retrieve a die from the box and clear some space on the kitchen table. The environment is now capable of supporting the event. And I notice that I have a half hour before *SpongeBob* comes on, so I have enough time to make the number of attempts required to roll a one. Let's say it takes me eight attempts to get a one. Thus, the resources were available to give dumb luck the opportunity to work. So, in this instance, dumb luck is a reasonable conclusion as a cause for the result.

2. **Applying the principles**: So let's apply what we've just learned to the origin of life and see what happens.

✓ **"Okay, what are the odds that life arose by chance?"** Mathematicians tell us that an event with greater odds than 1 in 10^{50} (a 1 with 50 zeros after it) is impossible or would be considered a bona fide miracle at the very least. To further underscore the absurdity of the following calculations, scientists have estimated the number of electrons, protons, and neutrons in the known universe to be 10^{80}.[32]

A modest protein has a chain of about 150 amino acids. We know that twenty different amino acids make up the proteins that occur in living things. So there are 10^{195} possible combinations, most of which are not functional proteins. There are also many kinds of chemical bonds that take place between amino acids, but peptide bonds are the only ones in living things. The odds of this occurring by chance are 1 in 10^{45}. All of the amino acids must be left-handed—the odds are 1 in 10^{45}. The protein must be able to fold into a stable form—the chances are 1 in 10^{77}. Even if we allow for some tolerance for variations we find that the odds of a modest functioning protein forming by chance in the primordial soup is 1 in 10^{164}. Oh, but that's just a protein. We need a whole bacterium!

Assuming that a modest bacterium would need at least 250 of these functioning proteins in order to survive—the chances are roughly 1 in $10^{41,000}$. This number is confirmed by British astronomer, Sir Fredrick Hoyle, who also calculated the odds that the proteins necessary to build a single bacterium could be spontaneously generated in primitive soup. He came up with 1 chance in $10^{40,000}$. Commenting on this he wrote, "It is enough to bury Darwin and his whole theory of evolution. There was no primeval soup, neither on this planet nor on any other, and if the beginnings of life were not random they must therefore have been the product of purposeful intelligence."[33]

These numbers are impressive. But they only consider the odds that the proteins could be formed. They didn't figure in the construction of the DNA or the cell wall or the cytoplasm or the pili or the flagella or the ribosomes or the microbots and all the rest by dumb luck. A more accurate assessment was made by Yale physicist Harold Morowitz. He figured that even if all of the necessary materials were present, the odds that they would combine into a living bacterium by dumb luck would be 1 in $10^{100,000,000,000}$![34] That is a number so great that it would take several thousand encyclopedia volumes just write out all the zeros…in very tiny print!

✓ **"But wait, we forgot to consider the probabilistic resources!"** Okay, let's give evolutionists the benefit of the doubt and say that the universe is fourteen billion orbital years old. If this were true, the number of seconds since the big bang would be roughly 10^{17}. The smallest unit of time is Planck time, which is 10^{-43} seconds. So, the maximum number of events that can take place in the universe leading to a specific result since the big bang is 10^{140}, which isn't even enough time to roll a single, modest, functioning protein!

And consider the environment. Is our universe a giant primeval soup, 100 percent dedicated to forming a working protein? Even if it were, it would still take a trillion-trillion more universes-worth of primeval soup to form just one cell!

Add to all of this the fact that geologists studying pre-life rocks have concluded that Earth's atmosphere and oceans were hostile to the chance formation of proteins. James Brooks made this observation, "The nitrogen content of early Pre-Cambrian organic matter is relatively low. From this we can be reasonably certain that: there never was any substantial amount of 'primitive soup' on earth when Pre-Cambrian sediments were formed; if such a soup ever existed it was only for a brief period of time."[35] Maybe Sir Hoyle was right.

But remember the expansion factor that we talked about earlier? And remember the discovery that the speed of light has been slowing down? These and other discoveries now prove that the Earth and universe are less than ten thousand years old. Sir Hoyle *was* right! It doesn't matter if the universe is fourteen billion or ten thousand years old. The probabilistic resources needed to evolve a simple cell even in a favorable environment are just not there!

"Oh, that proves that there must be a multiverse..."

Really? So a bacterium evolved in another universe somewhere and was transported here by pixies? Don't you see how absurd this is getting?

✓ **Is there evidence for engineering genius?** *"'Come now, and let us reason together,' says the Lord."* (Isa 1:18a, NKJV) Is there any evidence that this unsimple bacterium that we have been examining was designed on purpose by a brilliant Creator? Well, let's apply Dembski's tests. We have just demonstrated the extremely low probability, or impossibility, that it could have happened by dumb luck. So, is there any specific meaning present?

Let's consider the DNA molecule once again. You have to remember that even if a DNA molecule could generate by chance, it would only be the equivalent of a blank computer hard drive. The simplest DNA strand contains programming hundreds of times more complex than the biggest supercomputer yet developed by man. If all of the letters in a human DNA strand were printed in one-thousand 500-page books, it would still require a microscope to read them! How did all of that programming get there? And since the cell can't live without that programming, isn't it reasonable to assume that it represents specific meaning? But wait! There's more...

Let's consider the genetic code itself. Information scientists tell us that language conventions are always the result of intelligent, purposeful design. Never, under any circumstances, can they possibly arise by dumb luck because languages were invented as a means for one intelligent being to communicate with another. They only occur within the world of intelligent beings. They assign meaning to certain symbols and/or sounds and more meaning to specific arrangements of them. And, meaning happens to be an *exclusive* product of intelligence!

For example, if we find the figure *l* written on a tablet, what does it mean? In English, it could be a lowercase *L* or the number *1*. But it might mean something else in another language. You see, without an intelligent entity to assign some meaning to the figure and communicate that meaning to another intelligent being, the figure is, in fact, *meaningless*. Furthermore, if we somehow discover that the figure does have meaning, it also *proves* the existence of the intelligent entity that assigned the figure meaning in the first place, does it not?

This presents a huge boulder of kryptonite for the evolutionary superhero because the programming on the DNA molecule is written in a language convention that we call the genetic code. As we have already seen, it is complete with alphabet, punctuation and by far the most complex rules of grammar and syntax of any programming language ever devised by man! This brilliant masterpiece of highly advanced, sophisticated engineering didn't just require intelligence. You can't just pull some kid off the street and expect him or her to invent the code and successfully duplicate the information in the DNA molecule of our unsimple bacterium can you? No, this is the work of *engineering genius!* This same code is used in the programming of all living things. Since we are dealing with a language convention, we are forced to ask, *who* assigned the meaning of the alphabet and rules of syntax in the genetic code? Put me down for the record: I believe that the very existence of the genetic code with its alphabet and syntax is scientific *proof* of the existence of our Creator!

3. Are you a gambler?

"*So then, what are the odds that God created life on Earth?*"

We just saw that Yale physicist Harold Morowitz figured that the odds that all of the materials would combine into a living bacterium by dumb luck would be 1 in $10^{100,000,000,000}$. So, what are the odds that it was put together on purpose? Exactly the opposite! Try $10^{100,000,000,000}$ in 1 on for size! Are you a gambler? On which of these scenarios will you bet your eternity?

The Evidence is In!

Some Brilliant Scientists Weigh In:

1. **Francis Crick:** The famous co-discoverer of the DNA helix said, "An honest man, armed with all the knowledge available to us now, could only state that in some sense, the origin of life appears at the moment to be almost a miracle, so many are the conditions which would have had to have been satisfied to get it going."[36]

2. **Klaus Dose:** President of the Institute of Biochemistry at the University of Johannes Gutenberg states that research efforts until now have "led to a better perception of the immensity of the problem of the origin of life on earth rather than to its solution. At present, all discussions on principal theories and experiments in the field either end in a stalemate or a confession of ignorance."[37]

3. **An anonymous Cambridge supervisor:** "The field is becoming increasingly populated with cranks. Everyone knows everybody else's theory doesn't work, but no one is willing to admit it about his own."[38]

Does evolution really disprove the Bible?
Now we return to our original question. Has science really proven that we evolved by dumb luck? Has it proven the Bible to be scientifically inaccurate? Or has it proven that life is the result of engineering genius so incredible it staggers the imagination, just as the Bible has said all along? But if scientists know all of this, why do they still cling to evolution? There are several reasons:

1. **Evolution Mania: It's my team!** One influence is undoubtedly a human trait that we are all guilty of in one way or another. That is what I call the sports-fan mentality. I happen to like football and, yes, I am a fan of my local NFL team. Through thick and thin, good times and bad, I remain loyal to my team! But this is a heart decision, not a head decision. I could just as easily choose to love a different team. Unfortunately, we all have a tendency to let our heart make decisions for us. It happens in politics. "Why I was born a Republocrat, just like my daddy, and his daddy before him! So I will vote Republocrat till I die!" Once our heart gets involved, we stop researching the issues and examining individual character. We just get out the pom-poms and start jumping up and down, rooting for our team or party or whatever it may be. And the same is true of religion and evolution. Some people have embraced the evolution team; they love it with all their heart, they've worked all their lives for it, and they aren't going to stop, no matter what the evidence or odds.

2. **Evolution Mania: It's a philosophy.** A statement made by Harvard biochemist George Wald is also telling:

> There are only two possibilities as to how life arose. One is spontaneous generation arising to evolution; the other is a supernatural creative act of God. There is no third possibility. Spontaneous

generation, that life arose from non-living matter was scientifically disproved 120 years ago by Louis Pasteur and others. That leaves us with the only possible conclusion that life arose as a supernatural creative act of God. I will not accept that philosophically because I do not want to believe in God. Therefore, I choose to believe in that which I know is scientifically impossible; spontaneous generation arising to evolution.[39]

3. **Evolution Mania: It's the law!** Creation, on the other hand, is classified by the government as religion, which means that it cannot be taught by any school funded by the government. Nor can it be tolerated as a conclusion of any scientific research funded by the government. And government funding, of some kind, is involved in almost all scientific research regarding the origin of life. So, if a scientist dared to "cave in" to the truth about evolution, he could lose his job, his health insurance, his retirement plan, and everything he has worked all of his life to achieve for himself and his family. Evolution may not be the truth, but *it is the law!* This is why scientists believe they have a right to cheat and make so many unreasonable claims. They are mandated to do so by the government that provides their livelihood. I wonder…has our zeal to separate church from state inadvertently caused us to separate the truth from state?

4. **Evolution Mania: "But creation is not science!"** So what? I don't dispute that. But that's not even the issue! The issue is *whether creation is the truth!* Who says I have to live in a "science box" anyway? I'd rather live in "truth box." And whose "science box" am I supposed to live in? As Dr. Stephen Meyer points out,

To say that an idea, theory, concept, inference, or explanation is or isn't scientific requires a particular definition of science. Yet if different scientists and philosophers of science could not agree about what the scientific method is, how could they decide what did and did not qualify as science?[40]

Martin Eger agrees. "Demarcation arguments have collapsed. Philosophers of science don't hold them anymore. They may still enjoy acceptance in the popular world, but that's a different world."[41] And Dr. Meyer adds, "Theories are not rejected with definitions, but with evidence."[42]

What's in your heart?

So, we've looked at some of the evidence. But if you are an evolutionist, I'm sure you're still jumping up and down with your pom-poms cheering for your team. But I urge you to honestly consider whether your loyalty is based on the evidence or emotion. Honestly, the odds that dumb luck pulled off the origin of life are so staggering that dumb luck would have to be God! Truly, as David wrote, *"The fool has said in his heart, 'There is no God.'"* (Ps 14:1, NKJV) So, let me ask you, what's in your heart?

Here Lies
Darwin's Theory of
EVOLUTION
assassinated by
Missing "Missing Links"
Speed of Light Slowdown
The "Goldilocks Zone"
The Un-"Simple Cell"
DNA & the Genetic Code

Evolution is dead!

The Bible is Alive!

Flora Nienaber © 2013

"The sword of the spirit is living and powerful!"

CHECK IT OUT

As we have seen, God has taken care to embed the Bible with characteristics that set it apart from all other holy books. The unity it displays is miraculous considering the number and variety of authors and the time span involved. He made it a history book, so that its accuracy could be tested and proved. He filled it with prophecy so that history could verify its dependability. And science has yet to catch up to the depth of truth in its pages, proving that the God of the Bible is, indeed, our Creator. But there is one final factor that sets the Bible apart from all of the other holy books. It is a living love letter to each of us, individually, from a living God who is eager to be a part of our lives. Since he has gone to such great lengths to deliver his message to us, it only stands to reason that he would accompany it with his own presence and power. Indeed, the Holy Spirit has chosen to use the words in this book to do his miraculous work in our lives. The Holy Spirit breathes a life-giving quality into it, such that the writer of Hebrews even says that it's alive! *"For the word of God is alive and powerful. It is sharper than the sharpest two-edged sword, cutting between soul and spirit, between joint and marrow. It exposes our innermost thoughts and desires."* (Heb 4:12, NLT) Paul even calls it, *"the sword of the Spirit, which is the word of God."* (Eph 6:17b, NKJV) Now that doesn't mean that your Bible is going to sprout legs and start walking around. It means that the one and only true *living* God will meet with us face to face, as it were, when we seek him in its pages. God said this about the effectiveness of his word, through the prophet Isaiah.

> *For as the rain comes down, and the snow from heaven, and do not return there, but water the earth, and make it bring forth and bud, that it may give seed to the sower and bread to the eater, so shall My word be that goes forth from My mouth; it shall not return to Me void, but it shall accomplish what I please, and it shall prosper in the thing for which I sent it.* (Isa 55:10-11 NKJV)

So, the Bible is infused with the miraculous, life-changing power of the Holy Spirit Himself! It is not just a book. In a very real sense, it's alive with the very presence of God for those who are seeking to meet him! And Christians everywhere are living evidence of this fact. With this in mind, I submit the final exhibit in this book.

PRESENTING FOR EVIDENCE, EXHIBIT 10:
"Oh, taste and see that the Lord is good." (Ps 34:8a, NKJV)

Yes, this is a try-him-you'll-like-him challenge issued by David centuries ago. One of the awesome things about God's Word is that, no matter what situation we find ourselves in, it meets us where we are. A great example of this is the book of Psalms. It's not all ice cream and cake, you know! The psalmists express all of life's emotions you can think of, including the negative ones: apprehension, confusion, anxiety, fear, depression, and doubt. It's all there. Of course the positive ones are there as well: love, thanksgiving, forgiveness, victory, praise, and more. Another great example is the Book of Proverbs. You can find wisdom there for many of the situations and issues we find ourselves dealing with today. God has not abandoned us! Far from it; he wants to be a part of our lives, if we will only let him.

And that's where the try-him-you'll-like-him challenge comes in. We have validated the Bible in the previous chapters as being the container of God's message. Now, in this chapter I want to look at the message itself. Although the Bible contains many messages that meet the individual needs of our lives, it contains two general messages to two different kinds of people. The first message is to those who do not yet have a personal relationship with the Author; and the second is to those who do.

Exhibit 10a: God's Invitation to the Pre-Saved

If you have not yet accepted Christ as your Savior, you need to understand some things before you begin reading the Bible. Although there is much written to you, the very first message is an invitation for you to establish a personal relationship with God. This requires faith, and Paul said, "So then faith comes by hearing, and hearing by the word of God." (Rom 10:17, NKJV) Peter adds that we can be "born again not from some seed that will decay, but from one that cannot decay, through the living Word of God that lasts forever." (1Pet 1:23, CJB) The Bible's message to you has the potential to change your life in a very positive way for all eternity. But there is an issue that needs to be addressed first.

Spiritual ears are required.
"What does that mean?"
I will let Paul explain:

> We (who have been born again) *have not received the spirit of the world but the Spirit that is from God, so that we may understand the things freely given us by God. And we speak about them not with words taught by human wisdom, but with words taught by the Spirit, describing spiritual realities in spiritual terms. Now the natural* (pre-saved) *person does not accept what pertains to the Spirit of God, for to him it is foolishness, and he cannot understand it, because it is judged spiritually.* (1Cor 2:12-14, NABRE)

In other words, until you give your life to Christ, or are at least sincerely open to listening for his still, small voice, you will not be able to understand what you read. My son and I have spent some time working in the field of information technology. (Yes, we're computer geeks.) So when we get together we tend to "talk shop" about the latest computers and technologies. My wife gets very frustrated at this. She complains that she doesn't understand anything we are talking about. Well, it's the same with reading the Bible. Unless God gives you spiritual ears, so to speak, it will be much like listening to a conversation between two computer geeks—it will be nothing but gobbledygook to you. On the other hand if you are a fellow computer geek, you will not only understand but you will be excited to join in the conversation. That's the way it is with the Bible. God gives his kids spiritual ears and eyes, so they can understand the message he has written and join him in an eternal adventure.

God's Message to Pre-Saved People

So, if you will accept Jesus as your Savior, (which has nothing to do with joining a denomination or church) the Holy Spirit will be delighted to open up the riches of this powerful book to you. He has purposely made it so easy that even a child can be embraced in his arms. (He loves kids!) All it takes is a simple prayer that contains three elements:

1. **First, admit you are a sinner.**
   "Hey, wait a minute! I'm a good person! I'm confident God will see that I've done a whole lot more good things than bad and let me into heaven!"

   Well, before you throw this book away, let me at least explain what the Bible means by that. I have no problem admitting that I'm a sinner but if you are offended by this idea, it's important to understand that even though you may be a good person by human reckoning, God's standard is absolute, perfect, lifelong goodness. Consider the words of Jesus. *"Therefore you shall be perfect, just as your Father in heaven is perfect."* (Mat 5:48, NKJV) That means more than just not doing bad things. It also means always doing good things at every opportunity. There are very few of us humans who would have the guts to make a claim of perfection like that, especially while standing before God, because he's got the video on all of us. And to make matters worse, he knows our motives. We can't hide anything from him. *"God would surely have known it, for he knows the secrets of every heart."* (Ps 44:21, NLT)

   Earlier we learned that God created time and, therefore, lives outside of it. That means that when he looks at our lives, he doesn't see it the way you and I experience it, in moment-by-moment slices. He sees the whole thing, beginning to end, as a complete unit. And since God is holy (the super extreme world champion perfectionist of all time), it's all or nothin'! If you're in the hospital with a lung infection they don't say, "Well it's just your lungs that are the problem, so the rest of you can go home." No, the rest of you ain't goin' nowhere till your lungs are clear! That's the same way God views your life. If there ever was and/or will ever be one thought, word, or deed that was or will be selfish, or if you ever failed and/or will ever fail to be kind to anyone when you had or will have the opportunity, even if you haven't committed and won't commit any serious sins, like murder, I'm sorry. You do not measure up to God's standard of absolute lifelong perfect goodness, and you have no hope of being allowed into his heaven based on that. Of course that doesn't mean we shouldn't try to be good people. But that's not God's point. The point is that, in the eyes of a holy God, *all* of us are sinners and cannot achieve the perfect lifelong goodness he demands. Paul makes it very clear that this is a universal human condition. *"All have sinned and come short of earning God's praise."* (Rom 3:23, CJB)

"Well, what happens if I don't admit I'm a sinner?"

There are a number of places in the Bible that describe God's character in terms of light. *"God is light, and there is no darkness in him at all."* (1Jn 1:5b, NCT) And conversely, the Bible describes pre-saved people as darkness. *"For you used to be darkness; but now, united with the Lord, you are light. Live like children of light, for the fruit of the light is in every kind of goodness, rightness and truth."* (Eph 5:8-9, CJB) So what happens to darkness when the light is turned on? Darkness can't survive in the presence of light, can it? Paul wrote, *"For the wages of sin is death, but the free gift of God is eternal life in Christ Jesus our Lord."* (Rom 6:23, ESV) Eternal death or separation from God is not going to be fun. Since God is good, it means separation from all that is good. Since God is love, it means separation from all that is love. Jesus describes it as a place where *"there will be weeping and gnashing of teeth."* (Matt 8:12b, NKJV)

But this is not what God wants! When Paul was telling the story of how he was saved, he says that Jesus called him to be an apostle to the gentiles *"to open their eyes, so they may turn from darkness to light and from the power of Satan to God. Then they will receive forgiveness for their sins and be given a place among God's people, who are set apart by faith in me."* (Acts 26:18, NLT) John summarizes all of this for us like this:

> *This is the message we heard from Jesus and now declare to you: God is light, and there is no darkness in him at all. So we are lying if we say we have fellowship with God but go on living in spiritual darkness; we are not practicing the truth. But if we are living in the light, as God is in the light, then we have fellowship with each other, and the blood of Jesus, his Son, cleanses us from all sin. If we claim we have no sin, we are only fooling ourselves and not living in the truth. But if we confess our sins to him* (agree with him about them)*, he is faithful and just to forgive us our sins and to cleanse us from all wickedness. If we claim we have not sinned, we are calling God a liar and showing that his word has no place in our hearts.* (1Jn 1:5-10, NLT)

So, if you want into God's heaven, the first step is to admit that you are a sinner.

2. Second, put your trust in Jesus's payment for your sins.
The next step is to believe that Jesus died to pay God's judicial penalty for your sins, which, as we just saw, is eternal death or separation from him. Jesus said,

> *For God so loved the world that He gave* (a sacrificial term) *His only begotten Son, that whoever believes* (see the glossary entry for "believe" for an important definition) *in Him should not perish but have everlasting life. For God did not send His Son into the world to*

condemn the world, but that the world through Him might be saved. He who believes in Him is not condemned; but he who does not believe is condemned already, because he has not believed in the name of the only begotten Son of God. And this is the condemnation, that the light has come into the world, and men loved darkness rather than light, because their deeds were evil. (Jn 3:16-19, NKJV)

And Paul wrote,

Once we, too, were foolish and disobedient. We were misled and became slaves to many lusts and pleasures. Our lives were full of evil and envy, and we hated each other. But—"When God our Savior revealed his kindness and love, he saved us, not because of the righteous things we had done, but because of his mercy. He washed away our sins, giving us a new birth and new life through the Holy Spirit. He generously poured out the Spirit upon us through Jesus Christ our Savior. Because of his grace he declared us righteous and gave us confidence that we will inherit eternal life." (Titus 3:3-7 NLT)

And, "Jesus said to him, 'I am the way, the truth, and the life. No one comes to the Father except through Me.'" (Jn 14:6, NKJV)

3. **And finally make him *your*Lord and Savior.** Jesus said, "Look! I have been standing at the door, and I am constantly knocking. If anyone hears me calling him and opens the door, I will come in and fellowship with him and he with me" (Rev 3:20, TLB) When you open the door of your life to him, the Holy Spirit enters you and you are "born again." Jesus explains:

Jesus answered and said to him, 'Most assuredly, I say to you, unless one is born again, he cannot see the kingdom of God.' Nicodemus said to Him, 'How can a man be born when he is old? Can he enter a second time into his mother's womb and be born?' Jesus answered, 'Most assuredly, I say to you, unless one is born of water (physical birth) and the Spirit, he cannot enter the kingdom of God. That which is born of the flesh is flesh, and that which is born of the Spirit is spirit. Do not marvel that I said to you, 'You must be born again.' (Jn 3:3-7 NKJV)

"Okay, so, what am I supposed to do?"
First of all, salvation cannot be earned through any deed that we perform. Crawling around a mountain on your hands and knees will not earn you any brownie points with God. As Paul stated, "not by works of righteousness which we have done, but according to His mercy He saved us." (Titus 3:5a, NKJV) This is because God does not want us to be able to boast in how good we are or how much we have given up or denied ourselves. Paul tells us "For by grace you have been saved through faith, and that not of yourselves; it is the gift of God, not of works, lest anyone should boast." (Eph 2:8-9, NKJV) A simple prayer is all that is needed to receive this awesome gift.

Praying is not a complicated thing. God is not at all impressed with religious-sounding words. What he wants is sincerity of heart. So, you don't have to worry about getting all of your words technically correct. He sees your heart, and that is all that matters to him. But, if you would like to use it, here is...

A Model Prayer
Dear God,
I realize that, in your eyes, I am a sinner and have no hope of spending eternity with you based on being good. But I also know that you saw my need and sent your son, Jesus Christ, to die on the cross in my place. So, I now receive him as my Savior and invite the Holy Spirit to come and live in me and make me your child. Thank you for your free gift of salvation.

Help me, by the strength of your Holy Spirit, to live a life pleasing to you. In Jesus's name, I pray. Amen.

If you have prayed that prayer for the first time, it is my privilege to welcome you into the family of God! See Appendix B for some important tips on maintaining your new relationship with him. And then continue reading because the next part applies to you and your new "spiritual ears."

Exhibit 10b: God's challenge to "Born Againers"
The second kind of person that God writes to in his Word, are those who have been saved. For the most part, the Bible was written to you.

> *For this reason we also thank God without ceasing, because when you received the word of God which you heard from us, you welcomed it not as the word of men, but as it is in truth, the word of God, which also effectively works in you who believe.* (1Thes 2:13, NKJV)

So, God uses the Bible to do his work in the lives of believers, as well. Jesus himself links it to the process of Christian growth when he prays, *"Sanctify them by Your truth. Your word is truth."* (Jn 17:17, NKJV) Sanctification is "theologian-speak" for the continuing process of growing in Christian faith and behavior. Peter explains further:

> *For as you know him better, he will give you, through his great power, everything you need for living a truly good life: he even shares his own glory and his own goodness with us! And by that same mighty power he has given us all the other rich and wonderful blessings he promised; for instance, the promise to save us from the lust and rottenness all around us, and to give us his own character.* (2Pet 1:3-4, TLB)

Now, that doesn't mean Christians are perfect (just ask my wife). But it does mean that we can at least look forward to some continuous and measurable improvement.

The Normal Christian Life

The Bible gives us a blueprint for the role it should play in our lives as Christians. *"All Scripture is given by inspiration of God, and is profitable for doctrine, for reproof, for correction, for instruction in righteousness, that the man of God may be complete, thoroughly equipped for every good work."* (2 Tim 3:16-17, NKJV) Let's have a closer look at the four things Paul mentions here.

1. **Doctrine:** This is a dirty word to many people, but doctrine is simply what a group or person teaches about something. For example, the Bible has much to say about the nature of God—who he is and what he is like. Theologians call this the doctrine of God. The Bible also explains, among many other things, the meaning of our own lives:

   - ✓ **"Was I created on purpose, or did I just evolve?"** *"Know that the LORD, He is God; it is He who has made us, and not we ourselves; we are His people and the sheep of His pasture."* (Ps 100:3, NKJV)
   - ✓ **"Is there a reason I'm here?"** I'm not talking about *here* as in your house or school or wherever you happen to be right now. I'm talking about your purpose in life. *"Thou hast created all things, and for thy pleasure they are and were created."* (Rev 4:11b, KJV) We are created for God's pleasure in the same way that parents are excited about bringing children into the world because it pleases them to start a family. God is really into family building. *"The last word, when all is heard: Fear God and keep his commandments, for this concerns all humankind; because God will bring to judgment every work, with all its hidden qualities, whether good or bad."* (Eccl 12:13-14, NABRE)

✓ **"Where will I end up?"** I'm not talking about needing a GPS (although my wife thinks that might be a good idea for me). I'm talking about heaven or hell. *"And anyone not found written in the Book of Life was cast into the lake of fire."* (Rev 20:15, NKJV) And Jesus said, *"Don't be so surprised! Indeed, the time is coming when all the dead in their graves will hear the voice of God's Son, and they will rise again. Those who have done good (receiving Christ as Savior) will rise to experience eternal life, and those who have continued in evil will rise to experience judgment."* (Jn 5:28-29, NLT)

2. **Reproof:** Ouch! This is another bad word to a lot of people. After all, who likes being chewed out for doing something wrong? But when God calls something sin, it's because it has a destructive effect on us or others. For example, stealing something that doesn't belong to me not only hurts the person I stole from and ruins my relationship with them, it also heaps a load of guilt on my heart, which is bad for me. But God loves us both the same and wants me to behave in a way that is best for both of us. So I need to be willing to let God show me when I'm doing something wrong like that and also be willing to stop. Or if I've already done it, I need to be willing to make it right. That's what God's reproof is all about.

In this way, the Bible acts like a scalpel. *"For the word of God is living and powerful, and sharper than any two-edged sword, piercing even to the division of soul and spirit, and of joints and marrow, and is a discerner of the thoughts and intents of the heart."* (Heb 4:12, NKJV) Even though God's reproofs may cut, like a knife, if he gets the cancer out, so to speak, the result will be life for me rather than sickness and death. Of course, God already sees the thoughts and intents of our hearts. We can't hide anything from him. But he uses his Word to expose them for us to see. Once we see what we are really like, we have the opportunity to do what comes next.

3. **Correction:** God uses his Word to challenge us to change our behavior. It works much like a mirror in a spiritual sense.

> *For if you listen to the word and don't obey, it is like glancing at your face in a mirror. You see yourself, walk away, and forget what you look like. But if you look carefully into the perfect law that sets you free, and if you do what it says and don't forget what you heard, then God will bless you for doing it. (James 1:23-25, NLT)*

Think of the Holy Spirit as coach for the game of life. Coaches usually yell a lot, but the Holy Spirit is a quiet coach. What would happen if an athlete refused to listen to his coach? His game would deteriorate, wouldn't it? It may even cause him to be kicked off the team. But if an athlete makes the corrections that his coach gives him, his game will get better. The same is true of us. If we are chained down with bad habits or incorrect thinking, God's correction can set us free! *"Then Jesus said to those Jews who believed him, 'If you abide* (live your life immersed) *in My word, you are My disciples indeed. And you shall know the truth, and the truth shall make you free.'"* (Jn 8:31-32, NKJV)

The Bible also talks about our sins as if they were permanent stains on our lives. But as we listen to God's reproof and correction and repent (turn around and take the necessary steps to change), he scrubs our conscience clean. Jesus told his disciples, *"You are already clean because of the word which I have spoken to you."* (Jn 15:3, NKJV) And the Psalmist adds, *"How can a young man cleanse his way? By taking heed according to Your word. With my whole heart I have sought You; Oh, let me not wander from Your commandments! Your word I have hidden in my heart, that I might not sin against You!"* (Ps 119:9-11, NKJV)

4. **For instruction in righteousness:** Have you ever tried to navigate through your house during a power outage in the dark, trying to find a flashlight, stubbing your toes and knocking things over? I always prefer to see where I'm

going. Well, the Bible refers to God's Word as a lamp, figuratively speaking, because it enlightens us on how to live so that we stay at peace with him and with each other. *"For these commands are a lamp, this teaching is a light, and the corrections of discipline are the way to life."* (Prov 6:23, NIV) *"The teaching of your word gives light, so even the simple can understand."* (Ps 119:130, NLT)

Unfortunately, I love to eat, so much so that I have to control my food intake. Well, the Bible is described as food because it provides nourishment for our souls. And guess what? We can eat all we want! *"Like newborn babies, crave pure spiritual milk, so that by it you may grow up in your salvation, now that you have tasted that the Lord is good."* (1Pet 2:2-3 NIV)

When life happens and we experience pain and loss, God can use his Word to give us comfort. *"This is my comfort in my affliction, for Your word has given me life."* (Ps 119:50, NKJV) *"My soul is depressed; lift me up according to your word."* (Ps 119:28, NABRE)

When more life happens and the future doesn't look very good, the Bible can give us hope. *"For whatever things were written before were written for our learning, that we through the patience and comfort of the Scriptures might have hope."* (Rom 15:4, NKJV)

5. **Tools of the trade:** *"That the man (or woman) of God may be complete, thoroughly equipped for every good work."* (2Tim 3:17, NKJV) *"And you are complete in Him, who is the head of all principality and power."* (Col 2:10, NKJV)

So, God uses his Word to get us fixed up, coached up, scrubbed up, set free, enlightened, spiritually "ripped," and full of comfort and hope so we can tackle life in the power of the Holy Spirit, instead of just letting life happen to us!

It sounds like fun already, but wait....
There are even more good reasons to read and study the Bible.

1. **Because God wants us to.** When you text someone, or write them a letter or note, don't you want them to read it?
   "Of course."

So, the most obvious reason for us to read God's message to us is simply because he wants us to so he can bless us. This happens as we study to learn his ways and put them into practice in our lives. *"Study this Book of Instruction continually. Meditate on it day and night so you will be sure to obey everything written in it. Only then will you prosper and succeed in all you do."* (Josh 1:8, NLT) Jesus said, *"Man shall not live by bread alone, but by every word that proceeds from the mouth of God."* (Matt 4:4, NKJV)

"Oh, but I'm just so busy. I don't have time."

Too busy to be blessed? But I bet that if someone offered you a million bucks for reading the Bible cover to cover you'd have it done in less than two weeks despite your busy schedule! It really comes down to a matter of priorities, doesn't it? Just prayerfully read a little bit each day. Be persistent and ask for his help. And, he will bless you in ways that you wouldn't trade for a million bucks!

2. **Because our heavenly Father is the author.** If someone you knew, admired, and looked up to, wrote a book and dedicated it to you, would you read it? You would be honored to read such a book, wouldn't you? Well, your heavenly Father wrote every word of the Bible for your benefit and dedicated to you. And that's the point! It's not about a book, it's about a relationship with a real person—God! And Jesus said, *"He calls his own sheep by name."* (Jn 10:3, NKJV) That means he knows you by name. In a very real sense, you are God's muse, the inspiration that caused him to give his message to the prophets and apostles.

Unfortunately, some Christians encourage an anti-Bible attitude. They criticize what they think are "dead churches" that spend their time studying it. They believe that study is boring and church should be like a wild party all the time. They claim that these dead churches worship the book as if the members of the Trinity were Father, Son, and Holy Bible. They lead many to think that the Holy Spirit and his gifts replace God's written Word in our lives. What they fail to realize is that the Holy Spirit was the one who wrote the Bible in the first place by giving men his message! How can they claim to honor him while dishonoring the message he wrote to us?

3. **Because God values the Bible.** Have you ever wondered how much God values the message he wrote to us? David tells us *"For you have made your word [even] greater than the whole of your reputation."* (Ps 138:2, CJB) God is staking his reputation on his Word because it can only be fulfilled by his love, integrity, and faithfulness. And these qualities are exactly what he wants to show us!

4. **Because it is written with the blood of the martyrs.** God went through an awful lot of trouble to preserve the Bible for us. If you had a friend who died in the process of delivering an important message to you, would read it? Well, not only was Jesus's blood shed on the cross for us, but millions of martyrs were killed because they took steps to copy, translate, and keep the Bible safe. In that sense, every page was written with their blood, which they gladly gave to put this precious message into our hands! What value, then, should we give to God's Word? Perhaps we should be echoing the words of the psalmist. *"The words of the LORD are pure words, like silver tried in a furnace of earth, purified seven times."* (Ps 12:6, NKJV) *"More to be desired are they than gold, yea, than much fine gold."* (Ps 19:10a, NKJV)

5. **Because Satan can distort it.** Satan knows how to twist the words of the Bible for our destruction, and he has it memorized cover to cover! We need to know how to use it properly so we won't fall for his lies. He even tried to trick Jesus.

Then the devil took Him up into the holy city, set Him on the pinnacle of the temple and said to Him, "If You are the Son of God, throw Yourself down. For it is written: 'He shall give His angels charge over you,' and, 'In their hands they shall bear you up, lest you dash your foot against a stone.'

Jesus said to him, "It is written again, 'You shall not tempt the Lord your God.'" (Matt 4:5-7, NKJV)

Remember, at the beginning of the book we saw that Satan has presented us with many "alternate truths?" Well, that not only includes other religions that don't use the Bible, it also includes cults that *do* use the Bible, but misrepresent its teachings. For this reason every Christian should be "packin' heat" in the form of God's Word! *"I have written to you, young men, because you are strong, and the word of God abides in you, and you have overcome the wicked one."* (1Jn 2:14b, NKJV)

Taking the time to study the Bible to the extent that we know it well, is the only way to have victory over Satan's tricks! Paul echoed the same thing in 2 Corinthians. *"So that Satan will not outsmart us. For we are familiar with his evil schemes."* (2Cor 2:11, NLT)

But don't be overly concerned about Satan and his tricks to the point of fear. If you are seeking to know God better every day, he will prepare you for what's coming. God has given you this comforting promise, *"The temptations in your life are no different from what others experience. And God is faithful. He will not allow the temptation to be more than you can stand. When you are tempted, he will show you a way out so that you can endure."* (1Cor 10:13, NLT)

WHAT'S IN YOUR HEART?

If you have taken God up on his challenge, you are experiencing, firsthand, the fact that the Bible is not just a book—it's a doorway into the presence of the living Creator of the universe. Furthermore, he knows you by name and beckons you to enter for he loves you with an everlasting, infinite love. He is the one who made the door and has placed it before you in the first place. When you open the Bible, don't just open it to read. Open it to seek out the Author.

But regardless of whether you have taken God's challenge or not, it's time to take a look inside and assess our attitude toward his Word. So I ask you, what's in your heart?

Respect?

Since God has placed so much value on his message to us, shouldn't we, at the very least, treat it with a great deal of respect? This means that care should be taken when we study and interpret the Bible that the author's intent is respected. We study to find the truth and when it is found, we embrace it, even if it challenges our present ideas about things. *"Every word of God is pure; he is a shield to those who put their trust in Him. Do not add to His words, lest He rebuke you, and you be found a liar."* (Prov 30:5-6, NKJV)

> *For I testify to everyone who hears the words of the prophecy of this book: If anyone adds to these things, God will add to him the plagues that are written in this book; and if anyone takes away from the words of the book of this prophecy, God shall take away his part from the Book of Life, from the holy city, and from the things which are written in this book.* (Rev 22:18-19 NKJV)

Respecting God's Word really isn't that hard. All it takes is a little common sense and guidance by the Holy Spirit. The *Did God Really Say That? GPS Guide* has some great tips for properly interpreting God's Word. There is also a wealth of other resources available to help you. I list some in the next chapter.

Deep appreciation?

We've already seen that God wants us to seek him in his Word, like the psalmist, who sings, *"I rejoice at Your word as one who finds great treasure."* (Ps 119:162, NKJV) And Job, who declared, *"I have not* departed from the commandment of His lips; I have treasured the words of His mouth more than my necessary food." (Job 23:12, NKJV) In both of these verses we see the word *treasure*. Of course it implies great value. If you found a chest full of gold buried in your backyard, you'd probably be ecstatic, wouldn't you? You'd be jumping up and down, cheering. That's the idea that Job and the psalmist are trying to get across. That doesn't mean every Bible study should be a pep rally, but I suppose it wouldn't hurt every now and then.

Agreement?

Jesus said, "He who rejects Me, and does not receive My words, has that which judges him – the word that I have spoken will judge him in the last day. For I have not spoken on My own authority; but the Father who sent Me gave Me a command, what I should say and what I should speak." (Jn 12:48-49, NKJV) So every word comes to us with God's authority. And since that is true, our respect should work its way out in the form of agreement with the authority of his message. There are four critical areas where agreeing with God matters.

1. **Agree with God about our pea-brain thinking**: We need a Jesus "mind-meld" so we can see things with his eyes and know his mind and heart concerning the issues we face in life. God's Word is the key to that transformation. After all, going against the thinking of the brilliant engineer that created the universe and the unsimple cell is placing my hope in dumb luck! "'For My thoughts are not your thoughts, nor are your ways My ways,' says the LORD. 'For as the heavens are higher than the earth, so are My ways higher than your ways, and My thoughts than your thoughts.'" (Is 55:8-9, NKJV) "Trust in the LORD with all your heart, and lean not on your own understanding; In all your ways acknowledge Him, and He shall direct your paths. Do not be wise in your own eyes; fear the LORD and depart from evil. It will be health to your flesh, and strength to your bones." (Prov 3:5-8,

NKJV) Ah, but this takes faith and that's awfully hard for our proud pea-brains to swallow!

An example of this would be certain activist "Christians" who take violent vengeance on abortion clinic personnel and property. Even though the Bible teaches that life begins at conception and it is murder to kill an unborn child, it also teaches that murdering or harming an adult is wrong. Paul said, *"Beloved, do not avenge yourselves, but rather give place to wrath; for it is written, 'Vengeance is Mine, I will repay,' says the Lord.... Do not be overcome by evil, but overcome evil with good."* (Rom, 12:19-21 NKJV) So, we have to trust God with the souls of all the aborted children and trust him to work justice in his time. Giving in to frustration and a desire for revenge is, in itself, being overcome by evil. Another thing we learn in God's word is that he loves abortion doctors and nurses and is patiently waiting for them to repent so that he can forgive them! This doesn't make sense to human thinking, which is precisely why we cannot trust our own understanding and need to trust God instead.

2. **Agree with God about our unstable emotions:** Human feelings are notoriously unstable. They can thrash around all over the place from day to day and even hour to hour. Trusting them over God's Word is like building a house on sand. God's Word, on the other hand, is a solid rock!

> *Therefore whoever hears these sayings of Mine, and does them, I will liken him to a wise man who built his house on the rock: and the rain descended, the floods came, and the winds blew and beat on that house; and it did not fall, for it was founded on the rock. But everyone who hears these sayings of Mine, and does not do them, will be like a foolish man who built his house on the sand: and the rain descended, the floods came, and the winds blew and beat on that house; and it fell. And great was its fall.* (Matt 7:24-27, NKJV)

So, if we place our hope in God and his Word, we always have a reason to hope, regardless of the state of our emotions. *"Why are you cast down, O my soul, and why are you in turmoil within me? Hope in God; for I shall again praise him, my salvation."* (Ps 42:5, ESV)

3. **Agree with God about the world:** We are bombarded every day with messages from our society, our neighbors and friends, our loved ones, advertisers that want to sell us something, and on and on. One of the strongest temptations we can face is everybody's doing it or everybody has one. Not that everything in the world is bad, that's not the point. But Paul issues a warning that we would be wise to heed. *"Beware lest anyone cheat you through philosophy and empty deceit, according to the tradition of men, according to the basic principles of the world, and not according to Christ."* (Col 2:8, NKJV) I hate being cheated, don't you? John tells us that it's the love of world that gets us in trouble.

> *Do not love this world nor the things it offers you, for when you love the world, you do not have the love of the Father in you. For the world offers only a craving for physical pleasure, a craving for everything we see, and pride in our achievements and possessions. These are not from the Father, but are from this world. And this world is fading away, along with everything that people crave. But anyone who does what pleases God will live forever.* (1Jn 2:15-17, NLT)

Most people don't realize that this whole world system is profoundly influenced by Satan himself. John explains: *"We know that we are children of God, and that the whole world is under the control of the evil one."* (1Jn 5:19, NIV) This is why Paul tells us, *"Don't copy the behavior and customs of this world, but let God transform you into a new person by changing the way you think. Then you will learn to know God's will for you, which is good and pleasing and perfect."* (Rom 12:2, NLT)

4. **Agree with Jesus about his church:** Jesus is *alive!* He has risen from the dead and is seated at God the Father's right hand in heaven (Eph 1:20-23). This means that only he has authority over his Church. And all of the elders, preachers, pastors, apostles, bishops and even popes must submit themselves to his message to us in the Bible. *"And He is the head of the body, the church, who is the beginning, the firstborn from the dead, that in all things He may have the preeminence."* (Col 1:18, NKJV) Notice it doesn't say that he *was* the head of his Church. It says he *is* the head of his Church. Therefore, the Bible is our final authority for doctrine and practice in the church. (For more details on the Church and churches, see Appendix B.)

SPREAD THE GOOD NEWS!

And finally, if we love people the way we are supposed to, we should want to share God's Word with them. Jesus said, *"Go therefore and make disciples of all the nations, baptizing them in the name of the Father and of the Son and of the Holy Spirit, teaching them to observe all things that I have commanded you; and lo, I am with you always, even to the end of the age. Amen."* (Matt 28:19-20, NKJV) Paul told Timothy to *"Preach the word! Be ready in season and out of season. Convince, rebuke, exhort, with all longsuffering and teaching."* (2 Tim 4:2, NKJV) (See Appendix B for more on this, as well.)

Blessings...

And, here's the best part... *"Blessed is he who reads and those who hear the words of this prophecy, and keep those things which are written in it; for the time is near."* (Rev 1:3, NKJV)

THE EVIDENCE IS IN

Remember the opening illustration? Well, now you know quite a few things you could say when you are asked why you believe Christianity is the only way to God. You could tell them of the Bible's historical accuracy. It is full of specific dates, places, and names of people. You could say that no archaeological discovery has ever contradicted a single Bible reference, while hundreds have proved it correct. You could relate the Bible's record of fulfilled prophecy, and blow them away with a few examples. You could also tell them about the Bible's scientific accuracy and share some of the modern scientific knowledge found in its pages. And finally, you could cap it all off by relating the Bible's life-changing power. Tell them about your personal relationship with a living, loving Heavenly Father, and how he is actively participating with you in this miracle we call life. But wait, there's even more...

PRESENTING FOR EVIDENCE, EXHIBIT II:
The utterly unique, humanly incomprehensible nature and personality of the Living God of the Bible!

To be continued...

To Infinity and Beyond! Bible Study Tips and Additional Resources

"Man shall not live by bread alone." (Matt 4:4a, NKJV)

CHECK IT OUT

Not only is the Bible the most convincing proof of our faith, but it also has a vital role in maintaining it. And I think that Christians should make a lifetime habit of reading and studying it, not just for the sake of gaining academic knowledge, but in order to deepen a personal relationship with our infinite, all-powerful, all-knowing, and deeply loving heavenly Father. Such an adventure is truly one that will take us "to infinity and beyond!" But sadly, most believers are not aware of the rich bonanza of spiritual gems just waiting to be mined from the Bible's pages. Although they have read dozens, if not hundreds of other books, the vast majority of Christians have never read their Bible cover to cover even once. So, I would like to challenge you to do that, if you haven't already. And I also want to provide you with some basic resources and advice so you can get the most out of your reading and study time. Much more is available in the *Did God Really Say That? GPS Guide*.

ENGLISH TRANSLATIONS OF THE BIBLE

Mom warned me about doing risky things like this, but I am determined to take my life in my hands by discussing a controversial and divisive subject: English translations and versions of the Bible. Passions often run high when it comes to deciding...

Which version of the Bible is best?

There are quite a few churches and denominations that champion the King James Version of the Bible. And some even believe that it is the *only* English translation that has God's blessing. Now I am an enthusiastic supporter of this version for a number of reasons that I will go into shortly, and I do agree that it is a superior English translation for serious study. But the archaic language, which is one of its strengths, can also be confusing to someone who isn't familiar with it. This has given rise to an ark-load of translations that use modern English along with a corresponding ark-load of arguments and division over which one is good, better, or best. The serious arguments, however, are not even about the translations themselves, but over which "reading" of the Hebrew and Greek texts that was used.

"What is that supposed to mean?"

Remember back in "The Bible and History" when I said that there are some differences between the ancient manuscripts? Well a number of scholars have attempted to reconstruct the original text. The King James Version is based on the *Textus Receptus* or "Received Text" while most of the modern translations are based on newer readings, such as "Westcott and Hort," "USB," and others. The truth is, however, that the differences in these "readings" are limited to minor details. At the risk of prompting spontaneous demonstrations in front of my office, I stand by my statement in "The Bible and History." "The vast majority of these discrepancies are in the spelling of names and places, and the others are insignificant, making no difference to any essential fact or teaching." So with the exception of a few obviously spurious translations by some of the cults, orthodox evangelical Christian doctrine can be easily seen and taught not only through using the King James Version but also by using most of the modern translations as well.

There is a reason for this.

Some scholars have called God's design of the Bible holographic, and I agree. A hologram is a 3D photograph produced by a laser in a complicated process that I won't go into. But when the film is illuminated with the same laser that produced it, the 3D quality allows you to see behind objects in the foreground. But, when you look at the film in regular light, it just looks like a texture with no visible image. One of the unique things about a holographic picture is that the information is spread evenly across the entire piece of film. If you cut the film in half, you lose some clarity, but most of the image is still there. Cut it in half again and you lose some more clarity, but the basic photo is still intact.

Well, God, in his wisdom, designed the Bible in the same way. The information we need is spread evenly throughout the whole book. Think about it. Where is the chapter on water baptism? There isn't one place that has all of that information. In fact, the heritage of water baptism starts way back in Genesis and continues throughout the Old Testament into the New. Remember, the early Church didn't have the whole New Testament for nearly three hundred years. The collections of books were incomplete and varied from region to region, yet the Church survived just fine. Why? Because God made sure they had what they needed, even though they didn't have it all.

For example, one of the criticisms of the newer translations is that the doctrine of the Trinity is weakened. That might be true, but we're talking about a fraction of one percent. The Trinity is *everywhere* in scripture! Cut off the New Testament, and I can present a ton of evidence for the doctrine using nothing but the Old. Cut my Bible in half and give me thirty-three books randomly selected, and I can still present evidence for the Trinity. Give me just fifteen books, any fifteen books, in any modern translation and there is still plenty of evidence for the doctrine. Why? Because God has spread important information evenly throughout his message to us. And the same is true for all of the critical doctrines of the Bible. The deity of Christ might not be presented in one or two verses in a new translation, but not to worry, the rest of the verses on the subject present it just as strong as ever. To destroy the doctrine of the deity of Christ, they would have to gut the entire New Testament and change many key passages in the Old, which they failed miserably to do! So, accusations that the translators didn't believe in the deity of Christ based on the rendering of one or two verses are totally unfounded.

Therefore, even though there are a handful of small disputed passages and verses in certain translations, it's not enough to change anything. This means that the version you choose to use is mainly a matter of your own personal preference. But wait, there's more...

The English Language: "What did you say?"

The real issue with English translations is actually the English language itself. You see, there is no such thing as a truly word-for-word translation of the Bible from the original languages into English. No, not even the King James Version. This is because Hebrew is a graphically pictorial language, and Greek is deeply philosophical, while English is technical. You know the saying "A picture is worth a thousand words"? Unfortunately, this is very true when it comes to translating the Bible into English. The problem is that when the words are made to flow in English, the way we are used to, some of the meaning must be trimmed out of the Hebrew pictures and the depth of the Greek. The best "picture-for-word" translation in my opinion is the Amplified Bible because it uses several words and/or phrases to translate Hebrew and Greek words that have significant meaning. And there are still deeper levels of meaning to explore beyond that. But, the problem is, reading a story that spans a chapter or two in the Amplified Bible is like trudging through three feet of mud! The story gets so bogged down in layers of definitions that it doesn't flow right. This is why I use different versions for different purposes. Some are better for pure reading while others are great for serious, detailed study. So, for my money, there isn't one English translation that does everything. The best English translation is really a team approach, a selected collection of several. You will find my humble recommendations below.

Warning: A paraphrase is not a translation or version!
You need to know that there are quite a few Bibles that have not taken the time to consult the original languages. Or if they did, it didn't help. Instead, they take a shortcut and paraphrase an existing version. The Message and The Living Bible are examples of paraphrases. They are still useful for family devotions with kids, or for communicating specific thoughts, but you need to be careful not to rely solely on a paraphrase for serious study or for teaching. This is because they are usually watered down. It's not a good idea to quote a paraphrase if you are trying to argue a doctrinal position because it may not be an accurate representation of the original language. That being said, I have included a few quotes from The Living Bible in this book. But I've done so to emphasize a specific idea and only after checking other translations to make sure it represents the original text appropriately.

Recommendations

With all of this in mind, here are my humble recommendations (drumroll and fanfare please).

1. **For reading:** For children or youth I like the New Living Translation or The Living Bible and there are several other paraphrases that are suitable, so take your pick. For young adults and adults who are new believers I like the New Living Translation as it reads fluently and is easy to understand. I also like the New International Version for this purpose as well. For seasoned believers, I would start with the version that your pastor teaches from, but beyond that, use whatever version reads naturally to you.

2. **A general, all-purpose Bible:** For this, I have chosen the New King James Version. I like it for teaching because it is an acceptable compromise between the King James and most modern translations. It doesn't matter what Bible a

person in the congregation is using, if they want to follow along, they can. It is a little formal compared to many newer versions, but is still quite suitable for both reading and study. I also like it because it is one of the few modern versions based on the "Received Text" (see my comments on the King James Version below).

3. **For serious study:** As I said before, it really is necessary to have more than one version in order to have success in serious study. Add some of the following to those mentioned above, and you'll be good to go!

- **The Amplified Bible:** For quickly finding the basic meaning of key words in a passage without resorting to a Greek or Hebrew dictionary, I like the Amplified Bible.
- **Young's Literal Translation:** I like Young's for the same purpose. It will take you a level or two deeper than a reading translation will.
- **The King James Version:** No Bible research library is complete without a copy of the King James Version. Let me share with you why I believe this.

  As I stated earlier, there are a few differences in the ancient manuscripts of the New Testament. Scholars noticed that the differences tend to be regional—that is, the copies found in a specific region are generally similar to each other. So they categorized them according to the region they were found in. They traced the differences to see if they could find out where they came from and then attempted to reconstruct the original texts. There are now several different versions of the Greek New Testament that are called "readings."

  The "reading" that was used for the King James Version is called the Received Text. It is, in my opinion, the superior reading for a number of reasons. The main arguments against it are that the most ancient and best manuscripts, in terms of completeness and condition, differ on several passages. The newer readings rely heavily on the Alexandrian strain of texts because the oldest and most complete copies come from that group. The Received Text is from the Byzantine strain, which is several centuries younger as far as the age of copies is concerned. However, important evidence supporting the Byzantine strain comes from quotes by the early Church fathers. I'll give just one example. One of the contested passages is a handful of verses at the end of Mark's gospel, which are not present in the Alexandrian copies. But these verses are quoted from at least three times by early Church fathers in documents that pre-date the best and oldest Alexandrian manuscripts by two centuries. So it is clear that the passage was lost or removed by Alexandrian copyists, rather than added by the Byzantine copyists. This may have been an accident, but still raises some slight concerns about the purity of the strain. If they edited that passage, they naturally fall under suspicion for editing the other disputed passages as well. Thus, the Received Text is superior, regardless of the age and condition of copies used by the other readings. However, as I stated above, whether the verses in dispute are present or missing or contested words are changed or not makes absolutely no difference in establishing accepted Christian doctrine.

Another powerful argument in support of the King James Version is the fact that God is able to preserve his word and deliver it to us in the form he chooses. And there is no question that his blessing has been upon this regal version for centuries.

The KJV also tries to distinguish words that have significant meaning. An example of this is the use of *charity* instead of *love* in 1 Corinthians 13. The word *agapao* is usually translated "love," but Jesus consistently uses it to express God's perfect, selfless love that expects nothing in return. This is the kind of love that Paul is talking about in that passage, hence the switch to *charity*, which is closer to his intended meaning.

The King James Version also has a lyrical, Shakespearian meter to its phrasing that makes it easier to memorize than many modern translations. You might say it's fit for a king.

Along with it, however, you should add a copy of *Webster's Unabridged Dictionary* published in 1913. It includes all of the words used in the King James Version and gives the old-time definitions, which can be eye popping!

- **The New American Standard Version:** I also recommend the New American Standard Version. One of my college professors was on the committee that translated this version. He would often share in class the challenges they faced and the solutions they embraced. I am, therefore, personally acquainted with the translators' integrity and the utmost care they took to be as accurate as the modern English language would allow. I might add that he had great respect for the King James Version. He said that whenever they ran into a problem, they would consult the KJV. It got them out of many translational jams. He even thought it was inspired.

- **Others:** I also like the English Standard Version, the Complete Jewish Bible (although it often uses Jewish names and phrases), the Geneva Bible (The Pilgrims used this one, if you can get one with the original notes, do so!), the New American Bible (Although this is a Catholic-sponsored translation, it is superb.), and Noah Webster's Bible. There are many other good versions out there and more are being published all the time. So, my recommendations are not meant to put down the others. If you like a particular version, I only suggest that you do a little research on its background before investing in it.

BIBLE READING PLANS

There are a variety of ways that you can engage in daily Bible reading. Here is what I recommend.

1. **For New Believers:** New believers will benefit most by starting with Matthew and reading through the New Testament first. Then the Old Testament will make more sense.
2. **For Seasoned Believers**: If you've been a church-going Christian for a while but have never read through the Bible, why not start in Genesis and go straight through to Revelation? For those who have read the Bible through at least once, a chronological reading will open up many new insights. Most popular versions are now available in a chronological arrangement.
3. **Through the Bible in a Year**: There are also many "Through the Bible in a Year" plans that take you through both Testaments simultaneously, one reading in the morning and another in the evening. The ewordtoday (www.ewordtoday. com) offers an abundance of good plans (as of 6-30-14).

BIBLE STUDY ROCKS!

A great deal of benefit can be gained just by reading the Bible, as I just mentioned. But there is a difference between reading and studying. Reading is like digging with a shovel. Studying is like digging with a backhoe. And, just as there are many ways to read the Bible, there are also different approaches to studying it. You can explore the lives of prominent biblical characters, such as Abraham, David, Paul, or Jesus. Book studies are also popular. And there are many study helps and guides available for these as many Christian authors publish books that explore Bible topics, books, or characters. At the end of this chapter, I will make some suggestions based on three levels of interest. The *GPS Guide* associated with this book includes exercises that will show you how to use them to best advantage.

Additional Resources

Here is a short list (an ark-load could be added) of helpful resources for Bible study arranged according to your level of interest:

Level 1: Beginner or Light Study

Choose a study Bible. This alone can keep you busy at Bible study for years. Here are a few good ones, most of which are available in a variety of translations:

- *Life Application Study Bible*, Zondervan Publishing
- *MacArthur Study Bible*, Thomas Nelson Publishing
- *New Inductive Study Bible*, Harvest House Publishing
- *Ryrie Study Bible*, Moody Publishing
- *Thompson Chain Reference Bible*, BB Kirkbride Publishers
- www.ewordtoday.com for a Bible reading plan

Level 2: Intermediate

Add a few basic tools:

- Add an additional translation or two, like the *Amplified Bible*, Zondervan (mini-word studies on important theological terms)
- *Halley's Bible Handbook* by Henry Halley, Zondervan (includes an abbreviated commentary)
- *Nave's Topical Bible*, Orville J. Nave, Zondervan Publishing
- *Nelson's New Illustrated Bible Dictionary*, Thomas Nelson Publishing

- *Wycliffe Bible Commentary*, by Charles Pfeiffer, Hendrickson Publishing

Level 3: Advanced

Now let's get serious:

- *Holman Illustrated Bible Dictionary*, C. Brand, C. W. Draper, A. England, B&H Publishing
- *Matthew Henry's Bible Commentary*, Hendrickson Publishing
- *Strong's Exhaustive Concordance with Hebrew and Greek Dictionaries* (for the King James Version), Hendrickson Publishing
- *The Treasury of Scripture Knowledge* (an exhaustive cross-referencing tool), R.A. Torrey, Hendrickson Publishing
- *Thru the Bible Commentary*, J. Vernon McGee, Thomas Nelson Publishing
- *Vine's Complete Expository Dictionary of Old and New Testament Words*, W.E. Vine, Merrill Unger, William White Jr., Thomas Nelson Publishing
- *Willmington's Guide to the Bible*, H.L. Willmington, Tyndale House Publishers
- *Zondervan Pictorial Encyclopedia of the Bible*, Moises Silva, Merrill C. Tenney, Zondervan Publishing House
- *PC Study Bible* by Biblesoft, Inc. This is computer software that I use and recommend. It can be customized with any number of reference works. Visit www.biblesoft.com (as of 6-30-14). There are a number of other software apps for Bible study that are exceptional as well.

The Inductive Bible Study Method

Also, for the more serious Bible student, I heartily recommend the Inductive Bible Study Method. Here are some great books that will fill you in on all of its techniques. *The Did God Really Say That? GPS Guide* offers a summary, so you can see what it's like before investing in one of these books. I also include some exercises, so you can get your feet wet.

- *The New Inductive Study Bible* by Harvest House Publishing (available in several translations)
- *The New How to Study Your Bible* by Kay & David Arthur, Harvest House Publishing
- *Living by the Book* by Howard & William Hendricks, Moody Publishing

There are many more excellent resources, but these will get you off to a flying start! Also, if you want to "test drive" some awesome study books before investing in them, visit the Blue Letter Bible online. It features the whole Bible in many translations with dictionaries, commentaries, cross-references, and much more. You can find it at www.blueletterbible.org (as of 7-2-14).

ADDITIONAL INFO ON THE SUBJECTS IN THIS BOOK

- *A General Introduction to the Bible*, Norman L. Geisler and William E. Nix, Moody Press, Chicago IL (warning: the language is very academic)
- *Answering Islam*, Norman L. Geisler and Abdul Saleeb, BakerBooks, Grand Rapids
- *Beyond Series Briefing Pack* (CD or MP3), Dr. Chuck Missler, http://www.khouse.org (as of 1-8-14)
- *Creator Series* Audio Book (MP3), Dr. Chuck Missler and Dr. Mark Eastman, www.khouse.org (as of 7-2-14)
- *Evidence That Demands a Verdict Vol. 1,* Josh McDowell, Thomas Nelson Publishing
- *Flood by Design*, Michael Oard, Master Books

- *Handbook of Today's Religions*, Josh McDowell and Don Stewart, Thomas Nelson Publishing
- Institute for Creation Research, www.icr.org, for many books and DVDs on evolution vs. creation (as of 7-2-14).
- *Many Infallible Proofs*, Henry H. Morris & Henry Morris III, New Leaf Publishing Group
- *Mere Christianity*, C. S. Lewis, Harper One Publishing
- *Popular Handbook of Archaeology and the Bible*, Norman L. Geisler and Joseph M. Holden, Harvest House Publishers
- *Prophecy Knowledge Handbook*, John F. Walvoord, Victor Books
- *The Design Inference*, William Dembski, Cambridge: Cambridge University Press
- *Which Bible? A Guide to English Translations*, David Dewey, Inter-Varsity Press
- *World Religions in a Nutshell*, Ray Comfort, Bridge-Logos Publishing
- www.answeringislam.org/, many resources comparing the Koran with the Bible (as of 7-2-14).
- www.carm.org, Christian Apologetics & Research Ministry has much information on world religions and cults (as of 6-6-14).
- www.creationevidence.org for more information on creation vs. evolution (as of 7-2-14).
- www.genesispark.com for more information on creation vs. evolution (as of 7-2-14).
- www.setterfield.org has a ton of scientific info on the speed of light slowing, the plasma model for creation and the geologic column (as of 7-2-14).
- www.thechapelstore.com, resources by Chuck Smith and other Calvary Chapel pastors (as of 7-2-14).

Any good Bible bookstore is sure to have many other valuable titles on these subjects. Also, for an online resource, check out www.christianbook.com (as of 7-2-14). May God richly bless you as you continue to study his Word!

Glossary

Note: Words, places and people adequately defined and identified where they are mentioned and words explained in the notes section are not included in the glossary. For more information on any of these entries or any term or person not listed here or in notes, consult a Bible dictionary, Bible encyclopedia, commentary on the passage in question, regular dictionary, science dictionary or textbook, or search the Internet.

Abhor—related words are *horror* and *horrible*, so the idea is frightening repulsion.

Abraham (1967 BC-1792 BC)—Whole books have been written about this guy, but I'll keep it short. Abraham is a megastar of several religions because he is at the root of the family trees of many Near Eastern peoples, Jews and the Arabs being two of them. What makes him special is that he and his wife, Sarah, were senior citizens that couldn't have kids. God chose them because he wanted to show off their faith and do a miracle. As I said in the chapter on prophecy, God promised him that he would be the father of many nations. God also promised that he would give Abraham's descendants the land that we know as Israel today. Abraham's faith was tested, first because God told him to leave his home but didn't tell him where to go. And second, because God waited and waited and waited until he was almost a hundred years old before having the kid

(Isaac) that was promised. For more on his many exciting adventures read his life story in Genesis 11:27-25:10.

Ahab—After King Solomon died, Israel was split in two. His son, Rehoboam, continued Solomon's line in the southern kingdom, which was called Judah (this is where the word "Jew" is from). But the northern tribes kept the name Israel for themselves. Ahab was the eighth king of this northern kingdom and reigned for twenty-two years from 874 BC to 853 BC. His capital was a city called Samaria. He married a heathen princess named Jezebel from the neighboring country of Phoenicia. She was strongwilled, manipulative woman who soon convinced weak-willed Ahab to build temples to her nation's idols. He and she had many run-ins with the prophet Elijah. Read his life story in 1 Kings chapters 16-22.[1]

Alexander the Great (356 BC-323 BC)—This guy possessed one of the greatest military minds in history. His thirteen year blitzkrieg of the known world was the original shock and awe! He united most of the Greek city-states, conquered the vast Persian Empire, and spread his kingdom south around the Mediterranean Sea through the Middle East to Egypt. After he died of an illness at age thirty-three, his four generals divided the empire among themselves. But Alexander's policies of establishing Greek colonies as trading and cultural centers throughout the reaches of the known world were faithfully carried out in spite of political upheaval. The online *Encyclopedia Britanica* summarizes his influence:

His career led to the moving of the great centres of civilization eastward and initiated the new age of the Greek territorial monarchies; it spread Hellenism (Greek Culture) in a vast colonizing wave throughout the Middle East and created, if not politically at least economically and culturally, a single world stretching from Gibraltar to the Punjab, open to trade and social intercourse and with a considerable overlay of common civilization and the Greek *koinē* as a lingua franca (a common cultural and trade language). It is not untrue to say that the Roman Empire, the spread of Christianity as a world religion, and the long centuries of Byzantium (the Eastern half of the Roman Empire, which continued for a thousand years after the Western half fell apart) were all in some degree the fruits of Alexander's achievement.[2]

Alexandria—For Christianity and Judaism, Alexandria, Egypt, is the most significant of the Greek cultural colonies founded by Alexander the Great. Jews were encouraged to move there, and many were happy to oblige. Since the city quickly became a center of learning and research, many rabbis and other Jewish scholars and religious leaders were attracted. They became such an important part of the community that Ptolemy Philadelphus, the second king of Egypt after Alexander, commissioned seventy Jewish scribes to make a Greek translation of their Hebrew scriptures in about 300 BC. This is called the *Septuagint* and was the Bible that Jesus and his apostles used. An important Christian community was also established there by the apostle Mark. The oldest and most complete copies of the Bible, including the New Testament, were made and preserved by Alexandrian Christians.

Allah—The god of Islam was originally the idol moon god of Muhammad's tribe. This is why the crescent moon is one of Islam's holiest symbols. Allah is not to be confused with the God of the Bible in spite of Islam's insistence. The God of the Bible is a triune personage comprised of God the Father, God the Son (Jesus), and God the Holy Spirit. This is specifically denied of Allah in the Quran (Koran). There are other character differences as well.[3]

Alpha and Omega—These are the first and last letters in the Greek alphabet. It's like saying from A to Z in English. God gives himself this title as a way of stating that He is responsible for *everything* regarding our existence, from A to Z.

Andrew—One of the original twelve apostles (Matt 10:2-4, Mark 3:14-19, Lk 6:13-16, Acts 1:13-14) and was responsible for bringing his brother, Peter, to Jesus. At first, he was a disciple of John the Baptist, but after John pointed Jesus out to him, Andrew left and became one of the first of Christ's disciples (Jn 1:35-42). According to early church tradition, Andrew was a missionary to the region north of the Black Sea. That's why he was made the patron saint of Russia.[4]

Antichrist—The title of a person that means "against Christ" or a substitute Messiah. "Christ" in Greek is the equivalent of "Messiah" in Hebrew. Both Jesus and the apostle John use this term to describe false teachers who deny the deity of Christ (which Islam and all Christian cults do) and/or claim to be the Jewish Messiah instead of Jesus (Matt 24:5, 23-24, 1Jn 2:18, 22, 4:3, 2Jn 1:7). But John also uses it as the title of an important figure in end-time prophecy (1Jn 2:18). Therefore it is applied to this individual in a number of prophetic references, such as Daniel 7:23-24, 8:23-25, 9:26-27, 2 Thessalonians 2:3-4, 2:8-10, Revelation 13:1 and 13:17.[5]

Apocrypha—A collection of disputed religious books written during the years between the time that the Old Testament was completed and shortly after the New Testament was finished. Some church groups accept them as scripture, others don't.[6]

Apostle—This is the title of someone who is sent or commissioned to carry out a task or project. There are two kinds of apostles mentioned in the New Testament.

The first are the twelve men that Jesus chose from among his disciples and commissioned to be witnesses of his resurrection (Acts 1:21-22). These men exercised authority over the churches and organized evangelistic efforts. They also shaped official church doctrines and either wrote or placed their stamp of approval on the books and letters that became the New Testament. There are no apostles like this today who exercise this kind of authority over the Church, nor will there ever be again. This is because there aren't any more living eyewitnesses to Christ's resurrection that accompanied him during his Earthly ministry.

But Paul calls dozens of other men and women apostles, who do not meet the criteria Peter expressed in Acts 1:21-22. These people helped the primary apostles by traveling from church to church encouraging them in the Lord and teaching them the apostles' doctrine. The work that was done by this kind of apostle is still going on in the Church today. Missionaries, traveling teaching ministries and music groups, evangelists, denominational heads and administrative officials, and others could be labeled apostles in this sense.

I, however, discourage the use of the word for somebody's title because when people hear it, they automatically assume that the person has absolute authority over the entire worldwide body of Christ just like the original twelve had. And those that claim the title for themselves are usually trying to claim that kind of authority, when, in fact, they do not have it. We have the authority of the primary apostles handed down to us through their writings in the New Testament, not through living successors. Therefore, since the word *apostle* causes so much confusion and potentially dangerous activity, I believe it's wise to avoid the use of the word as someone's title in the Church today. Nobody has to have a title in order to do the work that God has called them to and gifted them for.

Artaxerxes Longimanus—(Try saying that ten times real fast!) "Art" ruled the Persian Empire from 465 BC to 425 BC. Although he had to put down several rebellions, which was common for kings in those days, his reign was fairly peaceful. In fact, he was known for being fair, wise, and peace loving. Nebuchadnezzar took many Jews to Babylon as slaves after the fall of Jerusalem. So when the Persians took control of the empire, there was a large Jewish population in Babylon. King Cyrus allowed the first wave of Jews to return to their homeland and start rebuilding their temple, which "Neb" had demolished. Art allowed the second wave, under Ezra, and the third wave, under Nehemiah, to return and rebuild the wall and city of Jerusalem.[7, 8]

Assyria—One of the world's earliest empires. It was named after its original capital of Assur, but the government was later moved to Nineveh. It was a cruel military state that existed for the purpose of total world domination. At the height of its power, the empire included modern Iraq, western Iran, eastern Turkey, Syria, Jordan, Israel, and eastern Egypt. It eventually fell to the Babylonians in 612 BC.

After King Solomon died, his kingdom was split in two. His son, Rehoboam, continued Solomon's line in the southern kingdom, which was called Judah. (This is where the word *Jew* is from.) But the northern tribes kept the name Israel for themselves. Assyria began attacking the fringes of the northern tribes of Israel in 750 BC. The book of 2 Kings, chapters 15-17, records the Assyrian advances as well as the siege of Samaria, Israel's capital, which fell in 722 BC. Israel had stopped worshipping God to worship idols, sacrificing their newborn babies to them and doing many other ghastly things to each other, so God allowed them to be taken as slaves to Assyria from which they never returned. But God delivered Judah from the Assyrians by miraculous means. You can read that story in 2 Kings, chapters 18-19.

Atomic clocks—Once upon a time, a year was determined by the time it took the Earth to make one complete revolution around the sun. And a day was determined by how much time it took the Earth to spin around once. And hours and minutes were divisions of that. But not anymore! We now go by (fanfare please…) *atomic time!* There are a whole slew of methods, so I won't get into that. But they all work by measuring the electromagnetic frequency emitted by the electrons of certain atoms at absolute zero degrees kelvin. There's just one problem. It's all based on the speed of light, which, as I noted in the chapter "The Bible and Science," has been slowing down. So atomic clocks have also been slowing down when compared to old-fashioned orbital clocks. At least now I don't feel so bad about the clock in our living room.

Babylon and Babylonia—Babylon was the capital city of the ancient empire of Babylonia. Its ruins are in central Iraq about fifty miles south of Baghdad. The extent of the empire at the height of its power included modern Iraq, western Iran, eastern Turkey, Syria, Jordan, Israel, and eastern Egypt. The city is also identified with the site of the tower of Babel by ancient traditions, but there is no certainty of that. Nebuchadnezzar was the most famous of its rulers.

After King Solomon died, his kingdom was split in two. His son, Rehoboam, continued Solomon's line in the southern kingdom, which was called Judah. (This is where the word *Jew* is from.) But the northern tribes kept the name Israel for themselves. Assyria took the northern tribes back to their country as slaves in 722 BC. Nebuchadnezzar conquered Judah in 587 BC and took the best and brightest of its people back to Babylon as slaves. After the Persians took control of the empire, King Cyrus allowed the first wave of Jews to return and start rebuilding their temple, which Neb had destroyed. Artaxerxes Longimanus allowed the second wave to return, under Ezra, and the third wave, under Nehemiah, who rebuilt the wall and the city of Jerusalem. Mentions of Babylon are too extensive to list here, but you can find out more by looking it up in a Bible encyclopedia.

Bartholomew—"Bart" was another of Jesus's original twelve apostles (Matt 10:2-4, Mark 3:14-19, Lk 6:13-16, Acts 1:13-14). He is probably the same person named Nathanael in John 1:45-51.

Behemoth—Creationists jump all over the description of this monster in Job 40:15-24 and excitedly claim that it is a dinosaur. The reasoning is that Job may have been the first book of the Bible that was written and he may have lived at a time when dinos were still around. But scholars who study ancient languages quickly point to a similar Egyptian word that means "water ox" or hippopotamus. To which the creationist exclaims, "Oh yeah! Well Palestine doesn't have any hippos!" And then the other guys answer, "Well the children of Israel spent four hundred years in Egypt and the Nile is fulll of 'em!" And so, sometimes I think, maybe, and sometimes I don't know for sure.⁹

Believe—When you see this word in a Bible verse that talks about being saved, it does *not* mean "mental acknowledgement." As James points out, "You say you have faith, for you believe that there is one God. Good for you! Even the demons believe this, and they tremble in terror" (James 2:19, NLT). So biblical belief or faith is more than just recognizing that something is true. That's only the first step. Let's say you come to my house for dinner, and you see a piece of paper on a place setting at the dinner table with your name on it. You wouldn't have any trouble "believing" that the chair in front of it is meant for you, right? But that's not biblical faith. You might even make a declaration to all those present, "This chair is mine!" But that's still not faith. You might even pick up the chair and carry it around with you, but that's still not the idea of biblical faith. You might even tell everyone, "I believe that this chair is strong enough to hold me," but that's still not faith. The biblical idea of faith, or belief doesn't occur until you actually sit in the chair, trusting your entire weight to it. So, as far as God is concerned, to believe in him means "to put your trust in and rely on" him and his promises to you. This is the kind of belief that is necessary for salvation.

Belshazzar—The crown prince of Babylon, second only to his father, Nabunaid (the son of Nebuchadnezzar), charged with the defense of the capital city. It was common for the sons of kings to be given smaller portions of the country to rule. They were called kings as well. This is why Belshazzar is given this title in chapters 5, 7, and 8 of Daniel. He really messed up his responsibilities bad! He was so busy partying that he didn't notice that the Medes and Persians had diverted the flow of the Euphrates, which normally went through the middle of the city of Babylon. Their armies snuck in unnoticed by means of the riverbed, killed Belshazzar, and took over the empire without a fight. You can read the story of his last night in Daniel chapter 5.[10]

Buddha, Buddhism, and Buddhist—Gautama Buddha was born in northern India around the year 560 BC. He founded the Buddhist religion. Although some of the concepts are borrowed from Hinduism, his religion is somewhat of a rebellion against its multitude of gods, the caste system and hopelessness brought on by the endless cycle of rebirths. Buddha sought a more practical way of avoiding life's pain and achieving peace through meditation. Buddhism denies the existence of a supreme, personal creator. It also denies the existence of sin, and, therefore, the possibility of a personal savior. It also wrongly assumes that the universe is eternal and infinite.[11]

Canaan—An ancient name used in the Bible for the land we know as Palestine.

Cirrhosis—This is a serious liver disease in which scar tissue slowly replaces the liver, preventing it from doing its job. Although the damage is permanent, there are many successful treatments for slowing or halting its progress.[12]

Communion—This is also called the Lord's Supper. Paul explains "For I received from the Lord that which I also delivered to you: that the Lord Jesus on the same night in which He was betrayed took bread; and when He had given thanks, He broke it and said, 'Take, eat; this is My body which is broken for you; do this in remembrance of Me.' In the same manner He also took the cup after supper, saying, 'This cup is the new covenant in My blood. This do, as often as you drink it, in remembrance of Me'" (1Cor 11:23-25, NKJV).

Compression—This is a computer-geek word that has to do with making data smaller. When a piece of data is too big for the space you have, say, on your computer's hard drive, you have the option of compressing it. That is, making it smaller so it doesn't take up so much room. They do this mathematically using a variety of methods. Compression formulas are used for a lot of things, including improved video performance over the Internet. But so far, they haven't figured out a way to mathematically compress my tummy... rats!

Confucius, Confucianism, and Confucianist—Confucius was one of the original wise guys. He lived in China from about 551 BC to 479 BC. At that time, China was embroiled in innumerable feudal wars. Confucius reacted to the horrors and cruelty around him by developing an ethical system of wisdom, honor, and good conduct. He believed in ancestor worship, which is one of the few spiritual aspects of his teachings. After his death, his followers deified him and set up shrines so that people could offer sacrifices and such. He taught that man is basically good and through strict adherence to wise, ethical, and moral practices, he can improve life for himself and others and earn the favor of the ancients. Although many of his sayings are, indeed, wise, his teachings amount to a life of law, similar to what the Pharisees practiced in Jesus's time. This is completely opposed to the principle of salvation by grace through faith taught in the New Testament.[13]

Cosmos and Cosmology—Cosmology won't make your face look any better, but it's pretty cool anyway. It's the study of the universe as a whole. An astronomer studies stars and planets and other spacey things. But a cosmologist looks at the big picture. Not that stars and galaxies aren't big, but I mean really big, like the whole-enchilada big! They probably would have called it universology, but that sounds too wierd.

Cult—An offshoot of Christianity that holds to beliefs that are not found in the Bible. These beliefs are usually from one or more "holy books" that they add as being equal to the Bible. They also deny the deity of Christ. And they are usually based on the false assumption that the universe is infinite and eternal or that God does not exist outside of the time domain.[14]

Daniel—A prime time Hebrew prophet and author of the book of (you guessed it...) Daniel. He was just a teen when he was made a slave and taken to Babylon by King Nebuchadnezzar, probably about 604 BC. He was, evidently, from a noble family for he was selected for service in Neb's court. Read his fascinating life story in the book of Daniel.[15]

Dark energy and dark matter—Sounds like mysterious stuff doesn't it? Well, it actually is! If you've read the chapter "The Bible and Science," you might remember that there are two models of cosmology. I try to explain the plasma model. But the one that is taught to school kids and that everyone understands is the gravity model. As I explain in the chapter, there are a number of issues that cannot be explained by gravity alone. To force the gravity model to work, scientists have to make believe there is something they call dark matter. But no one has ever seen it and there is no evidence for its existence except that they *need* it!

An exception can be made in the case of dark energy, however, because of the discovery of the zero-point energy (ZPE or black fire). For a full discussion of why zero-point energy and dark energy are the same, see this article at the Calphysics Institute website: www.calphysics.org/zpe.html (as of 7-2-14). And a more complete explanation of ZPE is available at www.setterfield.org/ZPE_layman.html (as of 7-2-14).

David—The second and most famous king of ancient Israel. Born around 1085 bc, he was an extraordinary man of many talents. He was a rockstar musician, songwriter, and poet who wrote most of the book of Psalms. He also served in King Saul's court, playing his harp to soothe the king's troubled mind. He was also a champion warrior, skilled in hand-to-hand combat. As a youth, he singlehandedly killed a lion and bear and became a legend by killing the giant Goliath with nothing more than a sling. He was also a wise statesman. After Saul was killed, he was made king of the tribe of Judah and eventually of all Israel. He was also an exceptional field general. As the king of united Israel, he defeated almost all of her enemies and expanded her borders, ushering in the golden age of the kingdom. And, he was a prophet as many of his psalms reveal. But he was not perfect. He committed adultery with Bathsheba and had her husband murdered to cover it up. But he repented publicly, expressing great sorrow, as several of his psalms attest, and God forgave him. But God did not remove the consequences of his sins. Read of his comic-book-like adventures in 1 Samuel and 1 Chronicles. They are truly stranger than fiction!

Dead Sea—The largest lake in southern Israel, forming part of the border between Israel and Jordan. It is fed by the Jordan River but has no outlet. This causes the lake to have a great deal of salinity, like the Great Salt Lake in the US. It is the lowest and saltiest place on Earth. The Dead Sea Scrolls were found in the vicinity.

Demarcation—This is like marking a boundary line. When applied to language, it means establishing clear definitions that distinguish one thing from another.

Denomination—These are man-made and man-administered divisions within Christianity consisting of like-minded churches. The divisions are due to differences in specific teachings, practices, different approaches or emphasis in ministry, and/or differences in the way the churches are governed. It might seem that division in Christ's Church is a bad thing, but in actuality, God has used the differences to appeal to different kinds of people, thus, bringing more to Jesus than would be possible if all churches were the same. For example, some churches are very formal—you should come dressed in a suit and tie or nice dress, the worship consists of classical music, the pastor wears a robe, and the service is very structured. Other churches are very informal, come as you are—the worship consists of contemporary music, the pastor wears a Hawaiian shirt and sandals, and the service is not structured. So, you can see that a person's personal preference plays a role in the kind of church or denomination he/she wants to become a part of.

Domain—A domain is another word for "kingdom" or "country." By extension, it is used to designate a group of things with similar features, such as the domain of reptiles. When used with time, it means everything that time has an influence over.

Elijah—A big-time prophet of Israel who stood up to the idolatry introduced by Ahab and Jezebel. He also trained Elisha to be his successor. He didn't die but was taken to heaven in a flaming chariot. What a ride! Read about his exploits starting in 1 Kings chapter 17 to 2 Kings chapter 2.

Elisha—Another superstar prophet of Israel. He was trained by Elijah and asked God for a double portion of the Spirit of God. God answered by doing twice the miracles through him that he did through Elijah. Read about them starting in 1 Kings chapter 19 to 2 Kings chapter 13.

Encryption—This isn't like a zombie being put in a tomb, it's yet another computer-geek word. Encryption is the great wizard of data security. As you may know, computer code is written in a language called binary, which means that there are only two letters, a one and zero, that's it. The code is also divided up into chunks called bits. The thing is, no matter what the code says in data, a bit can also mean a number. So what they do is apply a secret formula to the number value of the bits, so if a hacker steals it, he can't see what it really says. But when you access your data, the formula is applied in reverse, which restores it to what it was originally. Encryption makes your information magically vanish for everyone but you. And that could be a good thing in a zombie apocalypse.

Enzyme—An enzyme is a special kind of microbot that causes a chemical change inside of a living plant or animal. For example, enzymes take the vitamins and minerals out of the food we eat so our bodies can use them. Enzymes are vital for almost all functions inside living things. Without them, we wouldn't be around. So, if someone ever calls you an enzyme, thank them!

Ezekiel—While Daniel prophesied among the nobility in Babylon, Ezekiel ministered to the common people that were enslaved by them from about 594 BC to 573 BC. His story and prophecies are written in the Old Testament Book of (surprise, surprise) Ezekiel.

Ezra—The priest that led the second wave of exiled Jews back to Israel in 449 BC. You can read his story in the Book of Ezra.

Fission and Fusion—These are opposite nuclear reactions. Fission breaks a big atom into smaller pieces while fusion takes smaller atoms and mashes them together to make a big one. Both processes release megatons of energy, which is why they are used in atomic and hydrogen bombs.

Fuller's Club—Fulling was an old-time way of cleaning wool and preparing it for use. One of the processes was to beat the fabric with a flat club, which was called (you guessed it) a fuller's club.

Gabriel—The name of a messenger angel who appears several places in Scripture. He deliver's two visions to Daniel (Dan 8 and 9), announces the birth of John the Baptist to his father, Zacharias (Lk 1:5-22), and announces the birth of Jesus to Mary (Lk 1:26-38). So, he was a pretty busy guy.

Gas giants—These guys go into the hall of fame for... uh... never mind. Actually, this is a class of planet in our solar system, the big ones. Saturn, Jupiter, Neptune, and Uranus all have very small rock cores with super-sized atmospheres, which makes them bloated in size (because of all that gas).

Genome—This is a big-picture word that designates the genes and all of the other hereditary information of a living thing.

Gentile—Any and all persons who are not of Jewish descent. In the Bible, the word sometimes (but not always) has racial overtones. Just to show how generic the meaning is, the same Hebrew word is sometimes translated "nations."

Genus—No, this isn't what they call smart guys. This is a science word. Scientists have categorized all living things into groups, super groups, sub-groups, sub-sub-groups, sub-sub-sub-groups, etc. For example, the highest level divides animals from plants from fungi from some other microscopic things. The next group divides trees from grasses, etc. Each group has a name and has more groups under it. Genus is the group between family and species. For more specific information, look it up in a science dictionary, textbook, or do an Internet search.

Gilgamesh—No, this isn't a new kind of cereal. Gilgamesh was a real king who ruled a real city named Uruk, which was near Babylon. He lived a few hundred years after Noah's flood. An ancient Babylonian poem about him embellishes some historical facts with a lot of mythology. His comic-book style superhero adventures include slaying a demon, taking forbidden magic trees from a magic forest, fighting monsters, rejecting the advances of a goddess, and much more. When he starts to worry about his own mortality, he sets out on a quest to find the Babylonian Noah, seeking eternal life. Let me briefly jump back into reality here to say that since the real Noah lived for 350 years after the flood; it is really possible that the real king could have met and talked to him. In this version of the story, Noah tells Gilgamesh that the gods warned him of the coming flood and showed him how to build a dice-shaped boat big enough to save his family, some friends, and a bunch of animals. Thus they were saved and the gods granted Noah eternal life. When Noah is unable to grant Gilgamesh the same, he returns, satisfied with his mortality and content with the accomplishment of having built a magnificent city.[16] Of course, many of the details do not agree with the Bible, but isn't it odd that the earliest piece of secular human literature in existence includes an account of the great deluge? What is the best explanation for this?

Gluons—These sticky little guys are what glue quarks together to form protons and neutrons inside of an atom's nucleus. Hence the name, gluon. It must be short for "glue-on." For all you rocket scientists, they are the particle representatives of the strong nuclear force.

Godhead—This word is used by Paul three times when he is talking about God, as translated in the King James Version (Acts 17:29, Rom 1:20, Col 2:9). Other versions prefer the terms *divinity* or *divine nature*. So it is clearly a reference to all of the qualities that make him God, including his triunity (see entries for "Trinity", "God the Father", "Holy Spirit", and "Jesus").

God the Father—the first member of the triune Godhead or Trinity. He is normally the one we think of when we think of a Creator. But the Bible also says that God the Son (Jesus) and God the Holy Spirit were also involved. God the Father remains outside of the time domain, while God the Son (Jesus) entered it by putting on a human body in the physical realm; and God the Holy Spirit entered time in the spiritual realm. Thus, God is able to relate to us, because we inhabit time in both the physical and spiritual realms simultaneously.

Gospel—This is a great word! It literally means "good news." It is used in several senses in the Bible. The basic meaning is the message that Jesus, the Messiah, came and died for our sins on the cross, then rose again and offers us eternal life (salvation from eternal death in hell) through the forgiveness of our sins. Next, since the first four books of the New Testament—Matthew, Mark, Luke, and John—are eyewitness accounts of the life of Jesus and his message, they (the books) are referred to as gospels as in the Gospel of Mark. Another way that word is used is when Paul and others are warning the churches about false teachers bringing them "a different gospel". There are others, but I'd have to drag you into a bunch of theologically technical stuff. You can look that up in a Bible dictionary if you have a mind to.

Hepatitis—This is a general medical word describing the inflammation or swelling of the liver. It can result from a variety of different causes such as viral infections, bacterial infections, drug use, and other diseases.[17] It don't sound like much fun!

Herod's Temple—See Temple.

Heterogeneous—Mixed, not similar, and unconnected.... like my Internet service.

Hezekiah—After King Solomon died, his kingdom was split in two. His son, Rehoboam, continued Solomon's line in the southern kingdom, which was called Judah (this is where the word "Jew" is from). But the northern tribes kept the name Israel for themselves. Hezekiah was the twelfth king of Judah, reigning from 728 BC to 686 BC. He was one of the few good Jewish kings. He issued many religious reforms, destroyed idol temples, and resumed worship in the temple Solomon had built. He and his country were delivered miraculously from an Assyrian siege of Jerusalem when the Angel of the Lord wiped out the Assyrian army one night. Read about Hezekiah's heroic adventures in 2 Kings chapters 18-20, Isaiah chapters 36-39, and 2 Chronicles chapters 29-32.

Hill, Rowland—A popular, influential, non-denominational English preacher who lived from 1744 to 1833.[18]

Hindu and Hinduism—The primary religion in India. It is so complex that it is impossible to summarize here. It has even been described as an entire family of religions. There are thousands of gods and goddesses that a Hindu person can choose to be devoted to. So, there are thousands of sects within it. In addition to all of their gods, ancestor worship is also practiced and in some sects, is even more important than devotion to a god. Reincarnation is a primary belief, coupled with the law of karma, which teaches that the goodness and/or badness of your present life will determine what or who you are reincarnated as in the next. This also determines the caste (social class) you will belong to. Nirvana is the final goal, which can only achieved by being better and better in each life until you are liberated from this cycle and return to the universe, a state of non-existence that is void of suffering. The Christian teaching about Heaven is a foreign concept to Hinduism, as is the idea of salvation by grace through faith from the wrath of God. Mercy is not embraced either because, in their view, a person who is injured, sick, handicapped, or suffering in any way is only getting what they deserve because of sins in a former life. Therefore, helping someone like this (having mercy) is interfering with the law of karma. Different sects have conflicting views on these things as well as confusing ideas about morality.[19]

Hittites—An ancient kingdom occupying most of central Turkey during Old Testament times. It was a military state like Assyria and fought many wars with them.[20]

Holy Spirit—The third member of the triune Godhead or Trinity. God the Father remains outside of the time domain, while God the Son entered it by putting on a human body in the physical realm (Jesus); and God the Holy Spirit entered time in the spiritual realm. Thus he is able to relate to us because we inhabit time in both the physical and spiritual realms simultaneously. The Holy Spirit is specifically called the Helper and Comforter by Jesus. For more details on our live-in service rep, see Appendix B.

Implode—When something explodes, like a bomb, it does so because great pressure builds on the inside, causing the container to break into pieces and fly outwards. An implosion is just the opposite. It's an explosion in reverse. The pressure is on the outside pushing in, causing the container to collapse inward.

Indexed—Here's another computer-geek word that describes a method of increasing the performance of a computer's file system. It works the same as an index in a book. When you want to find the page that has the Gettysburg Address on it, you look it up in the index and voila! There is the page number so you can turn right to it without having to re-read the whole book. Well, modern computer operating systems have built-in apps that construct and maintain an index for your hard drive. That way, it doesn't have to scan the whole drive every time you want to share that photo of your new puppy. It just scans the index to find out where it is and grabs it for you—much faster and much more efficient!

Islam and Muslim—The Muslim religion, also known as Islam, is the major world religion that dominates the Middle East outside of Israel. A Muslim, is an adherent to Islam, a follower of the teachings of its founder and chief false prophet, Muhammad. Islam, however, is far more than just a religion. It is a life system that includes social, judiciary, governmental/political, and military components. Muhammad (AD 570—AD 632) governed and engaged in conquest in the same way that today's most radical Islamists do. He designed his religion as a theocracy with no separation of religion and state. Therefore, to disagree with the state (Muhammad) is to disagree with Allah and is often punishable by death. Evangelism is accomplished by violence. Conquered peoples were told to convert to Islam or die. Muhammad used his religion to gain submission to his political and military ambitions, all "for the glory of Allah" of course. Contrast this with Jesus's statement to Pilate, "My Kingdom is not an earthly kingdom. If it were, my followers would fight to keep me from being handed over to the Jewish leaders. But my Kingdom is not of this world" (Jn 18:36, NLT). Allah was originally the idol moon god of Muhammad's tribe. (See the glossary entry for "Allah".) Allah supposedly gave Muhammad messages and visions, which are recorded in Islam's holy book, the Koran or Quran. These messages specifically deny that the God of the Bible is, in fact, God. Therefore, the two are not the same. Additionally, the Allah of Islam is cold and aloof, devoid of the love, mercy, grace, and righteousness that are so much a part of the nature of the God of the Bible. Islam has been split into two major factions: the Sunnis and Shiites. There is also a moderated form of Islam practiced in countries that separate church and state.[21]

Jacob—The twin brother of Esau by Isaac and Rebekah and a grandson of Abraham. Esau, as the eldest brother, was in line to have the Messiah's lineage come through him in addition to the traditional double portion of his father's inheritance. But, being young and free-spirited, Esau didn't think much of his birthright. So, Jacob capitalized on his attitude and traded a bowl of chili for it. (It must have been some kinda chili!) That was Esau's first sin. The second was rebellion. God wanted the messianic line to be furthered by marrying within Abraham's family, but Esau married some local gals. As a result, God saw to it that Jacob received the blessing and the inheritance, which caused Esau to come unglued! Jacob had to run for his life and eventually made his way to his uncle Laban's place. There, he worked for two of his daughters, Leah and Rachel, to be his wives. God later changed Jacob's name to Israel. He had twelve sons, whose families became the twelve tribes of the nation of Israel. You can read his life story and the many escapades of he and his sons in Genesis chapters 25-50.

James the Great and James the Less—I decided to do these guys together because the descriptive parts of their names were intended to contrast with each other. You see, both were important to the early Church, but since they had the same names, they had to figure out some way of telling them apart. Who really knows what the "Great" and "Less" mean? It could be that one was taller or older or just plain fatter.

Anyway, James the Great was one of Jesus's original apostles (Matt 10:2-4, Mark 3:14-19, Lk 6:13-16, Acts 1:13-14), the brother of John the apostle and the first apostle to be martyred (Acts 12:2). You can read about him in Matthew, Mark, Luke, and John.

James the Less was the half-brother of Jesus (Matt 13:55 and Mark 6:3), leader of the church at Jerusalem (Acts 15:13 and 21:18), and author of the New Testament's Book of James. So, he did more, but they called him the less anyway.

Jean Dixon (1904-1997)—The queen of the tabloid junk prophets. Probably the most famous psychic of the twentieth century. She had a syndicated newspaper astrology column and dove headlong into the annual tabloid prediction derby without much success.[22]

Jeremiah—He was known as "the weeping prophet" because he cried a lot since his people rejected God, and he knew they had to go into captivity to Babylon as a result. He wrote the Book of Lamentations as well as the book of Jeremiah. These two books contain his harrowing experiences and writings. His ministry spanned the reigns of the last five kings of Judah (627 BC to 586 BC).[23]

Jesus—His name means "Jehovah saves." Jesus is God's "X-factor." Satan and his demons had a big party the night of his crucifixion. But while they were basking on their victory beach, Jesus shocked them by rising from the dead. They hadn't counted on that! The Bible says that when Satan got Adam to sin, he stole the keys to death and Hades. But when Jesus arose, he took them back. He even brags to John about it in Rev 1:18. Jesus made it possible for us to escape the second death (Rev 20:14) and go to heaven. All we have to do is take God up on his free offer of salvation. For more details see the chapter titled "The Bible is Alive" and Appendix B.

John (?—AD 98)—One of the original apostles of Jesus (Matt 10:2-4, Mark 3:14-19, Lk 6:13-16, Acts 1:13-14) and the only one to die a natural death. He also wrote the Gospel of John, Revelation, and the epistles (letters) of first, second, and third John. You can read about him in all of the Gospels (Matthew, Mark, Luke, and John) and in the early chapters of the Book of Acts.

John the Baptist—or "Johnie-B" as I like to call him, was the last, and, according to Jesus, the greatest of the Old Testament prophets (Lk 7:28). Yet he is one of the few prophets for which no miracle is recorded. He was the fulfillment of Isaiah 40:3, the forerunner of the Messiah, sent to prepare the way for his coming (see also Malachi 3:1). And, interestingly enough, Jesus waited until John's arrest before beginning his ministry. Johnie-B preached "a baptism of repentance for the remission of sins" (Lk 3:3, NKJV). A couple of his disciples became apostles of Christ: Andrew (Jn 1:40) and probably John the apostle, since he is the one who gives us the most detail about what John the Baptist said and did (Jn 1:19-42). You can read the rest of his exploits in Matthew chapter 3, Mark chapter 1, Luke chapters 1-3, and John chapter 1 as well as several other places in the Gospels.

Joseph Smith (1805-1844)—The founder and chief false prophet (there are actually a lot of them) of the Mormon Church, also called the Church of Jesus Christ of Latter Day Saints. For a brief summary of why Mormonism is not Christian, visit carm.org/is-mormonism-christian (as of 7-7-14).[24]

Josephus, Flavius (AD 37 to early second century)—He was a Jewish/Roman historian whose important works provide us with vital background of the life and times that Jesus lived in. They also give us corroborating evidence that substantiates a number of biblical statements, including events in the life of Jesus and his apostles. You can buy a copy of his works at any Bible book store.

Joshua (1475 BC—1365 BC)—Joshua was God's avenger. He was born in Egypt and became the assistant of and eventual successor to Moses. Joshua was a skilled field general and led Israel's armies in the conquest of the land that God promised them. That promise was given for a reason. The Cannanites were one of the most lawless, violent, and base anti-civilizations in all of history. Murder, gang rape, and other monstrous and unmentionable practices were commonplace and encouraged. They would sacrifice a living child to Baal, put its bones in a jar, and build the jar into the walls of their home for "good luck." They also buried children alive. What made it worse was that they knew better. If the person of Melchizedek (Gen 14:18-20), king and priest of Salem (Jerusalem) is a "Christophony" (Old Testament appearance of Christ), as many Bible scholars believe, then they had access to teaching that we should be jealous of! And, as Jesus said, "Everyone to whom much was given, of him much will be required" (Lk 12:48b, ESV). So God used Joshua to give them the punishment that he had determined against them and put a stop the atrocities they had been committing. The book of Joshua, in the Old Testament, gives us the lowdown on his victories and a few defeats. But he also appears in Exodus chapters 24 and 33 and Numbers chapter 13.

Jude—Author of the New Testament epistle (letter) that is named after him. He was the brother of James (Jude 1:1), probably referring to James the Less, half-brother of Jesus and leader of the church at Jerusalem. This would make Jude a half-brother of Jesus as well. Jesus's brothers didn't believe he was the Son of God until after his resurrection (Jn 7:5 and Acts 1:14). Jude may have identified himself this way so he wouldn't appear to be preempting his brother's authority. He may have even been commissioned by James to write this letter in the first place.

Keller, Timothy (1950)—The founding pastor of Redeemer Presbyterian Church in New York City; he is also an apologist, author, and speaker.[25]

Koran (Quran)—The holy book of the Muslim religion (Islam); it was dictated partially by Muhammad, himself, but was completed by his followers after his death.[26]

Krishna—One of the thousands of gods of the Hindu religion.[27]

Leviathan—Creationists get excited about this sea monster that appears in Job chapter 41 and say that it's a dinosaur. The reasoning is that Job was probably the first book of the Bible that was written, and he may have lived at a time when dinos were still around. But other scholars think it's a crocodile.

Luke (early to late first century?)—A physician and extremely accurate historian. Luke is one of the few gentiles (non-Jews) to author a portion of the Bible. He wrote the Gospel of Luke and then continued the narrative in the Book of Acts. He accompanied Paul on some of his missionary journeys. Read about his adventures with Paul as he narrates Acts chapters 16-28.

Maimonides (AD 1135-AD 1204)—A highly respected and influential Jewish rabbi, physician, and philosopher. He was born in Spain but moved to Egypt where he became one of the most prolific authors of Hebrew Scripture study in the Middle Ages.[28]

Manna—Literally means, "what's it?" Manna was something like flakes from heaven that God provided the Israelites for food on their forty-year trip from Egypt to Canaan. They never did figure out what it was, but it worked!

Mark (early to late first century?)—He wrote the Gospel of Mark and accompanied Paul, Barnabas, and Peter on numerous missionary expeditions around the Roman Empire. His Gospel was written from the recollections of Peter, who he was with in Rome for some time. He appears throughout the book of Acts and is mentioned in several epistles (letters) of Paul and Peter. He went with Paul and Barnabas on their first missionary journey, but left them to go home at some point. Barnabas wanted to take him again on a proposed second journey, but Paul would have nothing to do with him. So Paul took Silas with him, and Barnabas took Mark under his wing and gave him a second chance (Acts 15:36-39). It is to the patience and grace of Barnabas that we owe Mark's Gospel and later ministry in Alexandria, Egypt. And it is interesting that later in Paul's life, he specifically asks Timothy for Mark's companion-ship (2Tim 4:11). God is a God of second chances!

Matthew (early to late first century?)—The author of the Gospel named after him. He was originally a tax man, working for the Romans. His fellow Jews considered men like him to be traitors. But Matthew left his profession to follow Jesus and never looked back. Other than the time Jesus called him (Matt 9, Mark 2, and Luke 5), the Bible only mentions him in the lists of the apostles (Matt 10:2-4, Mark 3:14-19, Lk 6:13-16, Acts 1:13-14).

Matthias (early to late first century?)—Matthias was a dis-ciple of Jesus and followed him wherever he went. He was chosen to replace Judas as an apostle (Acts 1:15-26). Nothing more is mentioned of him in the Bible.

Muhammad (AD 570-AD 632)—The founder and false prophet of the Muslim religion, also known as Islam. For more details see the glossary entry for "Islam".

Muslim—See the entry for "Islam"

Nahmanides (AD 1194-AD 1270)—This highly respected and influential Jewish rabbi, physician, and philosopher was born in Spain but moved to the Holy Land (Israel) later in his life. Like Maimonides before him, he became one of the most prolific authors of Hebrew Scripture study in the Middle Ages.[29]

Naaman—A Syrian general who went to Elisha and was miraculously healed of his leprosy. Read the story in 2 Kings chapter 5.

Nebuchadnezzar—The most famous king of the Babylonian Empire (see the entry for Babylon). He reigned from 605 BC to 562 BC. Neb conquered Judah in 586 BC and took the best and brightest of its people back to Babylon as slaves.[30] Later in life, he actually converted and even wrote part of the Bible! You can read his testimony in Daniel chapter 4.

Nehemiah (?—413 BC)—Born in Babylon of Jewish slaves that had been taken captive by Nebuchadnezzar, Nehemiah was commissioned by Artaxerxes Longimanus to lead the third wave of Jews returning to their land. He gained permission to rebuild the wall and city of Jerusalem and became the governor of Judea until his death. You can read his hair-raising adventures in the book of Nehemiah.

Nero (AD 37-AD 68)—He was the fifth emperor of Rome and a confirmed wacko maniac. His actions were causing such an uproar that in AD 64 he set fire to Rome, blaming it on Christians, in an attempt to divert attention from his failures. The apostles Peter and Paul were victims of his fake wrath. Four years later, the Praetorian guard rebelled and forced him to flee the city. He committed suicide shortly after that.[31]

Nicodemus—A wealthy and powerful teacher and spiritual leader in Jerusalem at the time of Christ, Nic was also a member of a leadership council called the *Sanhedrin*. He went to Jesus secretly to learn more about his teaching (Jn 3). Evidently he became a follower as he sticks up for Jesus when the other members were plotting to kill him (Jn 7:45-52). He and a man named Joseph of Arimathea were the ones who claimed the body of Jesus after his crucifixion, wrapped it up and placed it in the tomb. Early Church traditions tell us that Nic was baptized by Peter and John. Eventually he was run out Jerusalem because of his faith.[32]

Nineveh—One of the most ancient cities on the planet, Nineveh may go back as far as 3000 BC. It was the capital of the Assyrian Empire and was located on the eastern bank of the Tigris River across from modern Mosul, Iraq. Nahum, Ezekiel, and Zephaniah are just a few of the Hebrew prophets who foretold the complete destruction of Nineveh and the Assyrian Empire.[33]

Nostradamus—A sixteenth century French astrologer and occult "seer" who published many "prophecies" in a prose-like style. His involvement with the occult arouses immediate suspicion that he may have been demon-possessed. But that still doesn't mean he could predict the future because only God lives outside of time and only he knows the future. The language of Nostradamus's prophecies is so vague that, even his most popular and supposedly "convincing" work is almost laughable when compared to the specific nature of Bible prophecy.[34]

Orthodox—Except when referring to the Eastern Orthodox Church, I use it to describe the standard beliefs that are generally accepted as true by evangelical Christian churches.

Oscillation—This is when something goes back and forth or up and down. In the case of the expansion of the universe it means that after reaching its maximum size, it contracted a little bit, then expanded again, then contracted, and continues going back and forth like that.

Papyrus—An ancient type of paper made from the papyrus reed that was used for making scrolls.

Parabolic curve—While it's true that some parables can throw you a curve, that's not what a parabolic curve is. If you kick a ball high in the air, it will go up to a point, make a relatively sharp turn, and come down. The path the ball takes is usually not a circle but a parabola. Another example is a dish antenna for satellite TV. The dish focuses the satellite signal on the receiver mounted in front of the dish. The dish is in the shape of a parabolic curve.

Patriarchs—Original ancestors or "fathers" of a family, tribe, or nation. As used in this book, it refers to Abraham, Isaac, and Jacob and his twelve sons.

Paul (?—AD 67)—The "apostle to the Gentiles" (Rom 11:13). Paul was his Greek name, while Saul was his Hebrew name. He was present at the stoning of Stephen (Acts 7) and afterwards undertook an organized persecution of Christians. Acts chapter 9 tells how he was converted and most of the rest of the Book of Acts is about his missionary trips around the known world. He is the author of most of the letters to churches that make up the bulk of the New Testament. He was beheaded by Nero in AD 67.[34]

Peter and Simon Peter (?—AD 67)—Peter's given name was Simon. It was Jesus who gave him the name Peter, which means "little rock" (I suppose that would make him a little rockstar instead of a big one.). He is one of the most famous of Jesus's apostles (Matt 10:2-4, Mark 3:14-19, Lk 6:13-16, Acts 1:13-14). All four of the Gospels have loads of material on him, as well as the first half of the book of Acts. The Gospel of Mark is reportedly from Peter's recollections. Other than that, he only authored first and second Peter. He was beheaded by Nero in AD 67.[35]

Philip (early to late first century?)—There are several Philips mentioned in the Bible. The two most notable being Philip the apostle of Jesus and Philip the evangelist. The second of these was chosen, along with Stephen and five other members of the church at Jerusalem to be a deacon. But the Book of Acts records that he was the original Billy Graham, engaging in wildly successful evangelism after he left Jerusalem. Read about his crusades in Acts chapters 8 and 21. But the Philip that is mentioned among the martyrs is the apostle of Jesus (Matt 10:2-4, Mark 3:14-19, Lk 6:13-16, Acts 1:13-14). Read about his adventures in the Gospels.

Presumptuously—To be presumptuous is to assume something is true when it may not be. A presumptuous person rushes ahead, doing or saying something that often turns out to be wrong. A presumptuous prophet is faking it, claiming that God told him something when he didn't, or mistaking his feelings for God's voice.

Primeval and primordial soup—This is a theoretical chemical mixture favorable to the formation of proteins and other necessary parts of living cells that evolutionists imagine was present on Earth during the Precambrian period.

No evidence has ever been found to support its existence. So, I guess this theory is really "in the soup!"

Rabbi—A Jewish religious leader and/or teacher, similar to a pastor or bishop in a Christian church.

Rabbinical—Describes something done, produced, said, or written by one or more rabbis.

Rashi (AD 1040—AD 1105)—A medieval French rabbi and major contributor to Hebrew Scripture study. His commentaries are still widely used by Jewish scholars to this day.[36]

Sea of Galilee—If you look at a map of Israel, you will see two large lakes. The southern one is the Dead Sea and the northern one is the Sea of Galilee. The Sea of Galilee is the lowest freshwater lake on Earth. Andrew, Peter, James, and John were partners in a fishing business on that lake until Jesus called them to be his disciples. Jesus spent a lot of time in the towns around this lake.

Secular—Something that is secular is not spiritual or religious. For example, Mark's gospel would be considered religious history because it deals with the life and teachings of Jesus, the founder of a world religion. A secular historian might not mention Jesus at all because he/she is not concerned with a particular religion. Or he/she might treat him as a historical figure and note his impact on world history in a very general sense.

Shintoism—The traditional ancient religion of Japan. It is based on the belief that the island of Japan is a divine creation and its people are descendants of the gods and therefore, superior to all other races. This is why it is limited to Japan and results in such fierce nationalism. Many Shintoists also mix in other religions such as Buddhism. The racism inherent in Shintoism is clearly against the teaching of the Bible.[37]

Simon—One of the original twelve apostles of Jesus (Matt 10:2-4, Mark 3:14-19, Lk 6:13-16, Acts 1:13-14).

Solomon—King Solomon was the son of King David and third of the kings of Israel before the kingdom split. Solomon was known for his wisdom and peace-making and brought Israel into her golden age of prominence. He is the author of Proverbs, Song of Solomon, Ecclesiastes, and a few of the Psalms. He also built the first temple in Jerusalem. Read about his wisdom and accomplishments in 1 Kings chapters 1-11 and 1 Chronicles chapter 22 to 2 Chronicles chapter 11 as well as in the books he wrote.

Solomon's Temple—see Temple.

Son of Man—There are two meanings for this term. First, it is used in the Old Testament generally to describe a man, emphasizing the frailty and weakness of his humanity. But it is also used a couple of times in reference to the Messiah (Ps 80:17 and Dan 7:13-14), indicating that, although he would be God, he is also coming as 100 percent man at the same time. (This also alludes to the virgin birth.) Jesus picks it up and applies it to himself about eighty times in the Gospels as sort of a humble and under-the-radar way of claiming to be the Messiah.[38]

Stephen (?—AD 37)—One of seven men chosen to be the first deacons in the church at Jerusalem. He also became the first Christian martyr after delivering a brilliant defense for Christianity. One of those who heard him and put him to death was Paul, who later converted. You can read his story in Acts chapters 6-7.

Supercollider—These things are extremely large experimental laboratories that specialize in sub-atomic particle physics. They go by a variety of names, but they all shoot particles at other particles to break them up and see what happens. Kinda like playing marbles. The only thing is, breaking atoms up can be risky—it could all go *boom*!

Synagogue—A Jewish house of meeting, similar to a Christian church building.

Tabernacle—This word literally means "tent" and is commonly used in the Bible to refer to someone's portable house. But the primary use is that the Tabernacle was a portable temple in tent form built by Moses at God's bidding. It served as a place of worship until Solomon built the permanent Temple in 960 BC. It housed the ark and other symbolic furniture. It was also the place where God's presence was, so it served as his house, so to speak. You can read a detailed description of it and its utensils and furniture in Exodus chapters 35-40. In Revelation 21, the word is used to say that God will eventually make his home with men.

Talmud—A collection of commentaries and teachings of the ancient rabbis concerning the Old Testament scriptures.

Temple—There were actually two and a half temples. King Solomon built the first one, which was magnificent and was completed about 960 BC. But Nebuchadnezzar destroyed it in 587 BC. Cyrus, the king of Persia, allowed the return of the exiled Jews that were taken captive by Neb and, at the same time, he allowed them to rebuild their temple, which was completed in 515 BC. This second temple was smaller and simpler than Solomon's. It served the people for five hundred years. But by the time King Herod was put in power by the Romans, it was in pretty sad shape. Since he wasn't a Jew, and the Jews didn't like him, he tried to buy them off by refurbishing and remodeling their temple. Work began in 19 BC and continued throughout the life of Christ. It was completed in AD 64. Herod not only beautified the existing temple buildings, but he expanded the courtyards and the outbuilding complex considerably. But it didn't last long as the Romans destroyed it all five years after it was completed. There will also be a third temple, which is prophesied by Ezekiel (chapters 40—43). The Antichrist will sign a treaty with the Jews that allows them to build it (Dan 9). The date of the signing of that treaty marks the beginning of the seven-year Tribulation period detailed in the Book of Revelation.

Tesserae—The small, colored pieces of something, like stone or glass, that are used to make a mosaic picture.

Testament—A written testimonial, covenant, or contract. The Old Testament is made up of the sacred Hebrew Scriptures. In them God provides for salvation by means of animal sacrifice, which foreshadowed the sacrifice of God's Son, Jesus, on the cross. The New Testament is a collection of the apostles' writings about the life and teachings of Jesus and provides for salvation by means of trusting in the completed sacrifice of God's Son, Jesus, on the cross.

Timothy—Probably the closest of Paul's missionary companions. They were a lot like Batman and Robin. After Paul's death, he became the bishop or head pastor of the church at Ephesus, a city in western Turkey near the Aegean Sea. Timothy is mentioned several times in the Book of Acts and in many of Paul's letters, especially the ones written to him—First and Second Timothy.

Thomas (early to late first century?)—Have you ever heard the expression "Doubting Thomas"? Well, this guy is the original. He was one of the initial twelve apostles (Matt 10:2-4, Mark 3:14-19, Lk 6:13-16, Acts 1:13-14). But he wasn't with the others the first time Jesus appeared to them after his resurrection. So when the others told him they had seen Jesus, Thomas thought they were pulling his leg. A few days later, Jesus appeared to them again when Thomas was there. Jesus challenged him to put his finger in the nail holes in his hands and put his hand in his side where the spear was thrust. Of course, Thomas didn't doubt Jesus anymore. Read the story in John 20:24-29.

Transcendent—To transcend something is to go way beyond its limits. A transcendent being is one whose existence goes beyond the four dimensions of our experience.

Trinity—The word *Trinity* is short for *triunity*. It means that God is eternally existent in the form of three persons. Jesus identifies them in the Book of Matthew. "Go therefore and make disciples of all the nations, baptizing them in the name of the Father and of the Son and of the Holy Spirit." (Matt 28:19, NKJV) It is humanly impossible to comprehend such a God, which is a powerful argument for the divine origin of this teaching. Since God created time, he exists outside of and independent of it in the person of God the Father. But he also created us inside the time domain with both physical and spiritual characteristics. Therefore, in order for him to relate to us completely, he must enter time with both physical and spiritual attributes. He does this in the physical realm in the person of Jesus Christ. He does this in the spiritual realm in the person of the Holy Spirit. It really is impossible for him to relate to us in any other form. And it is because of this that we can trust him. As the writer of Hebrews points out, "And it was necessary for Jesus to be like us, his brothers, so that he could be our merciful and faithful High Priest before God, a Priest who would be both merciful to us and faithful to God in dealing with the sins of the people. For since he himself has now been through suffering and temptation, he knows what it is like when we suffer and are tempted, and he is wonderfully able to help us" (Heb 2:17-18, TLB). It is beyond the scope of this book to present all of the Scriptural evidence for the doctrine of the Trinity as it is massive. But, if you want a complete explanation, you can look the term up in a *Bible dictionary*, *Bible encyclopedia*, or Systematic Theology textbook. I deal with it in more detail in *Is God Really Like That?*

Virgin Birth—The "virgin birth" of Jesus Christ solves a serious problem that God had in saving us. It was Jesus's blood, shed on the cross that paid the penalty for the sins of the entire human race, and therefore makes salvation available for anyone who chooses to take advantage of it. In order for that to happen, Jesus had to satisfy two criteria. First, he had to be part of our human race not some alien member of his own human race with Mary as the Catholics teach. Secondly, he couldn't have the "sin nature" that we inherit from Adam. Be honest, have you ever seen a child that had to be taught how to lie? It comes naturally, doesn't it? That's what I'm talking about when I say, "sin nature." So, how does the virgin birth solve it? Well, the egg of the female contributes the mass or body of a child, while the sperm of the male only contributes genetic information. The Bible tells us that "the life of the flesh is in the blood" (Lev 17:11, NKJV). It's interesting that the egg is not alive until it receives the genetic info that starts building the circulation system and the blood of the baby. Therefore, it is the sperm of the male that transmits the "sin nature" of Adam. So, all God had to do was bypass the sperm. The "virgin birth" provided a body for Jesus through Mary that was 100 percent a member of our human race. And the Holy Spirit simply performed microsurgery on the egg, adding the necessary genetic information to the DNA. So, Jesus did not inherit the "sin nature" that plagues the rest of us, making it possible for his blood to be holy and worthy to pay for our sins.

Appendix A:
Best Explanation Score Chart
After Reviewing the Evidence, What Is the Best Explanation for Each Exhibit Presented?

Exhibit	Name	Dumb Luck	Con Job	Space Aliens	Human Care	God	Need More Info	Comments
1	The Bible's Unity							
2	OT Historical Accuracy							
3	NT Historical Accuracy							
4	Fulfilled Prophecy							
5	Description of the Cosmos							
6	The "Goldilocks Zone"							
7	The Confined Cosmos							
8	Evolution Execution							
9	The Origin of Life							
10	The Bible is Alive							
	TOTALS:							

Appendix B:
Your New Life in Christ

CHECK IT OUT

From Deadness to Aliveness

Now that you have received Christ as your Savior, there are a few basic things you need to know about your new life. To begin with, the Bible tells us that death is not obliteration, but separation. So, physical death is when the soul is separated from the body. The Bible goes on to say that before trusting Jesus to save you, your spirit was dead—that is, separated from life in God. But after receiving Christ, your spirit was brought to life. That is, the connection to life in God is established. Paul explains:

> You were dead in sins, and your sinful desires were not yet cut away. Then he gave you a share in the very life of Christ, for he forgave all your sins, and blotted out the charges proved against you, the list of his commandments which you had not obeyed. He took this list of sins and destroyed it by nailing it to Christ's cross. In this way God took away Satan's power to accuse you of sin, and God openly displayed to the whole world Christ's triumph at the cross where your sins were all taken away. (Col 2:13-15, TLB)

A New Person is Created Inside You.

Jesus refers to it this way,

> *Jesus answered and said to him, 'Most assuredly, I say to you, unless one is born again, he cannot see the kingdom of God.' Nicodemus said to Him, 'How can a man be born when he is old? Can he enter a second time into his mother's womb and be born?' Jesus answered, 'Most assuredly, I say to you, unless one is born of water* (physical birth) *and the Spirit, he cannot enter the kingdom of God. That which is born of the flesh is flesh, and that which is born of the Spirit is spirit. Do not marvel that I said to you, 'You must be born again.'* (Jn 3:3-7 NKJV)

Paul tells us the same thing. *"Therefore, if anyone is in Christ, he is a new creation; old things have passed away; behold, all things have become new."* (2Cor 5:17, NKJV)

Now, There are Two Yous.

So, God gives you a new you at the moment you repent and express faith in Christ, but he doesn't zap our old, selfish, spiritually dead you right away; that comes later. This is a setup for a war between the old you and the new you. I'm sure you've seen those cartoons where the little angel is sitting on one shoulder telling the guy to be good, but there's also a little devil on the other telling him to be bad. Well, that's really not too far from the truth for a Christian. God allows this on purpose to strengthen the new you and gauge your love for him. It's much like a butterfly that struggles to get out of its cocoon. The struggle is what gives it the strength to fly. If you help a butterfly out of its cocoon, it will die in a matter of hours because it won't have the strength to fly and feed itself. Since God wants you to be strong enough to fly, in a spiritual sense, he has put you in a situation that requires the new you to fight and thereby become strong. But never fear—he has also given you some really cool tools to help out the new you.

FOUR TOOLS TO HELP YOU WITH YOUR NEW LIFE IN CHRIST

God has given you four tools to help you in life's struggles: an exhaustive owner's manual, a hotline to the manufacturer, a live-in service rep, and membership in a user support group.

The Owner's Manual is the Bible

I hate reading owner's manuals! I'd rather just see if I can wing it and get the thing working without going to all the trouble to read about it first. This is actually similar to the way you start out as a Christian. Your new life is in place and working before you even have a chance to do much reading. But, given the fact of the struggle I just mentioned and the constant presence of Satan's minions waiting for an opportunity to trip you up, reading the owner's manual is highly recommended. After all, your new life is about building and maintaining a relationship with God, not getting a new gadget to work. Personal Bible reading, hearing the Bible taught and preached by a pastor or teacher, and listening to other Christians as they share how God spoke to them through Scripture are the main ways God speaks to us. Notice that all of these are centered on Bible reading and study. Remember the verse we went through in "The Bible is Alive"? *"All Scripture is given by inspiration of God, and is profitable for doctrine, for reproof, for correction, for instruction in righteousness, that the man of God may be complete, thoroughly equipped for every good work."* (2 Tim 3:16-17, NKJV) Hearing from God about issues in our lives is dependent on our familiarity with scripture. The goal of all this Bible reading is to become familiar with God himself, as a person. Eventually you will know how he thinks and what he would have you do when life's issues come up.

The Hotline to the Manufacturer is Prayer

The Bible tells us, *"Now all of us can come to the Father through the same Holy Spirit because of what Christ has done for us."* (Eph 2:18, NLT) Book 2 in the *Biblical Christian Beliefs* series is a study of God's attributes (what he is like). One of the things I discuss is that God does not love in degrees, like we do. It's impossible for him to love one of his children more than another. So, when you pray you get the same loving attention that Billy Graham gets. That might be hard to believe, but it's absolutely true. You might not feel that way about praying at first, but it's important to realize that prayer works in the spiritual realm, so feelings may or may not be involved.

Communication is vital to maintaining any relationship. Obviously, there are two halves to it. I just mentioned that the Bible is the main way that God speaks to us. That's his half of the deal. And prayer is how we communicate with him, which is why it is so important. Jesus said, *"Men, always ought to pray and not lose heart."* (Lk 18:1b, NKJV)

"But why should I pray if God knows what I need before I ask?"

I once read a story about a king that had a son. The king loved his son and desired to spend time with him, but the only time he ever saw him was when he came to get his annual allowance. So, the king got an idea. Instead of giving his son his allowance once a year, he decided to make it a monthly event. It worked! The king saw his son every month. Then he again moved the timetable to every week. And finally, the king gave his son his allowance on a daily basis. This is how it is with God. It's true that he knows what we need before we ask. But the whole reason that he allows us to have needs in the first place is so we will bring them to him in prayer, thereby engaging in a relationship with him. That's what prayer is all about and why it is so important to God. Besides, there is more than one kind of prayer. It's not all about getting our needs met or wants satisfied.

Four Types of Prayer

There are four kinds of prayer: adoration, confession, thanksgiving, and supplication.

1. **Adoration** is a form of worship. It is simply expressing love and/or respect to God based on who he is and what he has done for us. Jesus gave us a model prayer, known as "The Lord's Prayer." He begins with adoration, *"Our Father in heaven, may your Name be kept holy."* (Matt 6:9, CJB) It's good for us to begin praying with adoration, because we are worshipping him for who he is first. This puts our needs and desires in the right perspective. The Psalms are full of wonderful examples of adoration. I encourage you to check them out.

   This is also why the song service is important in church. Many hymns and worship songs express love and adoration to God. And it is more important that you participate than that you enjoy the music itself or that you have a nice singing voice. The music is just a tool. It's not offered for your entertainment or for you to entertain, it's offered as a tool for you to use to express your love and adoration to God with your own lips.

2. **Confession:** God forgave all of your sins, past, present, and future, when you accepted Jesus as your Savior. What happened is that God, acting as your judge, dismissed all of the charges against you because Jesus paid the penalty himself. This is a judicial kind of forgiveness that established your relationship with him. Then God stepped down from his judge's bench, took off his judge's robe, and signed adoption papers making you a part of his family. This means

that he is no longer your judge and is now your Father. But, in order to maintain a continuing relationship with him, confession of your sins on an "as-needed" basis is also necessary. This is a fatherly kind of forgiveness. Confession is simply agreeing with God about our sin. Arguing with him or ignoring what he says about our behavior puts us at odds with him. John talks about this in 1 John."

> If we say that we have no sin, we are only fooling ourselves and refusing to accept the truth. But if we confess our sins to him, he can be depended on to forgive us and to cleanse us from every wrong. [And it is perfectly proper for God to do this for us because Christ died to wash away our sins.] If we claim we have not sinned, we are lying and calling God a liar, for he says we have sinned. (1Jn 1:8-10, TLB)

3. **Thanksgiving** is another form of worship. We should definitely be thankful for God's salvation and forgiveness, as well as all the other blessings we have in life. The Psalms are full of examples of thanksgiving. Being thankful is an attitude of choice that sometimes requires faith. But Paul said that if we choose this attitude, it will go a long way towards dispelling our anxieties and giving us peace.

> Don't worry about anything; instead, pray about everything. Tell God what you need, and thank him for all he has done. Then you will experience God's peace, which exceeds anything we can understand. His peace will guard your hearts and minds as you live in Christ Jesus. (Phil 4:6-7, NLT)

4. **Supplication:** Bringing our requests to God is what the Bible calls supplication. This should be the last part of our prayers, yet all too often it's the first and sometimes the only part. This, of course, is because of our inherent selfishness. Our prayers should not be just about us. We need to

spend time in adoration, confession, and thanksgiving, so that our prayers are balanced.

But don't misunderstand; God wants to hear our requests. James even chastises believers for not asking God for things. *"You do not have, because you do not ask God."* (*James 4:2b, NIV*) And God has promised to meet our needs. *"And my God shall supply all your need according to His riches in glory by Christ Jesus."* (*Phil 4:19, NKJV*) *"Casting all your care upon him; for he cares for you."* (*1Pet 5:7, NKJV*)

The catch in this is that he has not promised to fulfill all of our wants. James goes on in the next verse, to say, *"And even when you do ask you don't get it because your whole aim is wrong–you want only what will give you pleasure."* (*James 4:3, TLB*) That doesn't mean that God wants to squash all our fun. It means that prayer isn't like sitting on Santa's lap reading him our Christmas list. These kinds of requests reek with selfishness, which is not a quality of character that God wants us to have.

God also wants us to pray for the needs of others. This kind of supplication is called intercession. We should be praying for the salvation of friends and loved ones who don't know Jesus as their Savior yet. And, of course, we should be praying for the needs of our brothers and sisters in Christ as well as for the ministry of our local church. Praying for others increases our love and is one of the main ways we share God's love and compassion with them.

Rowland Hill (1744-1833) once said, "Prayer is the breath of the newborn soul, and there can be no Christian life without it."

The Live-In Service Rep is the Holy Spirit

Paul tells us in 1 Corinthians, *"Do you not know that you are the temple of God and that the Spirit of God dwells in you?"* (*1Cor 3:16, NKJV*)

Every believer is literally possessed by the indwelling Holy Spirit of God. He is a gentleman, however, and will never force you to do anything that you don't want to do. But, he graciously provides believers with many benefits like these:

1. **Assurance of Salvation:** The Holy Spirit provides us assurance that we belong to God and have eternal life. *"He has put his brand upon us his mark of ownership and given us his Holy Spirit in our hearts as guarantee that we belong to him and as the first installment of all that he is going to give us."* (2Cor 1:22, TLB)

2. **Wisdom:** The Holy Spirit gives us wisdom and enlightenment. *"I keep asking that the God of our Lord Jesus Christ, the glorious Father, may give you the Spirit of wisdom and revelation, so that you may know him better. I pray also that the eyes of your heart may be enlightened in order that you may know the hope to which he has called you, the riches of his glorious inheritance in the saints, and his incomparably great power for us who believe."* (Eph 1:17-19a, NIV)

3. **Love for God and Others:** The Holy Spirit helps us get along with each other. *"Try always to be led along together by the Holy Spirit and so be at peace with one another."* (Eph 4:3, TLB) *"And hope maketh not ashamed because the love of God is shed abroad in our hearts by the Holy Ghost which is given unto us."* (Rom 5:5, KJV)

4. **Inner Strength:** The Holy Spirit gives us inner strength. *"I pray that out of his glorious riches he may strengthen you with power through his Spirit in your inner being."* (Eph 3:16, NIV)

5. **Spiritual Maturity:** The Holy Spirit is making us more and more like Jesus. Paul writes, *"And we, who with unveiled faces all reflect the Lord's glory, are being transformed into his likeness with ever-increasing glory, which comes from the Lord, who is the Spirit."* (2Cor 3:18, NIV) *"But the fruit of the Spirit is love, joy, peace, patience, kindness, goodness, faithfulness, gentleness, and self-control. Against such things there is no law."* (Gal 5:22-23, NIV)

6. **Special Abilities:** The Holy Spirit gives us special abilities so we can help others. *"Now God gives us many kinds of special abilities, but it is the same Holy Spirit who is the source of them all.*

There are different kinds of service to God, but it is the same Lord we are serving. There are many ways in which God works in our lives, but it is the same God who does the work in and through all of us who are his. The Holy Spirit displays God's power through each of us as a means of helping the entire church." (1Cor 12:4-7, TLB) And this provides a perfect transition to the fourth thing that God gives us to help us in our struggles.

The User Support Group is His Church

Unfortunately, there are some denominations that think that their man-made, man-run organization is the only true church; but, let me be clear. God's Church is not a man-made, man-run organization, not that a denomination is wrong in and of itself. But God's Church is a spiritual *organism* made up of all believers from all churches and denominations throughout the entire world. This is the Church that you are automatically made a member of when you trust Christ as your Savior.

Nevertheless, God never intended for you to be a spiritual hermit. He wants you to associate with some of your fellow believers in a local church. I'd like to spend a few moments explaining why this is important. Since I have worked with and in many Christian denominations in my life, I can give some general, impartial wisdom on what to look for in a good church and warn you about what to stay away from.

"Why Should I Meet With Other Believers?"

The writer of Hebrews said, *"Let us consider how we may spur one another on toward love and good deeds. Let us not give up meeting together, as some are in the habit of doing, but let us encourage one another—and all the more as you see the Day approaching."* (Heb 10:24-25, NIV) That's it in a nutshell; God wants us to support each other through the ups and downs of life. Although helping each other out with things like doing chores around the house can be included in this idea, the writer of Hebrews is specifically talking about emotional and spiritual support. We all experience times of doubt and weak faith. When that happens, it's important to have a prayer partner to confide in, someone who will pray for you without judging. There is also the aspect of corporate worship. Personal worship is wonderful, but we need to know that we aren't alone in our adoration and thanksgiving. The teaching and preaching of God's Word is also vital to a healthy life in Christ. Accountability and pastoral care are also essential. All of these things are vital for maintaining a healthy walk with God. And he made it so that we can't have a healthy walk apart from our brothers and sisters in Christ. So, it's obviously his will for you to find a good church or Bible study to belong to.

"What Does a Good Church Look Like?"
The Book of Acts describes what the early Church was like. It turned the world "right-side-up" for Jesus, so it's a perfect example.

> They joined with the other believers in regular attendance at the apostles' teaching sessions and at the Communion services and prayer meetings. (Acts 2:42, TLB) And all the believers met together constantly and shared everything with each other, selling their possessions and dividing with those in need. They worshiped together regularly at the Temple each day, met in small groups in homes for Communion, and shared their meals with great joy and thankfulness, praising God. The whole city was favorable to them, and each day God added to them all who were being saved. (Acts 2 44-47, TLB)

So, they met regularly to hear the teaching of God's Word. They partook of communion regularly, as well, which is a way of remembering Jesus's sacrifice on the cross for our sins. It consists of eating a small piece of bread, symbolizing his broken body, and taking a sip of juice or wine, symbolizing his shed blood. They prayed together for each other and demonstrated God's love by taking care of each other's needs. They worshipped together. They were joyful and thankful. And there were new people constantly coming to Christ. Just as these characteristics were evident in the early church, they should also be evident in the church you select. No church is perfect, but if it can even come close to matching most of these qualities, it will likely be a healthy choice. Of course, the most important thing you can do is to pray for God's guidance. Ask him to lead you to the church family that he wants you to be a part of. He will! I should also add that the early church didn't have buildings to meet in. They usually met in each other's homes in small groups. This is also acceptable to God as long as the group is functioning in most of these areas.

Important Beliefs
There are a few important things that a healthy, Bible-based church should be teaching.

1. **Beliefs about the Bible**: A healthy local church uses the Bible as a source of that health. They will teach that the Bible is the only infallible, authoritative Word of God, as we have been proving in this book.
2. **Beliefs about God**: A healthy local church will have a biblical view of God. They will teach that God is eternally existent in the form of three persons: Father, Son and Holy Spirit. Jesus said, *"Therefore go and make disciples in all the nations, baptizing them into the name of the Father and of the Son and of the Holy Spirit."* (Mt 28:19, TCB) This is called the doctrine of the Trinity. And don't worry if you can't understand it. No mere human can fully comprehend the truth about an infinite God. A slightly more detailed explanation is given in the glossary.
Beliefs about Salvation: A healthy local church will teach that salvation is a free gift to all who will confess that they are sinners and receive Jesus Christ as Lord and Savior, which is the only way to come into a relationship with him.

"Jesus said to him, 'I am the way, the truth, and the life. No one comes to the Father except through Me.'" (Jn 14:6, NKJV) *"For it is by grace you have been saved, through faith–and this not from yourselves, it is the gift of God–not by works, so that no one can boast."* (Eph 2:8-9, NIV)

"What are the marks of a bad church?"

If you feel uncomfortable about a church, it may be the Holy Spirit telling you that something is wrong. If the characteristics do not match up with several of the things I just mentioned, it may not be a healthy environment for you. Pray and ask God for wisdom. You have his promise that he will answer. *"If any of you lacks wisdom, he should ask God, who gives generously to all without finding fault, and it will be given to him."* (James 1:5, NIV)

Avoid a church that teaches things that aren't in the Bible, including rituals and practices. This is especially true if they have additional books that they claim are equal in authority to the Bible. This is the mark of a cult. Also, steer clear if they add any kind of ritual or series of works that must be done in order to obtain salvation. Another "biggie" is if they deny that Jesus is God come down to us as a real man. And don't be fooled by the fact that most cult members and leaders are very nice, good, moral people. A lie is a lie, even when it's cloaked in love.

Here is a list of some of the most common cults:

- Latter-Day Saints or Mormons
- Jehovah's Witnesses
- Unification Church
- Unitarians
- Spiritists
- Christian Science
- Scientologists

Avoid all of these!

Some Final Considerations

Timothy Keller said, "The church is a hospital for sinners, not a museum for saints." The church that is right for you will be a place where you can "bloom" in the Lord, where you can grow and thrive and contribute. It will be a place where you can love and be loved, where there are people full of mercy, grace and forgiveness, yet balanced by encouragement and loving accountability.

Share Your New Life with Others

There is one last item I must mention. God wants you to share your new life with others. I'm not talking about beating everyone you know over the head with a giant twenty-pound-family Bible. I'm talking about being bold and honest enough to explain what has happened to you to the people who ask, "What is different about you now?" And believe me, they will notice! So, you need to be ready to share your faith. This doesn't have to be a big, scary ordeal. Just tell them the story of how you came to Christ and how your life is different now. You might be surprised to find out how many people also want to have a relationship with God like you!

May God bless you as you grow and share what Jesus Christ is doing for you in your new life!

Notes

Did God Really Say That?

1. Willmington, Dr. H. L. *Willmington's Guide to the Bible.* Tyndale, 1984. Pages xiv-xv. Used by permission.
2. Geisler, Norman and Abdul Saleeb, *Answering Islam.* Baker Books, 2002. Page 177.
3. McDowell, Josh and Don Stewart. *Handbook of Today's Religions.* Thomas Nelson Publishers, 1983. Pages 290-291.
4. Willmington, Dr. H. L. *Willmington's Guide to the Bible.* Tyndale, 1984. Page 811 Used by permission.
5. Orr, James. *The Christian View of God and the World.* Eerdmans, 1948.
6. This example is actually a gross over-simplification of God's incomprehensible relationship to time. It has more to do with who he is rather than what he does. But, I give it, nonetheless, to illustrate this truth in practical terms that can be understood by people like me, who are not rocket scientists. I hope it makes some sense to you.

The Bible and History

1. Morris, Dr. Henry M. *Many Infallible Proofs.* Master Books, 1974. Page 299.
2. God allowed this so that people wouldn't worship the manuscripts instead of him. For example, if the original stone tablets containing the Ten Commandments were

still with us, people would be tempted to worship them as a relic and attribute magic powers to them. Someone might think that if they touched one of the tablets that God would grant them some kind of request based solely on the supposed magical powers of the tablets. This is an occult practice that places a thing before having a relationship with God himself. He considers it idolatry.

3. Davidson, Samuel as quoted by McDowell, Josh. *Evidence That Demands A Verdict Vol. 1*. Campus Crusade for Christ Int., 1972. Page 57.

4. Connolly, W. Kenneth. *The Indestructible Book*. Baker Books, 1996. Pages 17-18.

5. Wikimedia Foundation. "Vedas." Wikipedia. http://en.wikipedia.org/wiki/Vedas (accessed June 19, 2014).

6. Halley, Dr. Henry. *Halley's Bible Handbook*. 24th ed. Zondervan Pub House, 1965. Pages 87-89.

7. Halley, Dr. Henry. *Halley's Bible Handbook*. 24th ed. Zondervan Pub House, 1965. Page 120.

8. Holden, Joseph M., and Norman L. Geisler. *The Popular Handbook of Archaeology and the Bible*. Harvest House Publishers, 2013. Pages 229-230.

9. Halley, Dr. Henry. *Halley's Bible Handbook*. 24th ed. Zondervan Pub House, 1965. Page 191.

10. Halley, Dr. Henry. *Halley's Bible Handbook*. 24th ed. Zondervan Pub House, 1965. Pages 199 & 206.

11. Halley, Dr. Henry. *Halley's Bible Handbook*. 24th ed. Zondervan Pub House, 1965. Page 225.

12. Willmington, Dr. H. L. *Willmington's Guide to the Bible*. Tyndale, 1984. Page 815.

13. Halley, Dr. Henry. *Halley's Bible Handbook*. 24th ed. Zondervan Pub House, 1965. Page 364.

14. Holden, Joseph M., and Norman L. Geisler. *The Popular Handbook of Archaeology and the Bible*. Harvest House Publishers, 2013. Page 202.

15. Gluek, Dr. Nelson. *Rivers in the Desert.* Farrar, Straus and Cudahy, 1959. Page 31.
16. Willmington, Dr. H. L. *Willmington's Guide to the Bible.* Tyndale, 1984. Page 813.
17. Sheler, Jeffery L. "Is the Bible True?". *U.S. News & World Report*, October 25, 1999. Page 52.
18. Halley, Dr. Henry. *Halley's Bible Handbook.* 24th ed. Zondervan Pub House, 1965. Pages 68-69.
19. Halley, Dr. Henry. *Halley's Bible Handbook.* 24th ed. Zondervan Pub House, 1965. Pages 48-49, 71-72.
20. Willmington, Dr. H. L. *Willmington's Guide to the Bible.* Tyndale, 1984. Page 814.
21. Halley, Dr. Henry. *Halley's Bible Handbook.* 24th ed. Zondervan Pub House, 1965. Pages 71-72, 76-80.
22. Oard, Michael. *Flood by Design.* Master Books, 2008. Kindle edition location 398-485.
23. Oard, Michael. *Flood by Design.* Master Books, 2008. Kindle edition location 485.
24. Oard, Michael. *Flood by Design.* Master Books, 2008. Kindle edition location 1396-1471.
25. Oard, Michael. *Flood by Design.* Master Books, 2008. Kindle edition location 1036-1125.
26. Oard, Michael. *Flood by Design.* Master Books, 2008. Kindle edition location 1518-1624.
27. Oard, Michael. *Flood by Design.* Master Books, 2008. Kindle edition location 2393-2421.
28. Holden, Joseph M., and Norman L. Geisler. *The Popular Handbook of Archaeology and the Bible.* Harvest House Publishers, 2013. Pages 214-220.
29. Willmington, Dr. H. L. *Willmington's Guide to the Bible.* Tyndale, 1984. Page 815.
30. Missler, Dr. Chuck. "Beyond Newton session 1." In *The Beyond Series Briefing Pack* (MP3 audio). Koinonia House, 2011.

31. answering-islam.org. "Chapter 7: Historical Errors of the Qur'an." *Behind the Veil.* http://answering-islam.org/BehindVeil/btv7.html (accessed June 19, 2014).
32. Willmington, Dr. H. L. *Willmington's Guide to the Bible.* Tyndale, 1984. Page 813 as quoted from Ramsey, Sir William *The Bearing of Recent Discovery on the Trustworthyness of the New Testament* 1923.
33. Dockery, David S. *Holman Bible Handbook.* Holman Bible Publishers, 1992. Page 73.
34. Halley, Dr. Henry. *Halley's Bible Handbook.* 24th ed. Zondervan Pub House, 1965. Pages 448-449.
35. Dockery, David S. *Holman Bible Handbook.* Holman Bible Publishers, 1992. Pages 72-73.
36. Josephus, Flavius, and William Whiston. *The Works of Josephus.* Hendrickson Publishers, 1981. Page 379.
37. Foxe, John. "Foxe's Book of Martyrs." In *PC Study Bible formatted electronic database* Biblesoft, Inc., 2006.
38. Greenleaf, Simon. *The Testimony of the Evangelists.* Baker Books, 1984. Pages 53-54.
39. The word, ascend, just means to go or move up. Acts 1:9-11 tells us how Jesus, after his resurrection, was taken up to heaven in a cloud. This event is called the ascension of Christ.
40. Simon is Peter's given name. Jesus gave him the name Peter, which means "little rock". Peter's dad's name was Jonah and "bar" means son. So Jesus called him "Simon, son of Jonah".
41. Lewis, C. S. *Mere Christianity.* The Macmillan Company, 1960. Pages 40-41.
42. Francis, Dr. James Allan. "Arise Sir Knight!" In *The Real Jesus and Other Sermons.* Judson Press, 1926. Pages 123-124.

The Bible and Fulfilled Prophecy

1. Antichrist is the title of a person that means "against Christ" or a substitute Messiah. "Christ" in Greek is the equivalent of "Messiah" in Hebrew. Muhammad probably adopted this term in the Koran because he wanted to attract Christians to convert to Islam and this was a major topic of their concern. But his prophecies concerning this guy are conflicting and confusing. He shows ignorance of what the title means in the Bible and, therefore, the Antichrist of Islam is different than the Antichrist of the Bible. For a brief rundown of the way the title is used in the Bible, see the entry in the glossary for "Antichrist".

2. Shamoun, Sam. "Muhammad's False Prophecies." At answering-islam.org. http://answering-islam.org/Shamoun/false_prophecies.htm (accessed June 19, 2014).

3. Myers, Philip. *General History for Colleges & High Schools.* Rev. ed. Ginn & Co., 1906. Page 55.

4. Eusebius. *Ecclesiastical History.* AD 320 Reprinted by Baker Book House, 1992. Pages 102-103.

5. It is well documented that the earliest Jewish and Babylonian calendars featured 360 days per year. Scientists believe that a natural cataclysm such as an asteroid impact changed the Earth's orbit at some point to the present 365¼ day period. But the Jews always kept the 360 day figure for the purpose of calculating prophecy. Eastman, Mark, and Chuck Missler. *The Creator Beyond Time and Space.* The Word For Today, 1996. page 137. See also *The Coming Prince*, Sir Robert Anderson.

6. Stoner, Peter W., and Robert C. Newman. *Science Speaks.* Moody Press, 1976. I used the free online version at http://sciencespeaks.dstoner.net/Christ_of_Prophecy.html#c9 (accessed June 19, 2014). He discusses all of the probability statistics at great length.

7. Meyer, Stephen C. *Signature in the Cell.* HarperCollins Publishers, 2009. Page 212.
8. Stoner, Peter W., and Robert C. Newman. *Science Speaks.* Moody Press, 1976. I used the free online version at http://sciencespeaks.dstoner.net/Christ_of_Prophecy.html#c9 (accessed June 19, 2014).

The Bible and Science

1. Arbesman, S. *The Half-life of Facts.* Penguin Group, 2012. Pages 28-29.
2. Meyer, Stephen C. *Signature in the Cell.* HarperCollins Publishers, 2009. Page 410.
3. Kitcher, P. *Living With Darwin.* Oxford University Press, 2007. Page 11.
4. Eastman, Mark, and Chuck Missler. *The Creator Beyond Time and Space.* The Word For Today, 1996. pages 97-98, used by permission.
5. Schroeder, Professor Gerald L. "The Age of the Universe." YouTube. www.youtube.com/watch?v=EhrdtTG0nTw (accessed June 23, 2014).
6. Schroeder, Gerald. "The Age of the Universe." Gerald Schroeder. http://geraldschroeder.com/wordpress/?page_id=53 (accessed June 28, 2014).
7. Setterfield, Barry. "ZPE-Plasma_model." www.setterfield.org/ZPE-Plasma_model.html (accessed June 23, 2014).
8. Schroeder, Professor Gerald L. "The Age of the Universe." YouTube. www.youtube.com/watch?v=EhrdtTG0nTw (accessed June 23, 2014).
9. For a full discussion of why zero-point energy and dark energy are the same, see this article at the Calphysics Institute website: www.calphysics.org/zpe.html (accessed June 23, 2014).

10. Setterfield, Barry. "ZPE-Plasma_model." www.setterfield. org/ZPE-Plasma_model.html (accessed June 23, 2014). This site provides much of the information in this section.
11. Eastman, Mark, and Chuck Missler. *The Creator Beyond Time and Space.* The Word For Today, 1996. Page 27.
12. Davies, Paul. *The Cosmic Blueprint.* Simon & Schuster, 1988. page 203.
13. Greenstein, George. *The Symbiotic Universe.* William Morrow, 1988. Page 27.
14. Lipson, H.S. "A Physacist Looks at Evolution." *Physics Bulletin.* Vol 31, May, 1980. page 138.
15. Jastrow, Robert. *God and the Astronomers.* W. W. Norton & Co., 1978. Page 116.
16. Darwin, Charles. *On the Origin of Species.* John Murray, 1872. Page 133.
17. Darwin, Charles. *On the Origin of Species.* John Murray, 1872. Page 133.
18. Jeremiah Films, Inc. "The Evolution Conspiracy." YouTube www.youtube.com/watch?v=mjoAhq1zs3E (accessed June 23, 2014).
19. Jeremiah Films, Inc. "The Evolution Conspiracy" YouTube www.youtube.com/watch?v=mjoAhq1zs3E (accessed June 23, 2014).
20. The Editors of Encyclopædia Britannica. "Ramapithecus (fossil primate genus)." Encyclopedia Britannica Online. www.britannica.com/EBchecked/topic/490510/ Ramapithecus (accessed June 23, 2014).
21. Oxnard, Charles E. *Fossils, Teeth and Sex—New Perspective on Human Evolution.* University of Washington Press, 1987. Page 227.
22. "Who was Neanderthal man?" biblestudy.org. www. biblestudy.org/basicart/who-was-neanderthal-man-was-he-the-missing-link.html (accessed June 23, 2014).
23. Gregory, W.K. " Hesperopithecus apparently not an ape nor a man". *Science*, 1927. Pages 579-581.

24. Setterfield, Barry. "ZPE-Plasma_model." www.setterfield. org/ZPE-Plasma_model.html (accessed June 23, 2014).
25. Josephus, Flavius, and William Whiston. *The Works of Josephus.* Hendrickson Publishers, 1981. Page 25.
26. Baugh, Carl. "The Crystalline Canopy Theory." Creation Evidence Museum of Texas. http://184.154.224.5/~creatio1/index.php?option=com_content&task=view&id=74&Itemid=29. (accessed June 23, 2014).
27. Clark, M.E. "The Clark Geologic Column." Creation Evidence Museum of Texas. http://184.154.224.5/~creatio1/images/wall_draft4_small.jpg (accessed July 1, 2014).
28. genesispark.com. "Historical Evidence" Genesis Park Historical Evidence Comments. www.genesispark.com/exhibits/evidence/historical/ (accessed June 23, 2014).
29. genesispark.com. "Cryptozoological Evidence." Genesis Park Cryptozoological Evidence Comments. www.genesispark.com/exhibits/evidence/cryptozoological/ (accessed June 23, 2014).
30. Goodsell, David. *The Machinery of Life.* Springer, 1998. Page 45.
31. Dembski, William. *The Design Inference.* Cambridge University Press, 1998.
32. Meyer, Stephen C. *Signature in the Cell.* HarperCollins Publishers, 2009. Page 212.
33. Hoyle, Sir Fredrick. *Nature*, volume 294:105, Nov. 12, 1981.
34. Morowitz, Harold. *Energy Flow in Biology.* Academic Press, 1968.
35. Brooks, James. *Origins of Life.* Lion, 1985. Page 118.
36. Crick, Francis. *Life Itself.* Simon & Schuster, 1981. Page 88.
37. Dose, Klaus. "The Origin of Life." *Interdisciplinary Science Review 13*, 1988 Pages 348-356.

38. Meyer, Stephen C. *Signature in the Cell.* HarperCollins Publishers, 2009. Page 321.
39. Wald, George. "Innovation and Biology." *Scientific American*, Vol. 199, Sept. 1958. Page 100.
40. Meyer, Stephen C. *Signature in the Cell.* HarperCollins Publishers, 2009. Page 401.
41. Eger, Martin quoted in Buell, "Broaden Science Curriculum." A21.
42. Meyer, Stephen C. *Signature in the Cell.* HarperCollins Publishers, 2009. Page 435.

Glossary

1. Unger, Merrill F., and R. K. Harrison. "The New Unger's Bible Dictionary." In *PC Study Bible formatted electronic data base.* Rev. and updated ed. Moody Press, 1988 and Biblesoft, Inc. 2006.
2. Walbank, Frank. "Alexander the Great." Encyclopedia Britannica Online. www.britannica.com/EBchecked/topic/14224/Alexander-the-Great (accessed June 30, 2014).
3. More info is available in the *Handbook of Today's Religions* detailed in the bibliography, or see Slick, Matt. "Is Allah, the God of Islam, the same as the Yahweh the God of the Bible?" CARM. at http://carm.org/god-islam-christianity-same (accessed June 30, 2014).
4. Lockyer, Herbert. *Nelson's Illustrated Bible Dictionary* in *PC Study Bible formatted electronic database.* Thomas Nelson Publishers, 1986 and Biblesoft, Inc., 2006.
5. Easton, M.G. *Easton's Bible Dictionary* in *PC Study Bible formatted electronic database.* Biblesoft, Inc., 2006.
6. More info is available in the *Handbook of Today's Religions* detailed in the bibliography, or see Slick, Matt. "The Apocrypha: Is it scripture?" CARM. http://carm.org/apocrypha-it-scripture (accessed June 30, 2014).

7. Bromiley, Geoffrey William. *International Standard Bible Encyclopedia* in *PC Study Bible formatted electronic database.* Fully rev. ed. W.B. Eerdmans, 1988 and Biblesoft, Inc., 2006.
8. Fausset, A.R. *Fausset's Bible Dictionary* in *PC Study Bible formatted electronic database.* Zondervan, 1949 and Biblesoft, Inc., 2006.
9. Bromiley, Geoffrey William. *International Standard Bible Encyclopedia* in *PC Study Bible formatted electronic database.* Fully rev. ed. W.B. Eerdmans, 1988 and Biblesoft, Inc., 2006.
10. The Editors of Encyclopædia Britannica. "Belshazzar." Encyclopedia Britannica Online. www.britannica.com/EBchecked/topic/60121/Belshazzar (accessed June 30, 2014).
11. More info is available in the *Handbook of Today's Religions* detailed in the bibliography.
12. American Liver Foundation. "Cirrhosis." American Liver Foundation. www.liverfoundation.org/abouttheliver/info/cirrhosis/ (accessed June 30, 2014).
13. More info is available in the *Handbook of Today's Religions* detailed in the bibliography.
14. More info is available in the *Handbook of Today's Religions* detailed in the bibliography, or see CARM "Cults." http://carm.org/cults (accessed June 30, 2014).
15. Smith, William. *Smith's Bible Dictionary* in *PC Study Bible formatted electronic database.* Barbour Books, 1987 and Biblesoft, Inc., 2006.
16. Faculty and students of Cuyahoga Community College Cleveland, OH. "Project Gilgamesh." www.tri-c.edu/enrichment/arts/ProjectGilgamesh/Documents/Gilgamesh%20Short%20Forms.pdf (accessed June 6, 2014).
17. Wikimedia Foundation. "Hepatitis." Wikipedia. http://en.wikipedia.org/wiki/Hepatitis (accessed June 30, 2014).

18. Wikimedia Foundation. "Rowland Hill (preacher)." Wikipedia. http://en.wikipedia.org/wiki/Rowland_Hill_ (preacher) (accessed June 30, 2014).

19. Much more info is available in the *Handbook of Today's Religions* detailed in the bibliography.

20. Wikimedia Foundation. "Hittites." Wikipedia. http://en.wikipedia.org/wiki/Hittites (accessed June 30, 2014).

21. More info is available in the *Handbook of Today's Religions* detailed in the bibliography. Another great source is *Answering Islam* by Norman Geisler and Abdul Saleeb listed in the last chapter.

22. More info is available in the *Handbook of Today's Religions* detailed in the bibliography.

23. Bromiley, Geoffrey William. *International Standard Bible Encyclopedia* in *PC Study Bible formatted electronic database.* Fully rev. ed. W.B. Eerdmans, 1988 and Biblesoft, Inc., 2006.

24. More info is available in the *Handbook of Today's Religions* detailed in the bibliography.

25. Wikimedia Foundation. "Timothy Keller (pastor)." Wikipedia. http://en.wikipedia.org/wiki/Timothy_Keller_(pastor) (accessed June 30, 2014).

26. More info is available in the *Handbook of Today's Religions* detailed in the bibliography and *Answering Islam* listed in the last chapter.

27. More info is available in the *Handbook of Today's Religions* detailed in the bibliography.

28. Wikimedia Foundation. "Maimonides." Wikipedia. http://en.wikipedia.org/wiki/Maimonides (accessed June 30, 2014).

29. The Editors of Encyclopædia Britannica. "Nahmanides (Spanish scholar and rabbi)." Encyclopedia Britannica Online. www.britannica.com/EBchecked/topic/401779/Nahmanides (accessed June 30, 2014).

30. Lockyer, Herbert. *Nelson's Illustrated Bible Dictionary* in *PC Study Bible formatted electronic database.* Thomas Nelson Publishers, 1986 and Biblesoft, Inc., 2006.
31. Bromiley, Geoffrey William. *International Standard Bible Encyclopedia* in *PC Study Bible formatted electronic database.* Fully rev. ed. W.B. Eerdmans, 1988 and Biblesoft, Inc., 2006.
32. Lockyer, Herbert. *Nelson's Illustrated Bible Dictionary* in *PC Study Bible formatted electronic database.* Thomas Nelson Publishers, 1986 and Biblesoft, Inc., 2006.
33. Bromiley, Geoffrey William. *International Standard Bible Encyclopedia* in *PC Study Bible formatted electronic database.* Fully rev. ed. W.B. Eerdmans, 1988 and Biblesoft, Inc., 2006.
34. More info is available in the *Handbook of Today's Religions* detailed in the bibliography.
35. Unger, Merrill F., and R. K. Harrison. *The New Unger's Bible Dictionary* in *PC Study Bible formatted electronic data base.* Rev. and updated ed. Moody Press, 1988 and Biblesoft, Inc. 2006.
36. Easton, M.G. *Easton's Bible Dictionary* in *PC Study Bible formatted electronic database.* Biblesoft, Inc., 2006.
37. Wikimedia Foundation. "Rashi." Wikipedia. http://en.wikipedia.org/wiki/Rashi (accessed June 30, 2014).
38. More info is available in the *Handbook of Today's Religions* detailed in the bibliography.
39. Easton, M.G. *Easton's Bible Dictionary* in *PC Study Bible formatted electronic database.* Biblesoft, Inc., 2006.

Bibliography

Besides the books and films listed in the endnotes, the following resources provided information for much of the content of this book.

Eastman, Mark, and Chuck Missler. *The Creator Beyond Time and Space*. Costa Mesa, CA: The Word for Today, 1996. Now available as *The Creator Series Audio Book* (CD or MP3), http://www.khouse.org (accessed June 28, 2014)

Editors of Encyclopædia Britannica. Encyclopedia Britannica Online. www.britannica.com (accessed June 28, 2014).

Editors of PC Study Bible. *PC Study Bible electronic database*. Biblesoft, Inc., 2006.

Geisler, Norman L., and William E. Nix. *A General Introduction to the Bible*. Chicago: Moody Press, 1986.

Geisler, Norman L., and Abdul Saleeb. *Answering Islam*. Grand Rapids: BakerBooks, 2002.

Halley, Henry H. *Halley's Bible Handbook*. Grand Rapids: Zondervan, 1965.

Holden, Joseph M., and Norman L. Geisler. *The Popular Handbook of Archaeology and the Bible*. Eugene: Harvest House Publishers, 2013.

Missler, Dr. Chuck. *The Beyond Series Briefing Pack (MP3 Audio)*. Coeur d'Alene: Koinonia House, 2010. Available at http://www.khouse.org (accessed June 28, 2014).

McDowell, Josh, and Don Douglas Stewart. *Handbook of Today's Religions*. Nashville, Atlanta, London, Vancouver: Thomas Nelson Publishers, 1983.

Meyer, Stephen C. *Signature in the Cell*. New York: HarperOne, 2009.

Morris, Henry M. *Many Infallible Proofs*. El Cajon, Calif.: Master Books, 1974.

Oard, Michael. *Flood by Design*. Green Forest: Master Books, 2008.

Setterfield, Barry, "Data and Creation", www.Setterfield.org, www.setterfield.org/Data_and_Creation/ZPE-Plasma_model.html (accessed June 28, 2014).

Schroeder, Professor Gerald L. "The Age of the Universe." YouTube. https://www.youtube.com/watch?v=EhrdtTG0nTw (accessed June 28, 2014).

Smith, Pastor Chuck. "Through The Bible C2000 Series (audio)." The Word for Today. http://twft.com/?page=C2000 (accessed June 28, 2014).

Willmington, Dr. H. L. *Willmington's Guide to the Bible*, Wheaton: Tyndale, 1984.

Index

dinosaurs (see also fossils), 130, 144-145, 151, 220, 236-237

Earth created cool, 142

evolution mania, 130, 168-171

fossils and fossilization, 47, 103, 132, 136-152

genetic processes, 133-135, 157

geologic ages, 138-149

human ancestors (not), 137-138

ice age, 149

man and dinosaurs coexisted, 145

methods of dating rocks, 98, 138-140, 149-152

missing links, 136-138

mutation, 133-135, 157

natural selection, 134-135

old Earth, what if, 151

relationships among species, 133-134

species, 131, 133-138, 140, 144, 152, 227

young Earth and universe, 101-103, 149-152, 165-166

Ezekiel, 82, 226, 239, 244

Ezra, 86, 218, 219, 226

God of the Bible (see also Jesus Christ and salvation)

Author, 20, 29, 175, 187-188, 190, 191

challenge to "junk" prophets, 74-75

character of, 21, 25-27, 31-33, 187-188

Creator, 28, 32, 45-46, 53, 74, 97-130, 129, 132, 133, 139, 142, 152, 166-168, 169-170, 174, 177, 183, 189, 221, 229, 246, 252

desire to communicate, 21, 27, 32-33, 180

existence of, 20, 25, 93, 117-129, 161-168

hope in, 22, 74, 127, 178, 181, 186, 191, 193, 258

Judge, 26-27, 43, 145, 178-179, 183, 184, 190, 191

knows us, 32, 177, 183-184, 187

light, 178-180

love of, 21, 26, 29, 32-33, 62-64, 91, 127, 130, 174, 177, 178-180, 188, 189, 192, 204-205, 232, 254, 257, 261

miracles of (see Old and New Testament)

not like us, 26, 191-194

outside of time, 26, 32, 73-74, 177, 223, 229, 231, 240, 246, 265

pray to, 31, 64, 177-182, 254-257, 260, 261, 262
reveals himself personally, 31-33, 174-175
truth about, 21-22, 23, 26-27, 33, 170-171
unchanging, 26, 97

"holy" books, other
Book of Mormon, 40, 51-52
Koran (Quran), 26, 51, 117, 210, 215, 232, 236, 269
Hindu Vedas, 40
unity of, 30
Holy Spirit, 27, 100, 110, 173, 174, 176, 177, 180, 181, 182, 185, 186, 187, 188, 190, 194, 215, 225, 228, 229, 231, 246, 247, 252, 254, 257-259, 261, 262
live-in service rep., 180, 257-259
sanctification, 182-186, 258

Isaiah, 73, 74, 85, 86, 90, 117, 174
Israel/Israelites, 27, 41, 42, 43, 44, 45, 50, 54, 74, 81, 85-87, 88, 89, 98, 213, 214, 218, 219, 220, 224, 225, 226, 230, 232, 233, 235, 237, 238, 242, 243

James, 56, 63, 65, 220, 233, 236, 242, 257
Jeremiah, 27, 82, 85, 116, 234

Jerusalem, 42, 59, 60, 63, 85, 86, 88, 89, 90, 128, 218, 219, 230, 233, 236, 239, 241, 243
Jesus Christ (see also salvation), 20, 26, 27, 32, 33, 36, 40, 44, 51, 52-54, 55, 57, 58, 59, 60, 61, 63, 65, 66, 67, 68, 69, 70, 77, 81, 82, 85, 87-92, 101, 125, 175, 176, 177, 178, 179, 180, 181, 182, 184, 185, 187, 188, 189, 191, 193, 194, 200, 204, 206, 215, 216, 217, 220, 222, 223, 225, 227, 228, 229, 231, 232, 233, 234, 235, 236, 238, 239, 241, 242, 243, 245, 246, 247, 251, 252, 253, 254, 255, 256, 257, 258, 259, 260, 261, 262, 263, 268
accepted the Old Testament, 52-54
authority of, 191-194
bizarre statements of, 67-70
character of, 61, 67-71, 234, 235, 246, 247
great moral teacher, 69-70
impact on history, 70
is alive, 194
Jewish Messiah, 60, 61, 87-92, 216, 229, 234, 235, 243, 269
lineage, 87
miracles of, 61-62, 66-67
offered as a sacrifice, 27, 91, 179-182, 245, 260
only way to God, 180
Palm Sunday, 88-92

born again, 175-176, 180-181, 182, 252
by grace through faith, 27, 180, 181, 223, 230, 262
cross of Christ, 51, 54, 58, 59, 60, 61, 67, 68, 70, 88, 89, 90-91, 179, 181, 188, 229, 234, 239, 245, 246-247, 251, 260
eternal, everlasting life, 74, 91, 127, 178, 179, 180, 184, 228, 229, 251, 258
forgiveness of sins, 62, 64, 68, 91, 175, 179-180, 192, 229, 235, 247, 251, 255-256
gospel, 63, 64, 65, 229
heaven and hell, 27, 53, 54, 66, 68, 69, 80, 99, 100, 128, 177, 178, 179, 184, 194, 225, 229, 230, 234, 237, 255, 268
not by perfect goodness (works), 27, 177-179, 181, 230, 230, 262
of creation, 127-129
resurrection of the dead, 69, 184
share your faith, 194, 253, 257, 263
sin and sinner, 26-27, 45, 61, 68, 90-91, 127, 145, 177-182, 184, 185, 221, 224, 229, 230, 233, 234, 235,

246, 247, 251, 255, 256, 260, 261, 263
sinner's prayer, 181-182
Satan, 21, 69, 179, 188-189, 193, 234, 251, 253
science and the Bible, 93-171
definition of science, 94-97, 131-132, 170-171
philosophers of science, 95-97, 131, 171
turnover of truth, 94-95, 97, 124
Solomon, 42, 85, 87, 214, 218, 219, 229-230, 243, 244
time, 99, 104, 106, 107, 122-123, 142
atomic clocks slowing, 102-103, 132, 218-219
created, 100-101
expansion of space-time, 100-102
God outside of, 26, 32, 73-74, 177, 223, 229, 231, 246, 265
limited, 122-123
quantized, 105-107
young Earth and universe, 102-103, 149-152, 165-166
truth, 20, 21, 22, 23-25, 26-27, 28-29, 33, 35, 37, 46, 53, 59, 60, 66, 68, 69, 76, 80, 83, 92, 93, 94-97, 103, 106, 107, 124, 128, 138, 140, 145, 149, 157, 161, 165, 169, 170, 174, 178,

Index of Cartoons/Illustrations

Index of Scripture References

Index of Quotations and Acknowledgments

Index of Websites